THE INVESTITURE CONTROVERSY

University of Pennsylvania Press
MIDDLE AGES SERIES
Edited by
EDWARD PETERS
Henry Charles Lea Professor of Medieval History
University of Pennsylvania

A complete listing of the books in this series
appears at the back of this volume

THE INVESTITURE CONTROVERSY

Church and Monarchy from the
Ninth to the Twelfth Century

UTA-RENATE BLUMENTHAL
Translation by the Author

upp
UNIVERSITY OF PENNSYLVANIA PRESS
Philadelphia

First paperback printing 1991

Library of Congress Cataloging-in-Publication Data

Blumenthal, Uta-Renate, 1935–
    [Investiturstreit. English]
    The investiture controversy: church and monarchy from the ninth
to the twelfth century / Uta-Renate Blumenthal; translation by the
author.
        p.   cm.—(Middle Ages)
    Translation of: Der Investiturstreit.
    Bibliography: p.
    Includes index.
    ISBN 0-8122-8112-8
    ISBN 0-8122-1386-6 (pbk)
    1. Investiture.   2. Monasticism and religious orders—Europe—
History.   3. Church and state—Europe—History.   4. Europe—Church
history—Middle Ages, 600–1500.   I. Title.   II. Series.
BX1198.B5813   1988
262'.12—dc19   88-10600
                                                          CIP

Maps by Anne Marie Palagano

FOR BARBARA

CONTENTS

PREFACE TO THE ENGLISH EDITION

As succinctly as possible this book describes the roots of a set of ideals that effected a radical transformation of eleventh-century European society that led to the confrontation between church and monarchy known as the investiture struggle or Gregorian reform. Ideas cannot be divorced from reality, especially not in the Middle Ages. I present them, therefore, in their contemporary political, social, and cultural context. Because of the brevity of this book, I was able in only a few instances to discuss the background in any detail, and I particularly regret that I could not give more space to social and urban developments. However, the bibliographies at the end of each chapter provide an introduction to the extensive historiography pertaining to the various topics touched on in the text. This book, a result of many years of research in connection with work on the later reform, does not intend to replace text- and handbooks. Some of them are excellent. The text indicates where my views are particularly influenced by the work of other scholars or where we disagree. Necessary translations of quotations into English are my own.

Chapter 5 and the bibliography of the original German edition have been extensively revised. *Der Investiturstreit* grew out of stimulating conversations with Professor Peter Herde, Würzburg, and I would like to thank him here once again. This English translation would never have been completed without the invaluable help and encouragement of my sister, Barbara Motyka. I dedicate the book to her with profound gratitude. I would also like to thank Professor Ed Peters, who kindly read the manuscript, and Mrs. Jo Mugnolo of the University of Pennsylvania Press.

Hyattsville, Maryland
June 1987

GENERAL BIBLIOGRAPHY

A voluminous literature demonstrates a lively interest in medieval history. The bibliographies at the end of each chapter, however, refer to only a small selection from recent or particularly important publications that have influenced me most. The selection is designed to permit a quick orientation for the reader with access to additional secondary literature as well as primary sources. Primary sources have been excluded from the bibliography. The outstanding *Guide to the Sources of Medieval History* by R. C. van Caenegem (with the collaboration of François L. Ganshof) (Amsterdam, 1978) is not only an excellent general introduction to the study of medieval history but also includes descriptions of the collections and series of primary sources in the different European countries (e.g., Rolls series, Bouquet's *Recueil des historiens des Gaules et de la France,* series of the *Monumenta Germaniae historica,* Muratori's *Scriptores rerum italicarum*). The bibliography of the German edition, *Der Investiturstreit* (Stuttgart, 1982), has been updated, but I have particularly tried to include publications in English. For books that are available in more than one language, especially those that were published first in German, I have given data only for the English edition. To save space I have also avoided duplication from one chapter to the next; therefore, literature listed at the end of one chapter will often be relevant to others as well.

A listing of introductory works of general interest follows.

Comparative History

Susan Reynolds, *Kingdoms and Communities in Western Europe, 900–1300* (Oxford, 1984); Heinrich Mitteis, *The State in the Middle Ages: A Comparative Constitutional History of Feudal Europe,* translated by H. F. Orton (Amsterdam, 1975) is still helpful; Fritz Kern, *Kingship and Law in the Middle Ages,* translated by S. B. Chrimes (New York, 1970); of the *Handbook of Church History,* edited by Hubert Jedin and John Dolan, vol. 3, *The Church in the Age of Feudalism* by Friedrich Kempf et al., translated by Anselm Biggs (New York, 1969), is an excellent guide to much more than just the church.

German History

The *Jahrbücher der Deutschen Geschichte* remain fundamental for chronology and primary sources, and the volumes by Gerold Meyer von Knonau for Henry IV and Henry V are particularly good; John B. Gillingham, *The Kingdom of Germany in the High Middle Ages* (Historical Association Pamphlet; London, 1971); Geoffrey Barraclough, *The Origins of Modern Germany* (2d ed. Oxford, 1947), unfortunately out of print, is more stimulating than the traditional history by Karl Hampe, translated by Ralph F. Bennett, *Germany Under the Salian and Hohenstaufen Emperors* (Totowa, N.J., 1973). B. Gebhardt, *Handbuch der Deutschen Geschichte,* edited by Herbert Grundmann (9th ed., 1970), must be consulted for the German bibliography. Particularly relevant for the period I cover are sections published in paperback by the Deutscher Taschenbuch Verlag (dtv) as vol. 3 (Josef Fleckenstein and Marie Luise Bulst, *Begründung und Aufstieg des deutschen Reiches* [1973]) and vol. 4 (Karl Jordan, *Investiturstreit und frühe Stauferzeit* [1973]). The more recent but briefer relevant volumes in the series *Deutsche Geschichte,* edited by Joachim Leuschner, have been translated into English: Josef Fleckenstein, *Early Medieval Germany,* translated by Bernard S. Smith (*Europe in the Middle Ages Selected Studies,* vol. 16 [Amsterdam, 1978]), and Horst Fuhrmann, *Germany in the High Middle Ages, c. 1050–1200,* translated by Timothy Reuter (Cambridge, 1986), a much more successful translation with an excellent critical bibliography restricted to English titles. Another useful guide in German is Hermann Jakobs, *Kirchenreform und Hochmittelalter, 1046–1215* (Oldenbourg, 1984).

English History

Frank M. Stenton, *Anglo-Saxon England* (Oxford History of England; 3d ed. Oxford, 1971) is unsurpassed albeit occasionally outdated; A. L. Poole, *From Domesday Book to Magna Carta: 1087–1216* (2d ed. rev. Oxford, 1955) in the same series has been replaced by Frank Barlow, *The Feudal Kingdom of England, 1042–1216* (3d ed. London, 1984) and Michael T. Clanchy, *England and Its Rulers: 1066–1272* (Totowa, N.J., 1983).

French History

Ferdinand Lot and Robert Fawtier, *Histoire des institutions françaises au moyen âge,* of which there are two volumes, *Institutions seigneuriales* (1) and *Institutions royales* (2); Robert Fawtier, *The Capetian Kings of France: Monarchy and Nation, 987–1328,* translated by Lionel Butler and R. J. Adam (London, 1960), presents basic information succinctly.

Handbooks

Finally, it may be helpful to mention at least a few handbooks, specifically in fields I was obliged to neglect: *Cambridge Economic History of Europe,* vol. 2 (2d ed. 1966); Robert-Henri Bautier and Janine Sornay, *Les sources de l'histoire économique et sociale du moyen âge,* 3 vols. (Paris, 1968); Michael M. Postan, *The Medieval Economy and Society: An Economic History of Britain in the Middle Ages* (Harmondsworth, 1972); *The Fontana Economic History of Europe,* vol. 1: *The Middle Ages,* edited by Carlo M. Cipolla (New York, 1972); Carlo M. Cipolla, *Before the Industrial Revolution: European Society and Economy, 1000–1700* (New York, 1976); Cyrille Vogel, *Medieval Liturgy: An Introduction to the Sources,* translated and extensively revised by William G. Story and Niels Krogh Rasmussen, O. P. (Washington, D.C., 1986); Giles Constable, *Medieval Monasticism: A Select Bibliography* (Toronto, 1976) offers a very judicious and helpful selection. A recent document collection of outstanding quality which continues the volumes by Haddan and Stubbs is *Councils & Synods with Other Documents Relating to the English Church,* edited by Dorothy Whitelock, Martin Brett, Christopher N. L. Brooke, 2 vols. (Oxford, 1978). Richard H. Rouse, *Serial Bibliographies for Medieval Studies,* is an invaluable key to 283 bibliographies. J. Paetow's *Guide to the Study of Medieval History* (2d ed. rev. 1973) has been continued with a bibliography in five volumes by Gray Cowan Boyce, *Literature of Medieval History, 1930–1975* (Millwood, N.Y., 1981).

Map 1: France, about 1035

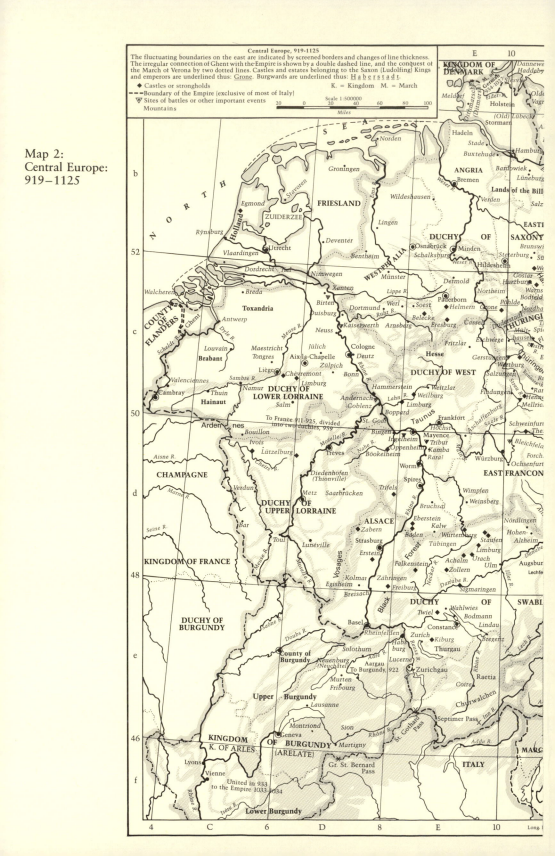

Map 2:
Central Europe:
919–1125

Central Europe, 919-1125

The fluctuating boundaries on the east are indicated by screened borders and changes of line thickness.
The irregular connection of Ghent with the Empire is shown by a double dashed line, and the conquest of
the March of Verona by two dotted lines. Castles and estates belonging to the Saxon (Ludolfing) Kings
and emperors are underlined thus: Grone. Burgwards are underlined thus: H a b e r s t a d t.

◆ Castles or strongholds   K. = Kingdom   M. = March
- - -Boundary of the Empire (exclusive of most of Italy)
▽ Sites of battles or other important events
   Mountains

Scale 1:500000
20   0   20   40   60   80   100
                Miles

KINGDOM OF DENMARK

NORTH SEA

KINGDOM OF DENMARK

Dannewe
Haddeb
Slesv

Meldorf

Holstein

(Old) Lübeck
Stormarn

Norden

Hadeln
Stade
Buxtehude

Hamburg
Bardowiek

Lüneburg

Groningen

Wildeshausen

ANGRIA
Bremen
Verden

Lands of the Bill

Salz

FRIESLAND

Egmond

Holland

Stavoren

ZUIDERZEE

Rynsburg

Lingen

DUCHY OF SAXONY

Osnabrück Minden
Schalksburg

Brunsw
Steterburg Sü
Hildesheim

Goslar
Harzburg
We

EASTE

Vlaardingen

Utrecht

Deventer

WESTPHALIA

Münster

Detmold

Northeim
Pöhlde

Warns
Bodfeld
Nordha

THURINGI

Dordrecht Iel

Nimwegen

Bentheim

Weser R.

Walcheren

Breda

Xanten
Birten
Duisburg

Lippe R.

Werl Soest
Dortmund
Ruhr R.

Paderborn
Helmern Grone
Belecke Cassel
Eresburg

Müh- Spi
hausen Eschwege

COUNTY OF FLANDERS

Ghent

Antwerp

Toxandria

Neuss
Kaiserwerth Arnsberg

Fritzlar

Gerstungen

Wartburg Ru
Salzungen

Thüringen
Neus tei
Sree R.

Louvain
Maestricht
Tongres

Dyle R.
Meuse R.

Jülich
Aix-la-Chapelle
Zülpich

Cologne
Deutz

Hesse

Hemme
Mellric.

Brabant

Liège
Chèvremont

Bonn
Rhine R.

DUCHY OF WEST

Scheldt R.
Sambre R.

Namur
Limburg

Hammerstein
Andernach
Coblenz

Weitzlar
Weilburg
Lahn R.

Salzungen
Fludungen

Valenciennes
Cambray

Thuin

DUCHY OF LOWER LORRAINE

Salm

Limburg
Boppard

Taunus

Aschaffenburg
Söele R.

Schweinfur
The.

Hainaut

Ardennes

Bouillon

To France 911-925, divided
into two duchies, 959

St. Goar

Hochst
Mayence
Ingelheim

Frankfort

Bleichfela
Forch.

Ivois

Moselle R.

Bingen

Tribur
Oppenheim Kamba
Böokelheim Raral

Würzburg
Ochsenfurt

Lützelburg

Trèves

Nahe R.

Worms

EAST FRANCON

CHAMPAGNE

Aisne R.

Chiers R.

Diedenhofen
(Thionville)

Metz Saarbrücken

Spires

Trifels

Wimpfen
Weinsberg

Bruchsal

Nördlingen

Marne R.

Verdun

DUCHY OF UPPER LORRAINE

ALSACE

Eberstein
Zabern Kalw

Baden
Tübingen

Wurtenberg
Staufen
Limburg

Hohen-
Altheim

Seine R.

Bar

Toul

Lunéville

Strasburg
Erstein

Black Forest

Falkenstein

Achalm
Zollern

Urach

Danube R.

Ulm

Augsbur
Lechfen

KINGDOM OF FRANCE

Meuse R.

Moselle R.

Vosages

Kolmar
Egisheim

Zähringen

Freibug

Neckar R.

Sigmaringen

Iller R.

Breisach

DUCHY OF SWABI

DUCHY OF BURGUNDY

Saône R.

Basel

Twiel Wahlwies
Bodmann

Constance
Lindau

Rheinfelden
Zurich

Rhine R.

Bregenz

Lech R.

Doubs R.

County of Burgundy

Habs-
burg

Solothurn
Aare R.

Lucerne

Kiburg
Thurgau

Zurichgau

Coire

Raetia

Neuenburg
(Neuchâtel)

Aargau

To Burgundy, 922

Reuss R.

Murten
Fribourg

Upper Burgundy

Lausanne

Churwalchen

Inn R.

Montriond

Sion

Rhône R.

St. Gothard Pass

Septimer Pass

Adda R.

KINGDOM
K. OF ARLES

Geneva
Martigny

OF BURGUNDY
(ARELATE)

ITALY

MARC

Lyons

Vienne

United in 933
to the Empire 1033-1034

Gr. St. Bernard Pass

Rhône R.

Isère R.

Lower Burgundy

Long

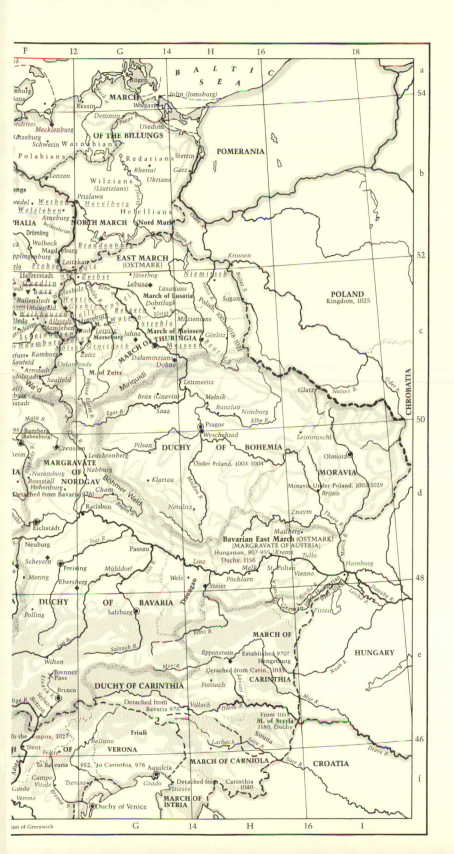

F　　12　　G　　14　H　　16　　18

a

B　A　L　T　I　C

S　E　A

54

Rügen

MARCH

Kessin · *Julin (Jomsburg)*

Demmin · Wolgast

OF THE BILLUNGS

Peene R.

Mecklenburg · *Usedom*

Ratzeburg

Schwerin W a r n a b i a n s

P o l a b i a n s

POMERANIA

Stettin

Lenzen

Redarians

Rhetra! · *Garz*

b

Wilzians

Ukrians

(Liutizians)

Prizlawa

Havelberg

Wedel · Werben

Walsleben

H e v e l l i a n s

Arneburg

NORTH MARCH　**Nord Mark**

Drömling

Belkesheim

Walbeck

Brandenburg

Oder R.

52

Magdeburg

Fpplingenburg

Leitzkau

Spree R.

Krossen

EAST MARCH

(OSTMARK)

Jüterbog

Zerbst

N i e m i t s c h

Lebusa

POLAND

Halberstadt

Lusatians

March of Lusatia

Kingdom, 1025

Quedlin-

Dobrilugk

Sagan

burg

Wettin

Bober R.

Ballenstedt

Elster R.

March of Meissen

c

Mansfeld

Allstedt

Milzienians

Strehla

Görlitz

MARCH OF

Merseburg

Jahna

THURINGIA

Meissen

M. of Zeitz

Dalaminzians

Dohna

M i r i q u i d i

Leitmeritz

Glatz　*Neisse R.*

CHROBATIA

Brüx (Gnevin)

Melnik

Saaz

Bunzlau

Nimburg

Eger R.　*Elbe R.*

50

Prague

DUCHY　**OF**　**BOHEMIA**

Wyschehrad

Leitomischl

Pilsen

Under Poland, 1003-1004

Olmütz

MARGRAVATE

Leuchtenberg

Nabburg

MORAVIA

OF

Klattau

Moravia Under Poland, 1003-1029

Hohenburg

Cham

Brünn

d

Detached from Bavaria 976!

Ratisbon

Netolitz

Znaym

Eichstädt

Mailberg

Neuburg

Passau

Bavarian East March (OSTMARK)

(MARGRAVATE OF AUSTRIA)

Scheyern

Freising

Linz

Hungarian, 907-955, *Krems*

Mering

Ebersberg

Wels

Duchy, 1156

Melk　St. Pölten

Steier

Pöchlarn

Vienna

Hainburg

48

DUCHY　**OF**　**BAVARIA**

German

Polling

Salzburg

Pitten

Enns R.

MARCH OF

Wilten

Salzach R.

HUNGARY

e

Brenner

Eppenstein

Established 970?

Pass

Mur R.

Hengstburg

Brixen

Detached from Carin., 1035

DUCHY OF CARINTHIA

Freisach

CARINTHIA

Bozen

Detached from

Villach

Drave R.

Bavaria 976

From 1055

Friuli

M. of Styria

46

VERONA

Laibach

1180, Duchy

Belluno

Sonna

Save R.

Drave R.

To the empire, 1027

Feltre

OF

To Bavaria　952,　to Carinthia, 976　Aquileia

MARCH OF CARNIOLA

CROATIA

Campo

Treviso

Grado

Sare R.

Vitale

Trieste

f

Verona

Detached from

Carinthia

1040

MARCH OF

Duchy of Venice

ISTRIA

G　　14　　H　　16　　I

Map 3: Italy, about 1050

Map 4: England, 1087–1154

ABBREVIATIONS

The Church in the Age of Feudalism	*Handbook of Church History.* Edited by Hubert Jedin and John Dolan. Vol. 3, *The Church in the Age of Feudalism,* by Hans Georg Beck, Josef A. Jungmann, Friedrich Kempf, and Hans Wolter. Translated by Anselm Biggs. New York and London, 1969
DA	*Deutsches Archiv für Erforschung des Mittelalters*
EHR	*English Historical Review*
HZ	*Historische Zeitschrift*
Investiturstreit und Reichsverfassung	*Vorträge und Forschungen* herausgegeben vom Konstanzer Arbeitskreis für mittelalterliche Geschichte 17, *Investiturstreit und Reichsverfassung,* edited by Peter Classen. Sigmaringen, 1973.
Medieval Germany	Geoffrey Barraclough. *Mediaeval Germany, 911–1250.* Vol. 2. Oxford, 1938.
MGH	*Monumenta Germaniae historica*
MIÖG	*Mitteilungen des Instituts für Österreichische Geschichtsforschung*
ZKG	*Zeitschrift für Kirchengeschichte*
ZRG Kan. Abt.	*Zeitschrift der Savigny Stiftung für Rechtsgeschichte, Kanonistische Abteilung*

The primary purpose of the Vikings was to amass booty, anything from gold and silver to weapons, cattle, and slaves. They looked upon Francia as an Eldorado, theirs to seize with little effort. The Saxon Count Kobbo, who had been sent by Louis the German as ambassador to the Danish King Orich in 845, was present when one adventurer named Ragnar returned to the Danish court from his successful assault on Paris in 843 and told his tale of fabulous riches to be found there undefended. Ragnar declared that never yet had he come across such a rich and fertile country, never yet a population so timid and fearful. It was true that the notables of the land, including its kings, at first saw flight and payment of tribute as the only means to escape from the Danes. But there were some exceptions: Abbot Gauzlin of Saint Denis, bishop of Paris since 884, defended the city in 885; Abbot Odo of Corbie was anxiously advised by Lupus of Ferrières to be more careful before throwing himself unarmed into combat accompanying his troops; and Archbishop Liutbert of Cologne, together with Count Henry, fought against the invaders in the valley of the Mosel River. Although canon law prohibited the clergy from bearing arms, a matter which Pope Nicholas I had again inculcated in his 860 letter to Bishop Humfried of Thérouanne, it was the bishops and abbots, more often than not, who issued the call to resistance. The most punishing incursions struck the Seine region during the years 856–62, and later—after the victory of Alfred the Great (871–99) over the "great army" of the Danes at Edington in 878—during the years 879–91. The fighting reached a turning point with the victory of the East Frankish King Arnulf (887–99) over the Vikings at Louvain in November 891. When Charles the Simple (893–922/29) agreed to allow Rollo and his Northmen to settle in the area of Rouen, the center of the region bearing their name, the Viking scourge subsided.

Throughout this period the heirs of Charlemagne found themselves under relentless assault not only from the north but also from the west, south, and east. A troop of Vikings returning from the Mediterranean advanced toward Orléans and Clermont and pillaged Nîmes, Arles, and Valence in 860, Pisa and Fiesole in 861. Bordeaux had been sacked earlier, in 848. The Saracens represented the more immediate danger in the Mediterranean basin, where Italy had to carry the brunt of their attacks. Saracen states set up on Sicily and in Apulia, with Palermo and Bari serving as the administrative centers, were mostly carved out of Byzantine and Lombard territories. The Byzantines, under General Nikephoros Phokas, succeeded in winning back Calabria in the 880s, but this same period also brought the destruction of Montecassino, in 882. The most famous Saracen citadel in the Alps, La Garde-Freinet in the bishopric of

Fréjus, served as a base for incursions into Provence and the region around Genoa, as well as for raids on unarmed pilgrims and other travelers crossing the Alps. The Saracens were not completely dislodged from their outposts until the tenth and eleventh centuries, when the Italian maritime cities gained strength through commerce and the Normans settled in the south of Italy. Although East Francia was spared from the Saracens, the Viking threat on its western frontier coincided, particularly during the tenth century, with eruptions by Hungarians and Slavs into the east and southeast. In part due to these military pressures, Conrad I (911–18) was elected king after the death in 911 of Louis the Child, the last Carolingian in East Francia. Similarly, the coronation of Otto the Great (936–73) in 962 as emperor and heir of Charlemagne would seem implausible without Otto's defeat of the Hungarians at the Lechfeld in 955.

The primary victims of the disruptions that characterized Europe in the second half of the ninth century were unarmed civilians and the churches and monasteries. Citing the duty incumbent upon a king, Archbishop Hincmar of Reims called on King Louis the Stammerer in 877 and soon thereafter, at the council of Fismes in 881, on the king's son, Louis III, to provide relief for the hard-pressed population suffering from relentless raids and the unbearably high taxes levied solely to buy off the Vikings. Not only had the simple people been impoverished, but heretofore wealthy churches and monasteries had also been reduced to near ruin. The king, Hincmar said, ought to see that justice is done so that God might fill the Franks with the courage to defend themselves against the heathen.

Hincmar's description of the circumstances appears credible. Current research seeks to evaluate the often implausible entries found in the monastic chronicles. Apart from coins and other archaeological evidence, these written records often are our only sources of information. Scholars are beginning to differentiate among the various regions of the country, not all of which were ravaged to the same degree. Although the answers to many questions are still uncertain, even the more recent findings leave no doubt that many monasteries and bishoprics suffered repeated destruction, and that the population, the churches, and the monasteries, even in such relatively secure regions as southern Lotharingia, were impoverished by the vast tribute payments to the Danes, raised, like the English Danegeld, in the form of taxes. Collection of such taxes has been established for the years 845, 853, 860/61, 862, 866, 877, 884, 897, 923/24, and 926. According to Albert D'Haenens, the sum of 39,000 pounds calculated to have been raised represents no more than one-third to one-half of the actual payments. The ransom and protection monies

that the monasteries and churches paid to the Danes directly must also be
added to these figures. For example, because the Parisian abbeys of Saint
Denis, Saint Etienne, and Saint-Germain-des-Prés made such payments,
they were the only churches of Paris not burned to the ground in 857.

The economic and intellectual-religious consequences of the Viking
onslaught proved devastating. Constant insecurity and desperate poverty
were not the only burdens weighing on the populace. Many of those who
managed to come away with their lives must have been left homeless. The
often epic wanderings of monks with the relics of their patron saints are
recounted in the chronicles and lives of the saints. Although the wanderings of the monks of Noirmoutier with the reliquary of Saint Philibert—
they found no permanent shelter for forty years until they were taken in
by Tournus in 875, and they did not return to their motherhouse for a
good hundred years—may not be typical, the monks of Saint Maixent
also crisscrossed the land from Brittany to Burgundy in constant flight
before the Northmen, until they were able to return to their monastery,
Maillezais, from an abbey near Poitiers in 942. In many instances flight
could be counted in a mere handful of years, or even months, particularly
once the monks had mastered the enemy tactics and learned that a well-
fortified hiding place counted for more than distance. This adaptability
was offset, however, by the fact that many monasteries and chapters
of canons had ceased to function as religious communities. Often, too,
the property of the absentee monks fell into the hands of nearby large
landowners, and so even after the Northmen had been driven out, the
returning monks were without means of support. Under such circumstances the rigorous monastic life envisioned by the reforms of Aachen
was impossible.

Dangers other than the Viking-Saracen raids threatened the monasteries and churches. The great abbeys in West Francia were made party to
civil strife in the struggle over the succession between the Carolingians
and the ancestors of the later Capetians. The proprietary church system
and the lay abbacies under the heirs of Louis the Pious were responsible
for this state of affairs. The proprietor and/or abbot would change with
every turn in military fortune. Often abbeys were turned into fortresses
and made to serve as domicile for the lord of the monastery with his
troops and his wife, children, dogs, and horses.

The researches of Ulrich Stutz remain the basis for any study of the
proprietary church, even though some of his conclusions have been superseded. In particular, his thesis of the Germanic origin of the proprietary church is generally rejected today. We now know that this form of
ownership also existed in non-Germanic areas of the former Roman Em-

pire and in similar guise among the Slavs and the Irish. In the Roman Empire the church had been centrally organized. All monasteries and churches of a diocese, including their personnel and the attached property, were subject to the bishop. A very different juridicial notion took hold in the Germanic successor states, as well as in East Rome, the later Byzantine Empire. A church or monastery founded by a landowner on his own grounds continued as part of the family property and, like its other properties, remained at the founder's disposition. The altar, erected above the relics of the saint to whom it was dedicated, was the legal anchor to which the buildings of church or monastery, the cemetery, its lands, tithes, and other fees were attached. On behalf of the saint, the landowner held title to the altar and everything associated with it, because his legal rights to the ground on which the altar stood continued unabated. If the proprietor so wished, he could dispose of the altar and thus of the income and property attached to it. He could sell, lend, or lease the altar, leave it to his heirs, use it for dower, or mortgage it, provided that a church, once dedicated, continued to be used as a church. The proprietor not only had the right to provide for appropriate divine services but was even duty bound to do so and to install and to support a priest for his foundation. With the rise of the proprietary church, the bishops lost much of their influence and many of their diocesan rights pertaining to churches and monasteries. The bishops' supervisory functions fell into abeyance, although the bishops theoretically never abandoned their rights. Their opposition failed to stem the new developments in the Frankish church that was shaken repeatedly by waves of secularization initiated by rulers to provide for adherents whose military support was the sine qua non of political power. Increasingly, side by side with new foundations, old churches and monasteries also came into the hands of the laity.

The great reforming councils of 802 and 818/19 under Charlemagne and Louis the Pious devised a compromise between the old and the new ecclesiastical orders. Proprietary churches were officially recognized, but capitularies eliminated some of the most glaring excesses associated with the proprietary church system. Laymen were no longer allowed to appoint or to depose priests without the permission of the diocesan bishop, or to ordain unfree persons. Moreover, every sufficiently wealthy church was to have its own priest, and every priest was to be provided with a manse free of seigneurial dues. For this land, for house and garden, for tithes and oblations, a lord could demand only spiritual services. The legislation, however, also protected the prerogatives of the lay founders. The councils specified on behalf of the proprietary lord that no bishop could refuse to ordain a cleric who had been nominated, provided the nominee's education and morals were satisfactory. Furthermore, bishops were obliged to grant the appropriate tithes to the new churches. These regulations were not applicable to monasteries unless they served as parish churches as well, but the legislation also protected proprietary rights in monasteries, usually by reserving abbatial elections to the founders and their descendants.

Since the time of Louis the Pious, the oldest and most renowned abbeys as well as certain churches were treated as dependent on the crown, even if they had not been founded by kings, had not been built on royal lands, or had not been transferred to kings by noble founders or confiscated by kings. Adhémar of Chabannes reports that Louis the Pious in conjunction with Benedict of Aniane confiscated all abbeys at the beginning of his reign to protect them from the intervention of counts and bishops. Since 815 royal protection had always been paired with immunity. Thus confiscated abbeys and churches pertained to the crown not only in fact but also by law (de jure). The royal protectorate was designed to insure the independence of monasteries and churches and to enable monks and canons to live in accordance with their respective rules. Royal rights and duties of surprising dimensions were derived from this arrangement, as revealed by capitularies and ninth-century conciliar canons. Archbishop Hincmar of Reims, for example, known for his polemics against royal domination of the church and especially against the royal nomination of bishops, repeatedly called upon the kings to have their *missi* investigate conditions in monasteries and abbeys, urging the imperial *missi* to prepare detailed inventories of all monastic property and to report on the numbers of monks and nuns and on their manner of life. In response to these inquests, the king was to undertake all necessary steps to insure that the proper number of monks and nuns be found everywhere, that the liturgy be celebrated appropriately, and that no monastery have either too much or too little temporal property. Strictly speaking, Louis the Pious had renounced in 818/19 the nomination of abbots for imperial abbeys where the *Ordo regularis* had been introduced, that is, the Rule of Saint Benedict as reformed by Benedict of Aniane. Louis, however, still reserved for himself consent to the election as well as the investiture of the elect and his right to examine electoral proceedings. In effect, therefore, abbatial elections after 819 were still determined by the king. Karl Voigt demonstrated long ago, however, that the negative implications of these regulations were negligible until the reign of Charles the Bald (840–77), who was the first to succumb to the pressure of the nobility and to bestow abbeys upon laymen. Gradually these laymen acquired the entire complex of royal rights. They became the familiar lay abbots or proprietary lords who dominated and exploited abbeys and churches in accordance with the customs of the proprietary church system. They claimed the right to live in the monastery and to use its militia for their private wars. It was of little significance that some lay abbots shared their rule with a regular abbot. Lay owners embroiled monasteries and collegiate churches in the disputes and wars over the succession to the West Frankish crown. Abbeys as well as churches became important pawns in the power politics of the prominent aristocratic families. In the late ninth and in the early tenth centuries, therefore, monastic peace and seclusion and observation of the Rule of Saint Benedict were rare.

2. The Beginnings of the Monastic Reform in Lotharingia

The religious longings and aspirations of mankind, however, were not to be thwarted so easily. Early in the tenth century the first stirrings of reform were seen in Lotharingia (Brogne, Gorze, Verdun) and Burgundy (Cluny). The spiritual inheritance of Benedict of Aniane fused with eremitical trends. A wave of renewal transformed monasteries, in particular, but also the houses of the secular regular clergy. Even in the second half of the ninth century new monasteries were founded, but Abbot Gerard of Brogne (d. 959) is probably the first representative of the new spirit of reform. In 913/14 he founded a monastic community on his inherited property and procured for it relics of Saint Eugenius from the little monastery of Deuil, a dependent of the abbey of Saint Denis in Paris. At the time Gerard was still a layman, and his actions were those of a proprietary lord. Gerard was a scion of the warlike Lotharingian nobility, as his father was a vassal of the great Capetian, Count Robert of Paris, king of France since 922. Gerard and his family were also on the best of terms with Count Berengar of Namur—Brogne is situated near Namur—and Bishop Stephen of Liège.

The *Vita Gerardi abbatis Broniensis* is unfortunately a "roman hagiographique" (De Smet) composed entirely with a view to the conditions of the diocese of Liège in the second half of the eleventh century. Thus we know little about Gerard's motivation, or about the early organization at Brogne. Not only is the *Vita Gerardi* almost pure legend, but also Brogne is among the best-known medieval centers of forgery, and surviving documents must be used with the greatest caution. It is agreed today, however, that Gerard, the proprietary lord, became a monk around 918/19, and joined the monastery of Saint Denis. In 921 the bishop of Paris, Theodulf, consecrated Gerard as subdeacon. A privilege of King Charles of France dating from the same year granted Brogne immunity. One year later, also in Paris, Gerard became a deacon, and after 923 privileges refer to him as abbot of Brogne, indicating that Brogne had then become an independent monastery. Gerard was ordained a priest in Paris in 927 but apparently did not spend the years from 923 to 927 there. He seems instead to have stayed at Brogne and, in particular, to have traveled and collected privileges for his beloved foundation from various parties whose influence waxed and waned. The reforms introduced by Gerard and the success of his renewal efforts must have been spectacular, for Duke Giselbert of Lotharingia (d. 939) asked Gerard as early as 931/32 to reform the monastery of Saint Ghislain (Hainault), which was in especially deplorable condition.

Gerard had founded Brogne with the intention of spending his life there in monastic solitude. Nevertheless, he did not refuse his aid to Margrave Arnulf of Flanders (918–65). In the early forties Arnulf asked Gerard to restore several famous Flemish abbeys: Saint Bavo and Saint Pierre of Mont-Blandain, better known as Blandigny, at Ghent as well as at Saint Bertin. The history of these monasteries provides an excellent commentary on contemporary conditions. In the ninth century Saint Bavo, a royal monastery, had been destroyed by the Normans. Subsequently, it became the property of the counts of Flanders, who apparently despoiled it of its possessions. The monastic community within its walls ceased to exist. Only its church was still used for worship services. At Saint Pierre of Mont-Blandain circumstances were similar, although the abbey still housed a group of canons who were replaced by monks when Margrave Arnulf asked Gerard to restore the abbey. Arnulf had inherited Saint Bertin from his brother and like him presided as lay abbot. Monks still lived there. When they objected to the reforms introduced by Gerard of Brogne, Arnulf expelled them, as he had the canons of Blandigny, and replaced them with newcomers. It is unlikely that the new monks came from Brogne, but their origin is unknown. To all three abbeys, on the occasion of the renewal of monastic observances within their walls, Margrave Arnulf returned as much of their former property as he considered adequate for the sustenance of monks. The remainder of the property he kept for himself. Arnulf continued as proprietary lord but gave up the office of lay abbot. The Flemish reform effort, which extended to the abbeys of Saint Vaast and Saint Amand, was intimately linked to Arnulf and Gerard of Brogne. It was arrested with the deaths of Gerard (960) and Arnulf (965), and had to be taken up anew at a later date by Richard of Saint Vanne and Poppo of Stablò-Malmédy.

Of greater permanence and influence was the almost contemporary reform radiating from the Lotharingian monastery of Gorze to Lower Lorraine and Germany. Here, too, reforms were usually inspired by proprietary lords, laymen as well as bishops, who generally were members of the high aristocracy. However, as Kassius Hallinger demonstrates, it is necessary to differentiate the Lotharingian/German movement from the general reform. Not all the elements of Hallinger's precise delimitation of the reform of Gorze from that of Cluny have withstood criticism, but apart from a few earlier studies, Hallinger's thesis is the first to provide a thorough description of the wide-ranging monastic reform movement spreading through Lotharingia and Germany with the strong support of the Ottonian and early Salian kings in the period before the investiture struggle. Hallinger's definitive work shows the scope and effects of a monastic reform initially lacking all direct ties to Cluny. It is now accepted that the reforms of Gorze were not derived from Cluny. Relying particularly on a new group of original sources and necrologies, and using them in connection with abbatial lists, Hallinger demonstrates the influence of Gorze through ten expansive groups of filiations: Gorze, Saint Maximin, Saint Emmeram, Niederaltaich, Lorsch, Fulda, the Mainz group, Einsiedeln, monasteries of the Lotharingian mixed observance, and monasteries associated with Young Gorze. But what precisely is the reform of Gorze?

In a privilege of 933, Bishop Adalbero of Metz reconstituted the completely devastated monastery of Gorze, founded by Chrodegand of Metz in the eighth century and situated just beyond the city gates. Adalbero handed it over to a group of zealous reformers, clergy from the area of Metz, Toul, and Verdun. The first abbot of Gorze, Einold, was the former archdeacon of Toul. As the *Vita* of John of Vanière, Adalbero's successor, relates, Adalbero required a great deal of persuasion to reconstitute Gorze. Earlier bishops of Metz had appropriated the possessions of Gorze, and it was difficult for a tenth-century bishop to surrender this property or to prevail upon his aristocratic relatives to do the same. The turning point came with the revelation of John's intention to emigrate to Benevento with his like-minded friends, including several clerics from Metz, the archdeacon and ascetic Einold of Toul, as well as the hermits Humbert of Verdun and Lauthbert from the Ardennes region. John had convinced them that life in the duchy of Benevento would provide the long-desired opportunity to live in a colony of hermits and to devote their lives entirely to God. Adalbero finally offered Gorze as habitation in order to keep his friends in Lotharingia. After some hesitation they accepted. But the beginnings were economically difficult, for Adalbero had been rather miserly in returning Gorze property. At one point the men, now Benedictine monks, were about to transfer to Saint Maximin at Trier, but matters improved and Gorze flourished. The monastery was soon ready to respond to requests for aid from other monasteries wishing to reintroduce strict Benedictine observances.

One of the first institutions to obtain such aid from Gorze was the abbey of Saint Maximin at Trier. In 934, at the request of Duke Giselbert of Lotharingia, the duke who had entrusted Gerard of Brogne with the reform of Saint Ghislain a year earlier, Gorze arranged to send two monks to Saint Maximin for a short time. The relations between Gorze and Saint Maximin remained friendly, but once the duke, lay abbot of Saint Maximin, had opened the door to reform, the monks of Trier completed the task on their own. Their new abbot was not a monk from Gorze. Instead, it was Ogo (934–45), mentioned in a document of 923 as a monk of Saint Maximin. Saint Maximin was probably more influential than Gorze in the spread of monastic reform. Otto the Great (936–73) relied on the monks of Trier to reform the imperial state church. A monk of Saint Maximin became abbot of Saint Maurice at Magdeburg, and another, Adalbert, already abbot of Weissenburg, was appointed archbishop of the see of Magdeburg, which was just being established in cooperation between king and emperor. At the request of Otto, Abbot Sandrat of Saint Maximin also reformed several imperial abbeys. Furthermore, the Bavarian monastic reform was linked to the monks of Trier, for Abbot Ramwold of Saint Emmeram, a close friend of Emperor Henry II (1002–24), formerly duke of Bavaria, was called from Saint Maximin to Regensburg by Bishop Wolfgang, earlier in charge of the cathedral school at Trier. Henry II also collaborated directly with Gorze, for example, when he called on Abbot Immo of Gorze, but in general the emperor relied on the circle around Ramwold for monastic reform.

In an exemplary study of the constitution of the monastery of Saint Evre at Toul, Heinrich Büttner, discussing the flourishing reform in Lotharingia and Germany, draws attention not only to Saint Maximin but also to Saint Evre, which he credits with similar influence. Most likely in 934, Bishop Gauzlin of Toul granted a noteworthy privilege to the reconstituted abbey of Saint Evre. It balanced the principle of internal monastic independence (*libertas monastica religionis*) with a carefully considered arrangement for the protection of this liberty. For this purpose the proprietary claims of the bishops of Toul were emphasized, but abuse of these rights could be appealed to the metropolitan, the archbishop of Trier, and if necessary to the king. Although it is tempting to think of the formula *libertas monastica religionis* as new and revolutionary, when considering the Saint Evre privilege in the context of the investiture struggle, it is far from being either. Gauzlin borrowed the terms for the 934 document, written for him by the ascetic Humbert of Gorze, from older ninth-century privileges for Saint Evre. Particularly important were several royal charters, and especially the privilege of Bishop Frothar of Toul, dating from about 836. This document, breathing the spirit of the world of Benedict of Aniane, became the model for subsequent restitutions. Büttner's careful analysis demonstrates with striking clarity that the desire for religious renewal was expressed in many forms. Individual monastic lords approached reform independently while being subject to the most varied influences. The bishop of Toul, for example, could draw for inspiration not only his own archive but also on the ideas represented by Brogne and Gorze. Gauzlin, furthermore, had connections to the abbey of Fleury (Saint-Benoît-sur-Loire), reformed around 930 by Abbot Odo of Cluny, and even if indirectly, was surely aware of the institutions and aims of the Burgundian abbey.

3. The Beginnings of Cluny

Cluny was a new foundation. Its purpose was the strict observation of the *Rule of Saint Benedict* as interpreted by Benedict of Aniane, and arrest of the decay of monastic customs. Early in the tenth century, William the Pious, duke of Aquitaine and count of Auvergne, asked Abbot Berno of Beaume, a man famous for his monastic asceticism and rigorous discipline, to establish and direct a new monastery. It was to be founded on William's property and endowed for the salvation of William's *senior*, King Odo, and William's relatives and himself. Berno chose Cluny, a hunting lodge of the duke in the vicinity of Mâcon, as the location for the new monastery. The foundation charter of William the Pious of 909 was rather unusual, for it immediately protected the monastery and its property from intervention and alienation by any secular power, insured independent abbatial elections, and subjected the monastery to the protection of the Holy See (*tuitio* and *defensio*). Every five years Cluny was to pay a census of ten *solidi* in recognition of this protection. Roman *tuitio* and *defensio* did not constitute an exemption from diocesan jurisdiction in the sense attributed to the term of the later eleventh and twelfth centuries, for at first the spiritual rights of the bishop of Mâcon over Cluny remained unimpaired. Still, thanks to its privilege, the monastery could develop and grow free from interference by either layman or bishop, at least in respect to its property. In the beginning, however, it seemed most unlikely that Cluny would ever be able to flourish, for the little monastery was perhaps the poorest of the six monasteries in the hands of Abbot Berno at the time of his death in 927. In his will Berno divided these monasteries between his nephew Wido and Odo. To Wido he gave Gigny, Beaume, and Ethice, and to Odo he gave his favorite monastery, Cluny, as well as Déols (founded in 917 with a privilege very much like that of Cluny) and Massay. The partition had become necessary because even in Berno's lifetime some of the monks objected to Odo's forbidding severity. Odo was the scion of an Aquitanian noble family with close ties to the abbey of Saint Martin at Tours. Under Odo as abbot (927–42), however, Cluny soon began to prosper. Owing to his family connections to the court of Aquitaine, and especially to his own sanctity, Cluny's reputation grew by leaps and bounds. Odo secured the status of his abbeys and repeatedly obtained privileges for them from the kings of France (Rudolf and Louis IV) and from the popes in Rome (John X, John XI, and Leo VII). One of the privileges was the confirmation of Cluny's foundation charter. Déols, on the petition of its founder, Ebbo of Déols, also obtained such a charter, confirmed now for the first time by the king of France (927) as well as by the pope (931).

Odo's extraordinary reputation for sanctity as well as his family connections soon involved him in the revival of other monastic centers, among them Fleury (Saint-Benoît-sur-Loire), Aurillac, and Saint Julien at Tours. At Fleury, Odo had to overcome strong opposition before he could pursue reform. A privilege granted to him in 931 by Pope John XI clearly reveals his passionate concern for reform. It grants Odo papal permission to reform monasteries should they be given to him by their owners ("ex voluntate illorum, ad quorum dispositionem pertinere videtur") and should he be willing to shoulder the task. Furthermore, Odo obtained permission to receive into his monasteries strange monks desiring to follow a stricter rule, provided they could not yet do so in their own monasteries. In 937 Odo obtained the same permission for Fleury, although Fleury nevertheless remained a royal proprietary monastery and maintained its independence from Cluny.

During these years, Italy also came under Odo's influence. Alberic, a son of Marozia and Theophylact, entrusted the abbot with the reform of several Roman monasteries. Monastic establishments situated along Odo's route to and from Italy were another point of contact between Italian and Burgundian forms of piety. But Odo was also moved by the concern to reconcile Alberic, the prince of Rome, with Hugh of Vienne, king of Italy from 926 to 947. Hugh and Alberic were engaged in a bitter struggle for the domination of Rome. The reconciliation of the two men was perhaps the original purpose of Odo's Italian journey. Although he was not particularly successful in Italy either as arbiter or as reformer, Odo's opinions about Christian, and particularly monastic, life left a deep and lasting impression on the Italians. In 971 one of his successors at Cluny, Abbot Majolus (954–94), was to found the monastery of San Salvatore at Pavia with the support of the Empress Adelheid. He reformed San Pietro in Ciel d'Oro at Pavia in 983, but it was not until the eleventh century that Cluny's influence on Italy was to increase spectacularly. Sometime between 1030 and 1048 the Abbey of Farfa assumed the *consuetudines* of Cluny, and still earlier, at the beginning of the century, a disciple of Abbot Odilo of Cluny, Alferius (994–1049), had founded La Cava in the vicinity of Salerno. In the second half of the eleventh century Cluniac influence also gained ground in northern Italy outside the Pavia region. One well-known example is the abbey of San Benedetto at Polirone.

In Italy, as well as in Burgundy and Aquitaine, Odo of Cluny insisted on a strict observance of the Rule of Saint Benedict as updated by Benedict of Aniane, prohibiting, for example, the eating of meat. Certain tendencies of the Carolingian version of the Rule received an even stronger emphasis. Odo introduced stricter rules of silence and extended the choir office. The exact observance of traditions was to Odo of the greatest importance—it was for him the most essential feature of true monasticism. First and foremost Odo was a monk, devoted to the welfare of the monasteries entrusted to his care. But he also attempted, as we would put it, to raise the Christian consciousness among the secular clergy and members of the nobility. For Odo, monasticism and flight from the world did not preclude but instead reinforced and supported efforts to convert the world.

Under Odo's successors, Cluny continued to develop in the direction set by him. The second of these, Abbot Majolus (954–94), wholly shared Odo's spirituality and outlook but perhaps combined them with greater human warmth. He was the first of the abbots of Cluny to be called a saint in a papal privilege granted only a few years after his death. A friend of the king of France, Majolus is said, furthermore, to have been the candidate of Emperor Otto II (973–83) for the papacy, a suggestion Majolus rejected. At the request of the emperor, Majolus, like Odo before him, was both reformer and mediator. He tried to reconcile the Romans and the counts of Tusculum. Abbot Odilo was a worthy successor of Saint Majolus. Fulbert of Chartres, author of the *Vita Odolonis,* held Odilo's reforming activity in such high regard that he named him archangel of the monks. It was Odilo who introduced, in about 1030, at Cluny and in other monasteries under his influence the annual celebration of All Souls' day on 2 November, the day after All Saints'. Memorial services for the dead, customary in churches and abbeys throughout Europe, held a place of particular distinction at Cluny. Liturgical celebrations of great solemnity and splendor reflect this particular concern of the abbey, as do the very extensive necrologies listing the names of the dead who were commemorated by prayer.

The fame of the Burgundian abbey spread in concert with the reputation of its remarkable and outstanding abbots. Cluny became ever wealthier and more powerful. The number of its monks increased continually. By 937 Odo directed seventeen houses of monks, loosely tied to Cluny by the institution known as *abbatia*. At the time of Abbot Odilo the number of monasteries depending on Cluny rose to approximately sixty. It is still frequently maintained that Odilo began to systematize the ties of dependence between Cluny, the mother abbey, and monasteries that Cluny had either reformed or founded, or that had been given to her. But strictly speaking, such a systematization first occurred under Odilo's successor, the great Abbot Hugh (1049–109). During his abbacy an estimated two thousand monasteries were legally dependent on Cluny. However, accurate lists of dependent institutions from that period have not been preserved, nor have scholars attempted to compile such lists. Nevertheless, though the approximate figure of two thousand is probably somewhat high, there is no denying that Cluny was world famous at the time of Odilo and Hugh. Numerous monasteries in France, Italy, Spain, Germany, and England either depended on the Burgundian abbey or were strongly influenced by it. Certain scholars use the terms *order* or *congregation* in connection with Cluny, but these terms would be misleading if understood in their modern sense. In any discussion of Cluny it is essential to distinguish dependent monasteries from those that were at one time or another influenced by Cluny.

For the tenth and the early eleventh centuries, Fleury, Farfa, and La Cava, as well as the abbeys directed by William of Volpiano are good illustrations of monasteries that were influenced by Cluny but retained their independence. William became a monk at Cluny in 987 under Abbot Majolus. The abbot had made an indelible impression on William when on his journey to and from Italy he had stayed at Lucedio, William's own monastery. William's biographer, Rodulf Glaber, reports that the young monk refused the ordination as deacon by the bishop of Vercelli, both diocesan and proprietary lord of Lucedio, because the bishop had demanded the customary oath of obedience. Ancient ecclesiastical traditions prohibited oaths for monks, and William upheld that tradition at any cost. Three years after William's arrival at Cluny, Bishop Bruno of Langres entrusted him with the reform of the abbey of Saint Bénigne at Dijon. He accomplished the task with great success. William's energy as well as his asceticism spread his fame, and the bishop of Metz soon approached him with the request to reform several monasteries in his diocese, monasteries that had been renewed earlier under the influence of Gorze. Among them were, besides Gorze herself, Saint Evre and Moyenmoutier. The duke of Normandy eventually appointed William abbot of Fécamp. William's overly strict observance of the Rule of Saint Benedict and of the customs of Cluny led to his nickname: William *super regulam*. The numerous charters and privileges that William acquired for Fruttuaria, his foundation near Vercelli on allodial or hereditary family property, are possibly the best indicators for his own perspective on reform. To avoid any kind of proprietary claims and simony, William obtained full exemption for Fruttuaria from the diocesan bishop, as well as full independence from all monasteries. The successor of an abbot at Fruttuaria was to be designated by the abbot himself and was to assume his office eventually through self-investiture. William's wise foresight and indefatigable efforts achieved these aims at a time (1015–22/25) of fuller and more extensive exemption of Cluny, notwithstanding the strong influence Cluny exerted on William *super regulam*.

How, then, did the congregation of Cluny develop, and what was the nature of the relationship between the abbey and its dependent houses? From the foundation of Cluny in 909 its abbot held an abbatiate, meaning that he was simultaneously abbot of several houses, a typical situation in the Carolingian period, when many abbots and lay abbots were in charge or in possession of more than one abbey at the same time. Einhard (d. 840), Charlemagne's biographer, is a well-known example. Under Louis the Pious he presided over several famous abbeys. The early abbots of Cluny usually reformed monasteries by introducing the observance of Cluniac customs. In some instances they acted as abbot of the monastery they were reforming. For example, when Odo was the abbot of Cluny, he remained for a time as abbot of Fleury, a royal abbey he reformed at the request of Count Elisiardus but against the will of its community of monks. Odo made no attempt to subordinate Fleury to Cluny, however, as illustrated by the 938 privilege that he obtained for the abbey from Pope Leo VII. The document indicates that Odo merely tried to secure his reforms and to give them permanence. Fleury remained a royal abbey with the right of free abbatial elections. Like Cluny and Déols in 931, Fleury was now also licensed to reform other monasteries. By the time of Abbot Hugh (1049–109) a system of subordination had finally developed. In theory, at least, every monastery that had been reformed by the abbots of Cluny became a priory dependent on Cluny. The prior at the head of each of these communities was appointed by the abbot of Cluny,

who could also depose him. Novices in the priories made profession to
the abbot at Cluny, who was thus directly responsible for all the monks.
The monks in turn owed obedience to Cluny's abbot. Some scholars suggest that this close relationship between the monks of dependent monasteries and the abbot of Cluny is analogous to the secular feudal system,
but in fact the ties between monks and abbots had nothing in common
with feudal ties. These monastic bonds were much closer than were the
links between lord and vassal; the vassal, for example, could simultaneously enter into several relationships. Priories under Cluny "were freed
from the feudal nexus and became part of a tight monarchical organization, far superior to the loose relations of the feudal system" (Hoffmann).
The following exceptions to the basic rule of subordination should be
noted:

1. Several well-known abbeys maintained the legal status of abbeys,
    but their abbot was appointed by Cluny and their houses adopted
    Cluniac *consuetudines*.
2. Other abbeys kept the right to elect their abbot, but the abbot-
    elect had to be approved by Cluny.
3. Some abbeys preserved their complete independence but observed
    the same customs and liturgies as Cluny. Thus they maintained
    loose spiritual bonds with Cluny.
4. Several abbeys were under the rule of an abbot who had been a
    monk at Cluny but who no longer had any links to it; these abbots
    might, however, have introduced some Cluniac customs.

Not all monasteries associated with Cluny necessarily enjoyed the same
independence as did Cluny regarding both secular and diocesan authority.
In short, even at the time of Abbot Hugh, when the ties between Cluny and
subordinated, reformed monasteries had been clothed in legal forms, it
cannot be said that Cluny constituted a monastic order transcending diocesan boundaries.

The exaggerated emphasis on Cluny's drive for exemption often results
in a one-sided description of Cluny as an opponent of the episcopacy and
of the prevailing mode of societal organization, usually all too briefly
identified simply as "feudal." As a matter of fact, Cluny enjoyed excellent
relationships with the nobility, the class of origin for most of the monks
at Cluny. Episcopal support for Cluny was essential for the growth of
the abbey and contributed greatly to the abbey's renown. The bishops of
Christian Europe, from Spain and Italy to France, Germany, and En-

gland, certainly did not think of Cluny as an institution that was fundamentally opposed to their interests. The collaboration of Cluniacs with kings and popes, with the nobility, and with the episcopacy, and Cluny's customary practice of diligent acquisition of proprietary churches illustrate how well Cluny fit in as part of the contemporary society without, however, allowing itself to become an indistinguishable component. Cluny obtained its independence from secular authority at the very time of its foundation when the abbey was also placed under papal protection. It is nonetheless true that the right of free abbatial elections, provided for in the same charter, at first contributed far more to Cluny's development than did papal protection. The earlier abbots understood the term *free elections* as their right to designate a worthy successor and thus to prevent any decline in reforming zeal or the strictness of life and morals. The later protection of Cluny by kings and popes eventually led to Cluny's complete exemption from diocesan authority through the papacy. The final step in the process was the privilege of 1024 bestowed by Pope John XIX on Cluny to terminate all the bitter disputes and struggles between the abbey and the bishop of Mâcon, who had lost large portions of his diocesan income because of Cluny's partial exemption.

Pope Gregory V confirmed in a privilege of 998 that no bishop or priest was permitted to confer ordinations or to celebrate mass at Cluny without an invitation from the abbot. Cluniac monks could be ordained by any bishop selected by the abbot, and the monks in their turn could select the bishop who was to consecrate their abbot. Pope John XIX completely suspended the spiritual rights of the bishop of Mâcon at Cluny, when he confirmed in the privilege of 1024 for Abbot Odilo that no bishop or priest could excommunicate or anathematize the Burgundian abbey itself, and that henceforth all monks of Cluny were exclusively under the jurisdiction of the Apostolic See. At the council of Anse of 1025 the archbishops of Vienne and Lyon vainly protested these regulations as contradicting canon law. In 1027, when Odilo was in Rome for the coronation of Emperor Conrad II, John XIX reconfirmed his privilege of three years earlier, emphasizing that Cluny was spiritually subject to Rome alone. Cluny's evolution under papal protection, from independence from secular authorities to an exemption from diocesan authority, was sometimes held up by reformers of the second half of the eleventh century as an example of the potential political evolution of any church that depended directly and exclusively on the papacy. Still, the reference to Cluny and the abbey's meteoric rise was only one more argument in the struggle for the liberty of the church. From the time of Leo IX on, but especially under Pope Gregory VII, the papacy claimed this liberty primarily on the basis of papal primacy and independence from the laity, as depicted in collections of canon law.

The expansion of Cluny reflects both widespread esteem for the abbey and widespread concern for reform. Pious laymen or bishops might even transfer to Cluny abbeys that either no longer were or never had been in need of reform, in some instances against the wishes of the monks who rose to a spirited defense of their own customs. At the time of William of Volpiano (d. 1031), Richard of Saint Vanne (d. 1046), and Richard's disciple, Poppo of Stablò (d. 1046), such attitudes brought about lateral connections between Cluniac and Lotharingian reforms. Such intermingling is behind the monastic affiliations described by Hallinger as the "Lotharingian mixed observance" and "Young Gorze." There continued to be noticeable differences, however, between Cluniac and the Lotharingian-German reform: autonomy of individual houses under the latter contrasted with the Cluniac system of priories. Furthermore, the protection by episcopal and royal proprietary lords provided the security in the Lotharingian reform that was provided in the other system by the exemption of Cluny and Cluny's subjection to Rome. There were also differences in habit, in the monastic schools, and in the liturgies that had partially replaced manual labor at Cluny. Primarily because of completely different political circumstances—the dissolving of all public central institutions in France contrasts with the strengthening of royal authority under the Ottonians in the East—Carolingian traditions that had been the original starting point in both East and West continued to be influential only in the East Frankish kingdom.

England, too, participated in this monastic renewal and expressed the renewal of ecclesiastical law side by side with the new piety of the tenth century. The Danish wars in England had nearly extinguished all trace of monastic life. Burgundian and Lotharingian elements of reform intermingled with native English monastic traditions to produce the famous flowering of late Anglo-Saxon monasticism. Saint Dunstan (d. 988) founded a new community at Glastonbury and became abbot there before 940. Dunstan was later bishop of Worcester, bishop of London, and from 960 archbishop of Canterbury. In 956 Dunstan spent some time in exile at the abbey of Saint Peter at Ghent, where he became familiar with Lotharingian ideas of reform that had been implanted there by Gerard of Brogne. Cluny's influence was felt in England earlier still. It reached the island nation indirectly through Fleury, where Archbishop Oda of Canterbury (d. 958) had been a monk. Oda's nephew Oswald spent several years at Fleury, as did Dunstan's most brilliant pupil, Aethelwold, who was interested in Fleury's customs. Oswald himself, however, was needed in England, where King Eadred (946–55) had entrusted him with the renewal of Abingdon abbey. He could therefore send only one of his pupils, Osgar, to Fleury. The best-known document of the English reform is the *Regularis Concordia,* committed to writing in 970 at the council of Winchester. Its author was Aethelwold in consultation with monks from Ghent and Fleury, both specifically named in the document.

4. Monastic Reform and the Eremitical Movement in Italy

During the ninth century, Italy, like the countries to the north of the Alps, suffered from invasions by Saracens and Magyars. There was little left that could be described as monastic life, and so in Italy, too, reform was attempted. In France, Burgundy, Lotharingia, and Germany reformers built on the foundations laid by Benedict of Aniane in the Carolingian period. In Italy, however, Benedict's reforms had never been firmly established. There were other differences between Italy and the north as well, in the strength of anchorites, and in the political situations. Anarchy was worse in Italy than in France and the border regions of Burgundy and Lorraine. Insecurity and uncertainty abounded. Lombard kingship in the north of the peninsula was exceedingly weak. From the death of Emperor Louis II in 875 to the coronation of Otto I in 951, the crown of Pavia enticed the rulers of Burgundy and Vienne, as well as the margraves of Ivrea. When Emperor Charles the Bald granted bishops the right in 876 to represent imperial authority side by side with ecclesiastical authority, northern Italian bishops began to expand their towns into minuscule states by conquering the neighboring countryside, the contado. Central Italy was dominated by the margraves of Tuscany and the great Roman families of the Crescentians and the Tusculans. Further to the south, Italy was divided into the duchies of Spoleto and Benevento, the principate of Salerno, the county of Capua, and the Greek themes of Calabria and Langobardia, from which the Byzantines had expelled the Arabs. Sicily had been conquered by an Islamic dynasty from North Africa and remained firmly under its control.

The travels of the abbots of Cluny in the tenth century had affected Italian cenobitism. Once even Gorze had been asked for help with monastic reform in Rome. Although we should not underestimate Cluny's influence on Italy, this influence was often asserted indirectly, at least before the second half of the eleventh century. The personal examples of the abbots of Cluny inspired local reformers to restore Italian monasteries and to make them once again into dignified centers of cenobitical life.

The first representatives of the Christian monastic ideal were the hermits of the Egyptian desert. Their ideal of strict asceticism and complete devotion to a life of penance and prayer in total solitude remained very influential in the eastern regions of the ancient Roman Empire as well as in southern Italy. Parts of this region were Byzantine into the late eleventh century, and even today a dialect derived from Greek is spoken in remote areas. The monastic communities of Calabria and Apulia, living most often as anchorites following the regulations of Basil the Great (330–79), increased in number during the ninth and tenth centuries. The newcomers were monks and hermits who had fled the Muslims and the wars in Sicily and in the deep south. The monastic heptarchy of Mercurion came to be particularly influential. Nilus, the most famous representative of this Italo-Byzantine monasticism, spent his formative years in its monasteries and retreated to a nearby cave in about 940 to begin his life as a hermit. His disciple and biographer, Bartholomew the Younger, showed that Nilus devoted his ascetic life entirely to prayer, penance, and the study of the Scriptures and the church fathers. When Saracen invasions forced him to flee the vicinity of the Mercurion, Nilus founded a monastery on family property in the vicinity of his birthplace, Rossano, but refused to accept the dignity of archbishop of Rossano. Renewed Saracen attacks eventually brought Nilus to Campania, where he built the monastery of Valleluce on land ceded to him by Abbot Aligerno of Montecassino. But his longing for yet greater solitude eventually drove him into the area near Gaeta where he founded the community of Serperi. The hermit made a profound impression on Emperor Otto III and his court. Was it mutual, we may wonder, for to please the emperor, Nilus briefly led the Roman abbey of Tre Fontane. Nilus later founded Grottaferrata, and he died there in 1004.

Because of Nilus, Greek aspects of Italian monasticism once again became prominent. Nilus sought to follow in the footsteps of the desert fathers of the third century. Another famous recluse, Romuald, was also inspired by their writings. A son of the duke of Ravenna, Romuald entered the abbey of Sant'Apollinare in Classe around 972 at the age of about twenty in order to do penance for a bloody crime committed by his father. Monastic life at Sant'Apollinare, however, did not satisfy Romuald, and he left to join a hermit in the marshes of Venice. In 978 Romuald entered the Catalonian monastery of Cuxa together with the hermit, his teacher, and several noble Venetians. He stayed on for about ten years and then returned to Italy. On his constant wanderings through central Italy, Romuald founded several monasteries and hermitages, among them Valdicastro and Camaldoli. Camaldoli, established around

1010 in the vicinity of Arezzo, is situated on a hilltop. It was conceived as a desert in accordance with Egyptian precedents and consisted of separate cells in the midst of a large area that was surrounded by a wall. The monks lived in their cells but met at certain hours for communal prayers and for meals in the church and in the refectory. Two years later, in 1012, Romuald constructed a cenobitical monastery below the eremus that followed a strictly interpreted Rule of Saint Benedict. Monks from the lower monastery could become members of the eremitical community, but a stay in the lower monastery was not a precondition for acceptance as a hermit. The lower monastery was not really seen as a place to prepare for the eremitical life; instead, it was set up to protect the hermitage. The monastery took care of administrative and economic chores to spare the hermits the distractions of a busy world.

Romuald died in 1027 at Valdicastro without leaving behind a written rule. His work was not everywhere permanent, but nonetheless it was of singular importance. He united both branches of monasticism, eremitism and cenobitism, in a single institution under a single prior, who had to be a hermit. Two generations after Romuald's death the traditions of Camaldoli were put down in writing as *Eremiticae Regulae* under Radulf (1074–89). The continued existence of Romuald's institutions was not really due to a written rule, however, but to the efforts of Peter Damian, who in 1034 entered another foundation of Romuald's, Fonte Avellana, and became its prior in 1043. Damian's reputation and his writings, among them one of the *vitae* of Romuald, furthered the cause of Fonte Avellana and of Camaldoli just as the outstanding character of the great abbots of Cluny had done earlier for the Burgundian abbey.

Shortly after Romuald's death, John Gualberti, born at Florence in 995, entered the Florentine abbey of San Miniato. Driven from the abbey because of quarrels with its abbot and the bishop of Florence, both of whom he accused of simony, John reached Camaldoli and eventually, in 1036, Vallombrosa. At Vallombrosa he joined two other hermits living there to form a cenobitical community that would lead a common life in accordance with the Rule of Saint Benedict. The Rule was interpreted with a degree of strictness that certainly exceeded the intention of Benedict. The monks lived in individual cells in accordance with the customs of Camaldoli and withdrew to a neighboring mountain, later called Paradisino, in search of solitude. The community of John Gualberti grew very quickly; most of the monks who joined came from San Miniato. At the request of Emperor Henry II, Bishop Rudolph of Paderborn dedicated the first church of the community. In 1051 Cardinal Humbert of Silva Candida consecrated a new church built in stone. John Gualberti followed the customs of Camaldoli when he erected a cenobitical monastery, charged with economic duties, at Vallombrosa. The inhabitants of this monastery were called *conversi* but differed from the *conversi* of Cluny in that their status seems to have been akin to that of the later lay brothers. Although the question of the origin of the institution of the *conversi* has not yet been fully answered, we do know that the *conversi* of Vallombrosa differed greatly from the old type of *conversi* of Cluny who were monks, as were the *nutriti*, the men who had grown up at the abbey from infancy.

The powerful religious sentiments that stirred up monastic reform throughout Europe also led to a revival of canon law. The deep piety of the proprietary lords of monasteries, usually nobles, of the bishops, and of the monks found a ready response among other population groups and eventually encompassed a renewal of the papacy under Emperor Henry III. The papacy was subsequently to emerge as the leader of reform in the church at large.

Bibliography for Chapter 1

Collected Papers

Chiesa, diritto e ordinamento della "societas christiana" nei secoli XI e XII. Atti della nona settimana internazionale di studio, Mendola 1983. Milan, 1986.

L'Eremitismo in occidente nei secoli XI e XII. Atti della seconda settimana internazionale di studio, Mendola 1962. Miscellanea del Centro di studi medioevali, no. 4. Milan, 1965.

Il monachesimo nell'alto medioevo e la formazione della civiltà occidentale. Settimane di studio del Centro italiano di studi sull'alto medioevo. Spoleto, 1957.

La vita commune del clero nei secoli XI e XII. Atti della settimana di studio, Mendola 1959. Miscellanea del Centro di studi medioevali, no. 3. 2 vols. Milan, 1962.

General

Amann, Emile, and A. Dumas. *L'eglise au pouvoir des laïques (888–1057).* Histoire de l'Eglise, vol. 7. Paris, 1948.

Constable, Giles. "Eremitical Forms of Monastic Life." In *Istituzioni monastiche e istituzioni canonicali.* Atti della settima settimana internazionale di studi medioevali Mendola, 239–64. Milan, 1980.

Geary, Patrick J. *Furta Sacra: Thefts of Relics in the Central Middle Ages.* Princeton, 1978.

Hallinger, Kassius. "Woher kommen die Laienbrüder?" *Analecta S. Ord. Cisterciensis* (1956):1–104.

Hauck, Albert. *Kirchengeschichte Deutschlands* 3:343–88, 443–515. Berlin, 1958.

Knowles, David. *From Pachomius to Ignatius: A Study in the Constitutional History of the Religious Orders.* Oxford, 1966.

Molitor, Rafael. *Aus der Rechtgeschichte benediktinischer Verbände.* Münster, 1928–33.

Noble, Thomas F. X. *The Republic of St. Peter: The Birth of the Papal State, 680–825.* Philadelphia, 1984. For the later period of the papal states see Peter Partner, *The Lands of St. Peter: The Papal State in the Middle Ages and the Early Renaissance* (Berkeley and Los Angeles, 1972).

Schmid, Karl. *Gebetsgedenken und adliges Selbstverständnis im Mittelalter: Ausgewählte Beiträge. Festgabe zu seinem 60. Geburtstag.* Sigmaringen, 1983.

Tomek, Ernst. *Studien zur Reform der deutschen Klöster im 11. Jahrhundert, I: Die Frühreform.* Graz, 1910.

Voigt, Karl. *Die karolingische Klosterpolitik und der Niedergang des westfränkischen Königtums.* Stuttgart, 1917.

Werner, Ernst. *Die gesellschaftlichen Grundlagen der Klosterreform im 11. Jahrhundert.* Berlin, 1953. For a response to this Marxist interpretation see Cinzio Violante, "Il monachesimo cluniacense di fronte al mondo politico ed ecclesiastico (secoli X e XI)," in *Convegni del centro di studi sulla spiritualità medioevale,* vol. 2 (Todi, 1960); reprinted in C. Violante, *Studi sulla Cristianità medioevale* (Milan, 1962).

Wisplinghoff, Erich. *Untersuchungen zur frühen Geschichte der Abtei St. Maximin bei Trier.* Mainz, 1970.

Wollasch, Joachim. *Mönchtum des Mittelalters zwischen Kirche und Welt.* Munich, 1973.

Viking Invasions

Ewig, Eugen. "Die Kirche im Abendland vom Tode Ludwigs des Frommen bis zum Ende der Karolingerzeit." In *The Church in the Age of Feudalism,* 144–78.

Fleming, Robin. "Monastic Lands and England's Defence in the Viking Age." *EHR* 100 (1985):247–65.

D'Haenens, Albert. *Les invasions normandes en Belgique au IXe siècle: Le phènomène et sa répercussion dans l'historiographie médiévale.* Louvain, 1967.

———. *Les invasions normandes, une catastrophe?* Questions d'histoire. Paris, 1970.

Jäschke, Kurt-Ulrich. *Die Anglonormannen.* Stuttgart, 1981.

Lawson, M. K. "The Collection of Danegeld and Heregeld in the Reign of Aethelred II and Cnut." *EHR* 99 (1984):721–38.

Lot, Ferdinand. *Le tribut aux Normands et l'Eglise de France au IXe siècle.* Paris, 1924.

Musset, Lucien. *Les invasions: Le second assaut contre l'Europe chrétienne.* Paris, 1965.

Sawyer, Peter. *The Age of the Vikings.* London, 1962.

Steenstrup, Johannes. *Les invasions normandes en France.* Paris, 1969.

Vogel, Walther. *Die Normannen und das fränkische Reich bis zur Gründung der Normandie (799–911).* Heidelberg, 1906.

Zettel, Horst. *Das Bild der Normannen und der Normanneneinfälle in west-*

fränkischen, ostfränkischen und angelsächsischen Quellen des 8. bis 11. Jahrhunderts. Munich, 1977.

Ecclesiastical Constitutions, the Proprietary Church, and Monastic Exemption

Appelt, Hans. "Die Anfänge des päpstlichen Schutzes." *MIÖG* 62 (1954):212ff.

Feine, Hans Erich. *Kirchliche Rechtsgeschichte.* 5th ed. Cologne, 1972. Especially pp. 160–82 (proprietary church) and pp. 205–13 (benefices).

————. "Kirchleihe und kirchliches Beneficium nach italienischen Rechtsquellen des frühen Mittelalters." *Historisches Jahrbuch* 72 (1953):101–11.

Hirsch, Hans. "Untersuchungen zur Geschichte des päpstlichen Schutzes." *MIÖG* 54 (1941):363–433.

————. *Die Klosterimmunität seit dem Investiturstreit.* Cologne, 1967.

Kempf, Friedrich, and Josef Jungmann. "Constitution of the Church, Worship, Pastoral Care, and Piety: 700 to 1050." In *The Church in the Age of Feudalism,* 258–350.

Lemarignier, Jean-François. "Le monachism et l'encadrement religieux des campagnes du royaume de France situées au nord de la Loire, de la fin du Xe à la fin du XI siècle." In *Le istituzioni ecclesiastiche della "societas christiana" dei secoli XI–XII: Diocesi, pievi e parrochie, Mendola 1974,* 357–94. Milan, 1978.

Mollat, Guy. "La restitution des églises privées au patrimoine écclésiastique en France du IXe au XIe siècle." *Revue historique du droit français et étranger* 67 (1949):399–423.

Schwarz, Wilhelm. "Jurisdicio und Condicio: Eine Untersuchung zu den Privilegia libertatis der Klöster." *ZRG Kan. Abt.* 45 (1959):34–98.

Semmler, Jakob. "Traditio und Königsschutz." *ZRG Kan. Abt.* 45 (1959):1–33.

Stutz, Ulrich. "The Proprietary Church as an Element of Mediaeval Germanic Ecclesiastical Law." In *Medieval Germany,* 35–70.

Szaivert, Wilhelm. "Die Entstehung und Entwicklung der Klosterexemtion bis zum Ausgang des 11. Jahrhunderts." *MIÖG* 59 (1951):265–98.

Monastic Reform

Hallinger, Kassius, O.S.B. *Gorze-Kluny: Studien zu den monastischen Lebensformen und Gegensätzen im Hochmittelalter.* With an introduction by Heinrich Schmidinger. 2 vols. 2d ed. Graz, 1971. The most important review of Hallinger's magisterial study is by Theodor Schieffer, "Cluniazensische oder Gorzische Reformbewegung?" *Archiv für mittelrheinische Kirchengeschichte* 4 (1952):24–44. This paper has been reprinted in Helmut Richter, ed., *Cluny: Beiträge zu Gestalt und Wirkung der cluniazensischen Reform,* 60–90, Wege der Forschung 241 (Darmstadt, 1975).

Sackur, Ernst. *Die Cluniacenser in ihrer kirchlichen und allgemeingeschichtlichen Wirksamkeit bis zur Mitte des 11. Jahrhunderts.* 2 vols. Darmstadt, 1965. Fundamental for the reform in general.

Schreiber, Georg. *Gemeinschaften des Mittelalters: Recht und Verfassung, Kult und Frömmigkeit.* Münster, 1948.

Lotharingia and Germany

Büttner, Heinrich. "Verfassungsgeschichte und lothringische Klosterreform." In *Aus Mittelalter und Neuzeit: Gerhard Kallen zum 70. Geburtstag,* edited by J. Engel and H. M. Klinkenberg, 17–27. Bonn, 1957.

Bulst, Neithart. *Untersuchungen zu den Klosterreformen Wilhelms von Dijon 962–1031.* Bonn, 1973.

Dauphin, Hubert. *Le bienheureux Richard, abbé de Saint-Vanne de Verdun (+1046).* Louvain, 1946.

Kaminsky, K. H. "Zur Gründung von Fruttuaria durch den Abt Wilhelm von Dijon." *ZKG* 77 (1966):238–67.

Revue bénédictine. Vol. 70. 1960. Contains the proceedings in honor of the nine hundredth anniversary of the death of Gérard de Brogne. Particularly important is the article by J. M. de Smet, "Recherches critiques sur la Vita Gerardi abbatis Broniensis," 5–61.

Wühr, Wilhelm. "Die Wiedergeburt Montecassinos unter seinem ersten Reform-abt Richer von Niederaltaich (†1055)." *Studi Gregoriani* 3 (1948):369–450.

Cluny

See also "Monastic Reform," above.

Antonelli, G. "L'Opera di Odone di Cluny in Italia." *Benedictina* 4 (1950): 19–40.

Constable, Giles. "Monasticism, Lordship, and Society in the Twelfth-Century Hesbaye: Five Documents on the Foundation of the Cluniac Priory of Bertrée." *Traditio* 33 (1977): 159–224.

———. *Cluniac Studies.* London, 1982. Collected papers.

Hallinger, Kassius. "Kluny's Bräuche zur Zeit Hugos des Grossen (1049–1109), Prolegomena zur Neuherausgabe des Bernhard und Udalrich von Kluny." *ZRG Kan. Abt.* 45 (1959):99–140.

Hourlier, Jacques. *Saint Odilon, Abbé de Cluny.* Louvain, 1964.

Hunt, Noreen. *Cluny Under Saint Hugh.* London, 1967.

Richter, Helmut, ed. *Cluny, Beiträge zu Gestalt und Wirkung der Cluniazensischen Reform,* Wege der Forschung 241 (Darmstadt, 1975). Contains a full bibliography.

Schmid, Karl, and Joachim Wollasch. "Die Gemeinschaft der Lebenden und Verstorbenen in Zeugnissen des Frühmittelalters." *Frühmittelalterliche Studien* 1 (1967):365–405.

Schwarzmaier, Hans. "Das Kloster S. Benedetto di Polirone in seiner cluniacensischen Umwelt." In *Adel und Kirche,* edited by Josef Fleckenstein and Karl Schmid. Freiburg, 1968.

Sitwell, Gerard. *St. Odo of Cluny.* London and New York, 1958.

Tellenbach, Gerhard, ed. *Neue Forschungen über Cluny und die Cluniacenser.* Freiburg, 1959. Includes very important articles by H. Diener, H. E. Mager, and J. Wollasch.

Valous, Guy de. *Le monachisme clunisien des origines au XVe siècle.* 2 vols. 2d ed. Paris, 1970.

Wollasch, Joachim. "Qu'a signifié Cluny pour l'abbaye de Moissac?" *Annales du Midi* 75 (1963):345–52.

Monastic Renewal in Italy

Boesch Gajano, Sofia. "Storia e tradizione vallombrosane." *Bullettino dell'Istituto storico italiano per il medio evo* 76 (1964):99–215.
Cappelli, B. "Il Mercurion." *Archivo storico per la Calabria e Lucania* 25 (1956):43–62.
Ferrari, Guy. *Early Roman Monasteries.* Vatican City, 1957.
Franke, Wilhelm. *Romuald von Camaldoli und seine Reformtätigkeit zur Zeit Ottos III.* Berlin, 1913.
Guillou, André. "Il monachesimo greco in Italia meridionale e in Sicilia." In *L'Eremitismo* (see above, "Collected Papers"), 355–79.
Hamilton, Bernhard. "The Monastic Revival in Tenth-Century Rome." *Studia Monastica* 4 (1962):35–68.
Kurze, Wilhelm. "Campus Malduli, Die Frühgeschichte Camaldolis." *Quellen und Forschungen aus italienischen Archiven und Bibliotheken* 44 (1964): 1–34.
Mattei Cerasoli, L. "La Badia di Cava e i monasteri greci della Calabria superiore." *Archivio storico per la Calabria e la Lucania* 8 (1938):167–85, 265–85; also 9 (1939):279–318.
Penco, Gregorio, O.S.B. *Storia del monachesimo in Italia dalle origini alla fine del Medio Evo.* Vols. 1 and 2. Rome, 1961 and 1968.

Monastic Renewal in England

Bethurum, Dorothy. *The Homilies of Wulfstan.* Oxford, 1957.
Dauphin, Hubert. "Le renouveau monastique en Angleterre au Xe siècle et ses rapports avec la réforme de Saint Gérard de Brogne." *Revue bénédictine* 70 (1960):177–96.
Deanesly, Margaret. "The Anglo-Saxon Church and the Papacy." In *The English Church and the Papacy in the Middle Ages,* edited by C. H. Lawrence and David Knowles, 29–62. London, 1965.
————. *Sidelights on the Anglo-Saxon Church.* London, 1962.
Gatch, Milton McC. *Preaching and Theology in Anglo-Saxon England: Aelfric and Wulfstan.* Toronto and Buffalo, 1977.
Godfrey, John. *The Church in Anglo-Saxon England.* Cambridge, 1962.
Jost, Karl. *Wulfstanstudien.* Bern, 1950.
Stenton, Sir Frank M. *Anglo-Saxon England.* 3d ed. Oxford, 1971.
Whitelock, Dorothy. "Archbishop Wulfstan, Homilist and Statesman." *Transactions of the Royal Historical Society,* 4th ser., 24 (1942):25–45.

Monastic Renewal in Other Countries

Bishko, G. Julian. "Salvius of Albelda and Frontier Monasticism in Tenth-Century Navarre." *Speculum* 23 (1948):559–90.

————. "The Cluniac Priories of Galicia and Portugal: Their Acquisition and Administration." *Studia Monastica* 7 (1965): 305–56.

Defourneaux, Marcelin. *Les Français en Espagne aux XIe et XIIe siècle*. Paris, 1949.

Lemarignier, Jean-François. "Structures monastiques et structures politiques dans la France de la fin du Xe et des débuts du XIe siècle." In *Il monachesimo* (see above, "Collected Papers"), 357–400.

Mundò, Anscario. "Moissac, Cluny et les mouvements monastiques de l'est des Pyrenées du Xe au XIIe siècles." *Annales du Midi* 75 (1963): 551–70.

Schmid, Paul. "Die Entstehung des Marseiller Kirchenstaates." *Archiv für Urkundenforschung* 10 (1928): 176–207, and 11 (1930): 138–52.

Segl, Peter. *Königtum und Klosterreform in Spanien: Untersuchungen über die Cluniacenserklöster in Kastilien-Leon vom Beginn des 11. bis zur Mitte des 12. Jahrhunderts*. Kallmünz, 1974.

Valous, Guy de. "Les monastères et la pénétration française en Espagne du XIe au XIIIe siècle." *Revue Mabillon* 30 (1940): 77–97.

CHAPTER 2

The German Emperors
and the Legacy of Rome

1. The Monarchy Under the Ottonian and Early Salian Dynasties

Although agriculture predominated and trade assumed increasing importance (as indicated by the discovery of coin hoards), the landed and military nobility, which counted the clergy among its members, gave tenth- and eleventh-century society the aristocratic imprint that sources reflect to the exclusion of almost anything else. In East Francia, where allodial or hereditary property continued to be important, feudal ties—often loosely described as the feudal system—constituted only one kind of link in the societal order. In this, Germany was set apart from many regions in France—and especially from England after 1066—where feudalism had gained general acceptance.

The term *feudalism*, following the classical definition by F. L. Ganshof, denotes the grant of income-producing property (usually land), the benefice, by the lord and protector (*dominus, senior;* French: *seigneur*) in return for the promise or oath of fealty by the vassal (*vasallus* or *homo*). After the late eleventh and early twelfth centuries, the oath of fealty was given in the ceremony known as *hominium* or *homagium*—whence *homage* in French and English. The promise encompassed not only loyalty or fidelity (*fidelitas,* as among the warband of Tacitus), but also advice and aid (*consilium* and *auxilium*), that is, a specific service. It was based on reciprocity, and nonobservance by either party was a legitimate cause for feud. Benefices, more commonly known as fiefs, were generally granted to the warlike sectors of the populace, not excluding peasants with even the smallest allodial property. The lord formally invested the vassal with the fief in the "investiture ceremony" (the name dates to the late eleventh century), usually by handing him a staff, sword, or spear as a symbol of the transfer. Such feudal ceremonial form and substance was also associated with initiation into office and was the lifeblood of politics. The eventual hereditability of the fief, repeatedly rejected by the lord, but again and again exacted by the vassal, makes plausible the claim that "feudalism in conjunction with public service could strengthen as well as endanger the public order" (T. Schieffer).

Peasants dependent on the great landowners made up the majority of the lower social classes. By the middle of the eleventh century, a new class of ministerials, or servants, who provided armed protection for their lord, had begun to differentiate itself from the peasantry. In areas of Germany where the manorial system prevailed—as it did not in Saxony and Bavaria, for example—unfree peasants were subject to customary manorial law, were counted among the *familia* of a secular or ecclesiastical landowner, and were represented through him to the public authorities. The oldest known record of German manorial customaries is that of Bishop Burchard I of Worms (d. 1025). Although the term *customary* implies serfdom, or villeinage, it is also described as something more akin to a contractual relationship between lord and peasant (Mitteis). This is one reason why European peasants could derive special benefits from the economic expansion of the eleventh and twelfth centuries.

It is against this background that the duchies and the monarchy in Germany evolved. By 900, the West Frankish kingdom had splintered into some thirty independent territories with at best only tenuous connections to the disputed crown. The king's influence had reached its nadir. His landed property and his offices, earlier granted as fiefs, had passed permanently into the hands of the noble families. Promises of service and fealty had become meaningless. The families, in pursuit of their own dynastic ambitions, mediatized the former royal vassals, the *vassi dominici*. In Lotharingia, the situation developed along similar lines. But this did not happen in the East Frankish kingdom, the later Germany. Here, instead of the usual plethora of independent lordships, four duchies evolved in the late ninth and early tenth centuries. The duchies, Bavaria, Franconia, Saxony-Thuringia, and Swabia, took root in the ancient tribal structures native to their regions, but they neither embraced as a whole nor confined themselves to one single or particular tribe or stem (Tellenbach). A stem was wont to crystallize around the power and authority of the most influential duke or count. He in turn conferred upon it the mantle of political unity. The dukes, typically not members of these stems or tribes themselves, all traced their lineage to the Carolingian nobility and were highly likely to call the Carolingian rulers kin and to have served them as lord marchers in a similar position. They derived their authority from their preeminent position among the local magnates. Primacy was based on landed property, military success, and legacies of high office. The preeminence of the Liudolfings in Saxony and of the Luitpoldings in Bavaria was never in dispute. In Franconia and in Swabia, however, where noble Carolingian families were more numerous, this preeminence had to be established in bloody confrontations with rivals.

While the Carolingians were in power, the growing influence of the duchies could not yet make itself felt. Even the illegitimate Arnulf of Carinthia (887–99), and his minor son, Louis the Child (899–911), could still depose a duke at will by treating his incumbency as wholly dependent on the king. Even so, tribal affiliations, which had already been a factor under Louis the German, could not be ignored altogether, at least not in a military context. The turning point came in 911 with the death of Louis the Child, the last of the East Frankish branch of the Carolingians reckoned through patrilineal descent, leaving a sole Carolingian, Charles the Simple (893–922, d. 929), to rule the West Frankish kingdom. The issue now turned on whether the tribes would recognize Charles or remain independent of the Western Franks. Lotharingia did recognize Charles, but the Eastern Franks did not. The dangers posed by the Magyar attacks in the East, linked to the realization that military aid would not be forthcoming from the king, are thought to have played the major role in the decision. Franks and Saxons elected Conrad I (911–18) of Franconia king in November 911, after his designation by Duke Otto of Saxony. The election was held in the Frankish town of Forchheim. Later, Bavaria and Swabia gave their assent. The consensus of historians is that Conrad was chosen because he was at least a Frank, if not a Carolingian. Moreover, his family could claim kinship with the last Carolingian through Uta, wife of Arnulf and mother of Louis the Child who had governed on the minor's behalf. The election should thus be interpreted as a conscious decision to continue Carolingian policy, albeit under a Frankish king. And Conrad I did see himself as heir to the Carolingian tradition embodied by Arnulf, not as first among a group of dukes with equal rights, his true position. But luck was not on King Conrad's side. He fought unsuccessfully for the restitution of Lotharingia and against the menace of the Hungarians. He provoked the enmity of the dukes, whose power he tried to break by every means at his disposal. But they, now finding strong backing within the stem—tribal assemblies now enter the record—were able to secure hereditary succession to ducal office, beginning with Arnulf of Bavaria. Conrad, however, did find support in the church. In 916, the synod of Hohenaltheim, attended by ecclesiastical representatives from all stem regions except Saxony, threatened with anathema anyone who attacked royal authority.

Conrad seems to have acknowledged the failure of his policies, for his designated successor was not his brother Eberhard but his most dangerous opponent, Duke Henry of Saxony. Upon the king's death, Eberhard faithfully delivered the royal insignia to the duke. Following brief negotiations, Henry was elected king by the Franks and Saxons in the Frankish town of Fritzlar. The Bavarians tried at first to have their duke, Arnulf, recognized. The Swabians and Lotharingians (in 920 once again independent from the West Frankish kingdom under Giselbert, who had been elected *princeps*) were also little inclined to go along with the election. Henry (919–36), however, showed wise restraint. He had not forgotten his own experience as duke of Saxony. By waiving ecclesiastical consecration and the royal prerogative of a palace chapel, he began by avoiding overt display of the qualitative differences between royal and ducal power. Unlike Conrad, Henry was also willing to acknowledge ducal rights, as long as these were seen as derived from the monarchy. Impressed also by Saxon might, Swabia declared its willingness to recognize Henry in 919. And after a victorious battle, Henry was also able to bring Bavaria into the fold in 921. Both Duke Burchard of Swabia (d. 926) and Duke Arnulf of Bavaria (d. 937) were invested with their duchies as vassals of the king. Henry used the occasion to reserve for himself the right to make the ecclesiastical appointments for Swabia but found himself constrained to confirm the protection of the Bavarian church to Arnulf. Such evidence suggests that Henry sought early to augment the power of the crown, notwithstanding his initial deemphasis of royal pomp.

A government which at its inception offered no more than "a faint reflection of Franco-Carolingian sacral and ministerial kingship" (T. Schieffer) was all the more surprising with its later successes. Indeed, Henry became the true founder of the medieval German empire. For despite initial rejection of certain aspects of royal tradition, Henry's politics soon moved in the old Carolingian, or Frankish, pattern. In 922/23 he revived the court-chapel as an institution and named Archbishop Heriger of Mainz arch-chaplain. A few years later, Henry took over Lotharingia, the region that was to become the fifth German duchy. The unification of Lotharingia with the East Frankish kingdom created a new balance of power and laid the territorial foundation for medieval Germany. Henry's farsighted politics and wise restraint are deservedly admired. The course of action leading to his celebrated victory over the Magyars, at the Unstrut River in 933, is one example. Securing the eastern borders took the establishment of a nine-year truce with the Hungarians in return for the payment of tribute, the construction of fortresses, and the creation of burgwards—probably based on Anglo-Saxon precedents under Alfred the Great (871–99)—in addition to a new emphasis on and revision of the ancient royal *heribannum,* the right of the king to call to arms.

A further example of the rewards of patience and wise management is Henry's Italian policy. The confused situation in Italy was strong inducement to intervene not only for the *regna* Provence and Burgundy but also for the duchies of Swabia, Bavaria, and Lotharingia. Ambition was nourished by the prospect of resurrecting Lothar's old middle kingdom, and of gaining the rich and fertile lands along with the crown. Any unification between Lotharingia, Burgundy, or one of the southern German duchies and Italy would have created a great new power block to the detriment of the existing balance of power. No king could therefore afford to lose sight of events in Italy. During much of Henry's reign the claim to Italy was contested between King Rudolph II (912–37) of Burgundy and Hugh of Provence (d. 948). Rudolf eventually recognized Hugh's rights to Italy in exchange for the cession of parts of lower Burgundy. Ruldolf, however, passed on the Holy Lance, or Constantine's Lance—to this day preserved in the imperial treasury of the Hofburg in Vienna—to King Henry I, probably at the diet (court) of Worms in 926. According to Luitprand of Cremona, courtier and ambassador of Otto I, the lance symbolized the right to Italy. It is clear that Henry valued the lance highly. He compensated Rudolf II with payments of gold and silver, as well as with the transfer of Basel and its environs. He also concluded a treaty of friendship with the Burgundian. When Henry met with Rudolf II in July 935 to renew the pact, a third king, Rudolf of West Francia (923–36), was included. The meeting of the three kings was a remarkable foreign policy feat for Henry which resulted in the consolidation of peace and stability in the West. It is conceivable that Henry planned an Italian campaign, with the imperial coronation as his aim, but death intervened in 936 at Memleben.

Henry had formally designated his son, Otto I (936–73), as successor at the diet of Erfurt in 936. An election confirmed the designation. Otto's brothers, Thankmar, the eldest, and Henry and Brun, the youngest, were excluded from the succession. It appears that the *regnum Francorum* was no longer considered family property that could be partitioned in accordance with Frankish custom but instead an indivisible public institution. The solemn coronation of Otto I provided immediate confirmation that the Saxon duke was heir to the Franco-Carolingian kingship tradition, owing largely to the restraint and purposeful government of Henry I. Significantly, the coronation took place at the Palace of Aachen, the intellectual and spiritual center of Charlemagne's realm, and the site of his tomb. The ceremony differentiated between the temporal and the spiritual aspects of the coronation: proclamation and acclamation by the representatives of the tribes occurred in the forecourt of the palace chapel, anointing and coronation by the clergy took place inside, followed by solemn enthronement and the coronation banquet. Otto was clad in Frankish robes. During the banquet, the dukes Giselbert of Lotharingia, Eberhard of Franconia, Herman of Swabia, and Arnulf of Bavaria did court service as vassals of the young king, serving as chamberlain, lord high steward, cupbearer, and marshal. The banquet thus symbolized recognition by the dukes of the kingship's claim to sovereignty in the sphere of public law.

The harmonious picture presented by the coronation festivities at Aachen, however, was deceptive. Two of the excluded brothers of Otto, Thankmar and Henry, as well as the dukes of Franconia, Bavaria, and Lotharingia in alliance with ecclesiastical princes, and even with the West Frankish Carolingian, King Louis IV, rebelled against Otto, at times singly, at other times in unison. The uprisings were in reaction to the expansion of royal authority under Henry I. The first crisis of 937–38 was followed by two more insurrections in 939 and and 953–55. Since Otto I emerged victorious from each, the fighting only resulted in a further strengthening of the kingship at the expense of the particularism of the nobility. The fate of Bavaria is an example. Duke Arnulf had designated his son Eberhard as successor, who was accordingly "elected" by the tribe and became duke of Bavaria upon his father's death in 937. When Eberhard refused to obey a summons to court, Otto deposed him and proceeded to appoint Arnulf's brother, Berchthold of Carinthia, to the Bavarian office, passing over Arnulf's other sons. Berchthold, however, had to cede to Otto the right to nominate all bishops and counts for Bavaria. Furthermore, the royal estates in the duchy were now once again administered on behalf of the royal house by a count palatine, who functioned as assistant to the duke. Otto's successes in Bavaria were not yet permanent, and their effectiveness, for example with the counts, is still disputed by historians, but they nevertheless demonstrate that the rebellion of Eberhard of Bavaria provided Otto with the opportunity to force recognition of royal authority over Bavaria. Like Henry I, Otto recognized the dukes, but not as hereditary princes of tribes, independent of the crown. In 948, after the death of Berchthold (947), for example, Otto raised his own brother Henry to the position of duke of Bavaria. It is also significant that Berchthold had accepted in principle the right of the king to fill episcopal vacancies, a right that the king had exercised in the other duchies since the time of Henry I.

The insurrection of 953–55 is generally ranked as equal in importance to the earlier uprisings, because it involved a family dispute. It was proof of the failure of Otto's policy to appoint as duke a member of his own family whenever possible as a means of strengthening his official power with the help of family ties. His eldest son, Liudolf, duke of Swabia since 950, and already designated to succeed his father in royal office, and his own brother Henry, duke of Bavaria since 948, were the chief instigators of the rebellion. Otto's son-in-law, Conrad of Lotharingia, also partici- pated. From among all of Otto's kin, only his youngest brother, Brun, chancellor since 940 and archbishop of Cologne since 953, remained faithful to the king. In the face of the Hungarian threat in the East, the rebels submitted to Otto in June/December 954. Still, the crisis gave the king pause. With renewed interest, he began to look once more toward the traditional cooperation between church and monarchy. Unable to pass on either office or property to direct descendants, the princes of the church tended to buttress royal power in counterweight to the particu- larist interests of the nobility.

The close cooperation between kings and ecclesiastics is often described as the "Ottonian-Salian imperial state-church system" (*Reichskirchen- system*), but this term is a misnomer. There was no institutionalized system in the technical sense, nor was the cooperation limited to the Ottonian and Salian dynasties. In France, too, as well as in England and what is today Spain, the ties between ruler and church were exceedingly close during the Middle Ages, this was equally so in the Byzantine Empire. Political circumstances in Germany during the tenth and eleventh centuries rendered this cooperation especially significant, however, for it coincided with the evolution of the monarchy. The most visible expression of the cooperation was the nomination of bishops and abbots by the king, a right long ago claimed by the Merovingian rulers. This customary royal right contradicted canonical stipulations requiring the clergy and people of a diocese to elect its bishop, but it was as little contested as the royal convocation and presidency at the Frankish national synods of the Me- rovingian and Carolingian periods. The king was no ordinary layman. In- stead, he was the ruler elected by God, who had not only the right but also the responsibility to intervene in the church, since protection and supervision of the church in the sense of lordship were part of the *minis- terium* God had bestowed on him.

Under Louis the Pious and his successors such militant and highly edu- cated churchmen as Hincmar of Reims attempted to check royal influence within the church. These efforts came to nothing when control over epis- copal nominations passed almost entirely into the hands of the French nobility with the disintegration of royal power and public authority. The results were similar to those described earlier for the monasteries. The first German kings, by contrast, succeeded in reclaiming their right to lead and protect the church, and to enforce this right in their struggles with the dukes. Throughout, they proceeded with the agreement and full support of the church, which, for ideological but also eminently practical reasons, preferred royal to ducal domination. Adhémar of Chabannes, writing in the early eleventh century, reported that Louis the Pious placed all abbeys (*abbatia*) under his authority to protect them against the bishops and a rapacious nobility. The king's intent was to create a royal church such as had not existed under Charlemagne, but he was also concerned with reform, for he closely coordinated his efforts with those of Benedict of Aniane.

In the tenth and eleventh centuries, both royal episcopal nominations and royal protection (*tuitio*) of monasteries were seen as defensive measures against intervention by the nobility, especially in the form of alienation of property. Royal protection was a privilege, described as *libertas* (liberty), and until the 1050s constituted the highest degree of *libertates* attainable by a monastic founder for his institution. After the reign of Otto I, papal protection is also occasionally mentioned in monastic privileges but functioned merely as a complement to the royal *defensio* or *tuitio*, "and even the *traditio* (transfer) of a monastery to St. Peter in Rome receded into the background compared to the royal rights of defense and dominion (*Herrschaft*)" (Semmler). Since the reforms of Louis the Pious, royal protection and immunity were closely linked and yielded rights for the ruler equal to those provided by proprietary monasteries, even if a monastery had not been built on royal lands. Monasteries that had obtained royal protection conditionally, that is, with reservations on behalf of the founder, were the exception. Royal proprietary rights over episcopal sees were more limited than those over monasteries, but after 976 all episcopal sees in the Empire were subordinate to the king.

As a consequence—and a most important one—royal wishes prevailed in episcopal and abbatial elections. Even if the privileges of an abbey confirmed the right to free abbatial elections, when an imperial monastery was involved, royal sanction of abbot or abbess was required. Late ninth-century sources for Western Francia mention that the king presented the successful candidate with his bishopric by handing the bishop-elect a symbolic staff, described by at least one source as a shepherd's crook. German kings, especially from the time of Otto I, strongly emphasized this ceremony, which later sources describe as investiture (Middle High German: *gewere*, grant). Under Henry III (1039–56) the episcopal ring was added to the crosier. Originally, the officiating metropolitan had given the ring to the candidate at the time of consecration. The formula "receive the church" (*accipe ecclesiam*) was used by the king in the investiture ceremony to indicate that the concepts of office and appurtenances were not differentiated. The new bishop or abbot on his part promised fealty, in Germany at this time usually by swearing an oath. Episcopal consecration by the metropolitan bishop ordinarily followed investiture by the king. The formal aspects of initiation into ecclesiastical office had come to resemble closely the investiture of vassals with secular fiefs, but, as Albert Hauck pointed out long ago, this did not mean that ecclesiastical offices were considered fiefs. Investiture merely made evident that bishop or abbot was under royal protection, and that he in turn had certain obligations toward the king.

Both abbeys and bishoprics had become very important landowners, largely through royal and private donations. They were required to contribute their share to the duties levied throughout the empire. The king commanded as permanent impost the *dona annualia* (annual gifts), which were most often horses and arms, and the important *servitium regis,* composed of property taxes and hospitality and riding duties. Military and court service were other impositions from which only certain nunneries and monasteries were exempt. The obligations expanded under Ottonian rule and sometimes came to include high justice. In such instances, this jurisdiction was added to low justice, which had devolved on the abbots and bishops in the context of immunity, one of the facets of royal protection. Thus certain abbots and bishops were incorporated into the imperial administration where they were a position that, in the juridical sense, was equal to that of the counts. At the same time, rights derived from immunities were no longer tied to landownership, because comital rights and counties were now granted independently. As a result, *Bannleihbezirke* came into existence. These were districts where representatives of the bishop rather than of the count constituted public authority. Now and then complaints were raised that kings disposed of bishoprics, or that bishops were so overburdened with temporal affairs that they had barely any time for their pastoral activities. But on the whole, the harmonious cooperation between king and ecclesiastics was appreciated as a perfectly natural, mutual complementarity of two closely allied divine institutions. Not only was this state of affairs conducive to the accretion of territorial power in the hands of the episcopate but also it tended to lay the basis for the creation of a "state church" (Kempf) so dependent on the king that he would be able to expand it into "the leading central institution of the empire" (Mitteis). Both shifts could occur only in a period of history "which did not yet know the essential distinction between state and church, but merely the functional distinction between *sacerdotium* and *regnum*. Since both powers saw themselves as members of a single higher entity under the dominion of Christ, and as such pursued the same religio-political goal, royal service, secular administration, and divine service could all be conceived of as one and the same religious and moral accomplishment" (Kempf).

In many respects, Otto's youngest brother, Brun, is the typical ecclesiastical prince endowed simultaneously with far-reaching secular rights and their ensuing obligations. As the youngest son of King Henry I, Brun was destined for the clerical life from an early age. He was educated at the cathedral school of Utrecht until Otto invited him to his court. At age fifteen, in 940, he became chancellor; several years later he is described as abbot, and in 950 he was abbot of the abbey of Lorsch. In 953 he became archbishop of Cologne. Later that same year, with the outbreak of the insurrection of 953 and the participation of Otto's son-in-law, Conrad the Red, the king also appointed Brun duke of Lotharingia. Until his death in 965, Brun jointly administered both his ecclesiastical and secular offices and loyally supported Otto I. Brun was at once a successful duke and a serious bishop, with a spirituality that leaned toward monasticism.

A different example of the cooperation between the ecclesiastical and the secular powers in the Ottonian and the early Salian period is territorial expansion and missionary activity in the north, east, and southeast of Germany, and its further promotion under Otto I, after the victorious battle of Henry I near Lenzen (929), Henry's victories over the Danes (934) and the Hungarians (933), and the defeat of the Hungarians by Otto I himself in 955. Along the Slav frontier, two famous margraves, Herman, ancestor of the Billungs, and Gero were put in charge by Otto. To the north, probably in 947, the dioceses Schleswig, Ripen, and Aarhus were founded as suffragans of the archdiocese Hamburg-Bremen. Their bishops were among the participants at the synod of Ingelheim in 948. In the east, the dioceses of Meissen, Merseburg, and Zeitz were added in 968 to the bishoprics of Brandenburg and Havelberg, created in 948. The bishopric of Oldenburg was established for the Wagrians and Abodrites, probably also in 968. Brandenburg, Havelberg, Meissen, Merseburg, and Zeitz (located at Naumburg after about 1030) were suffragans of the archbishopric of Magdeburg, another new foundation sanctioned by Pope Agapete II in 955 in response to the urging of Otto I. Understandably, there was some opposition to the establishment of Magdeburg by the archbishops of Mainz and Halberstadt, who had hoped to increase the size of their dioceses in the course of German eastward expansion. Thus it was only in 968, after their opposition had been overcome, that

Pope John XIII (965–72) could solemnly proclaim the new archbishop-ric. At the time of Otto the Great, three kingdoms were also evolving along the southeastern border of Germany: Bohemia, Poland, and some-what later, Hungary. Under their Christian rulers, all three strove for as much independence as possible, given the existing ties to the East Frank-ish kingdom. Feudal homages to their rulers alternated with wars against them. Such wars were especially threatening when they coincided with internal German rebellions, as they did in Bohemia at the time of Otto I. The generally close relations between Germany and especially Poland and Bohemia were a significant factor in the Christianization of these coun-tries and their subsequent ecclesiastical organization. Ninth-century mis-sionary work in Bohemia had been largely carried out by the Bavarian church, but Otto successfully prevented the organizational expansion of the Bavarian church into Bohemia, which would have meant an increase in the power of the Bavarian dukes as well. Shortly after Otto's death, in 976, when the establishment of the see of Prague was definitive, Prague was attached to the archbishopric of Mainz, perhaps in order to indem-nify Mainz for having been supplanted in its missionary work among the Wends by Otto's favorite foundation, Magdeburg (Kempf). Poland was the most successful in its drive for independence. Its ecclesiastical organi-zation crystallized around the bishoprics of Poznan (probably developed without links to Magdeburg and missionary activity from Bohemia) and Gniezno. Gniezno, by virtue of a papal privilege personally delivered by Emperor Otto III, grandson of Otto I, while on pilgrimage to Poland in the year 1000, was elevated to an archbishopric with the suffragan sees of Cracow, Wroclaw, and Kolberg. Poznan was added somewhat later. Already a decade earlier, Mieszko I had donated Poland to Saint Peter to protect it against Germany and Bohemia; now, in 1000, with its own archbishopric, Poland's ecclesiastical independence from Magdeburg was complete.

Otto's victory over the Hungarians in 955 at the Lech symbolizes best the successes of Otto the Great both within Germany and in the East. Contemporaries saw this victory as final proof of divine sanction for the hegemony Otto had by then attained in the Christian occident. It was well-nigh inevitable that this hegemony should evoke memories of the im-perial might of the Frankish Charlemagne. As the chronicler Widukind reports, in 955 the army proclaimed Otto emperor on the very battlefield. Ever since the time of Henry I, Italy had influenced royal political consid-erations, and Otto I probably intended to resume Carolingian imperial policies as early as his first Italian expedition in 951, when he married Adelheid and was crowned king in Pavia. Indications are that he hoped for an imperial coronation in Rome as well, but when he encountered opposition from the Italian nobility and the pope, he returned to Germany. The imperial coronation of Otto I did eventually take place in 962. It was a fateful event that in the eyes of Otto and the world at large perfected the restoration of the *regnum Francorum*. The Saxon Otto had become the heir of the Frankish Emperor Charles, but changes had occurred. France, for example, was completely independent and was never thought of in any other light. But, as under Charlemagne so also under Otto, the imperial ruler was to be the sword of the church. For Otto, this meant in particular an obligation to defend the pope and the church, as well as to undertake missionary endeavors among the pagans. As we have seen, only the first task added new facets to Otto's duties. The defense of pope and church also carried with it substantial rights and responsibilities toward Italy, all associated with the imperial dignity. As heir to the Carolingian tradition, Otto I granted a privilege to the Roman church along the lines of the Donation of Pepin. It secured for the pope, as successor of the prince of the apostles, Saint Peter, parts of Italy that became the territorial foundation for what was later called the Papal States, although Otto, like Charles the Great before him, reserved for himself the secular supervision of these lands. The Italians were not exactly enchanted with the turn of events in 962. Where the writer Adam of Bremen saw restoration of the ancient Roman liberty by Otto the Great, they perceived enslavement of the Roman Empire, that is, Italy. Thus it is not surprising to encounter repeated uprisings in Italy to shake off the alien yoke, however gentle it may have been.

Byzantium, too, as in Charlemagne's time, was unwilling to recognize a second emperor and heir of the Roman tradition, at least not as long as other political and military options remained. Not until the replacement of the Byzantine ruling dynasty was Otto able to procure a favorable response to his courting of a Byzantine bride for his son, an accommodation the famous Luitprand of Cremona, Otto's ambassador, had sought in vain until then. In spite of all resistance, however, Otto succeeded to such an extent in securing the imperial dignity that at his death it descended without difficulty to his son, Otto II. The reign of Otto II ended in near disaster. He died in Rome in December 983 after a decisive defeat by the Saracens near Cotrone (Calabria) in July 982 and a devastating uprising by Danes and Slavs on Germany's eastern frontier in the early summer of 983. Nevertheless, in May 983 the diet of Verona elected Otto's three-year-old son to the kingship and thus secured the dynastic succession also for the imperial dignity, which Otto III attained in 996, not long after he had reached his majority (994). Thus the imperial con-

secration and coronation of 962 was the beginning of a tradition—all
difficulties concerning German hegemony in Italy notwithstanding—that
was to transform Germany into a Roman *imperium,* in principle also including Italy and Burgundy, and German kings into successors of the Roman and Frankish emperors. In many respects the qualitative significance
of this sovereign dignity is difficult to evaluate. Friedrich Kempf puts it
very well: "It would not have meant much unless it was destined for a
ruler endowed with power. . . . The quasi-imperial power of the German
monarchs and its hegemonial radiation gave importance and esteem to
the imperial dignity, while the imperial dignity surrounded what was basically a royal power with a mysterious glamour supported by a genuine
symbolic force and made it appear as an imperial power."

Italian circles in general supported this tradition, at least as long as the
German rulers did not try to alter the status quo created in the years after
888, when Italian nobles and towns usurped royal rights, and as long as
these rulers relied on Italian princes to represent their interests in Italy.
The foremost supporters of the Ottonian emperors were found among
the bishops and abbots, joined by princes like Pandulf of Capua and the
margraves of Tusculum. In the city of Rome, where the families of the
Crescentians and the Tusculans struggled for predominance, there was
likewise usually one party that sought imperial support and willingly
opened the city gates to the emperor at the head of his troops. Already
toward the end of the reign of Otto II, when Otto campaigned against
Muslim and Byzantine forces, a new expression, designed to emphasize
the legitimacy of the western imperial title, appeared in documents: *romanorum imperator augustus.*

When Otto's son Otto III (983–1002), began to govern in his own
right in 995, imperial ideology evolved as the predominant theme of his
administration, with a special emphasis on the universality of the dignity.
The young emperor, imaginative, highly gifted, and religiously inclined,
was familiar with Greek through his mother, the Greek Princess Theo-
phano. He surrounded himself with teachers and advisors such as John
Philagatos, a Greek from southern Italy who later was to disappoint him
severely, Bernward of Hildesheim, Leo of Vercelli, Adalbert of Prague,
and especially the famous scholar Gerbert of Aurillac, later Pope Sylvester II (d. 1003). Otto pursued the *renovatio* or *restitutio* of Rome, a
program that he had conceived. At the same time, the ideological linkage
between the traditions of Frankish Aachen and of ancient Rome was to
become a political reality. In Rome, Otto III lived on the Palatine hill, and
because of a Roman insurrection, he ruled the Eternal City himself. He
did not hesitate to elevate other non-Italians to high positions as well, and

in the process, he established firm lines of communication between Rome and Germany. Ancient Roman-Byzantine titles appeared often among the court officials in his entourage. The legend on Otto's seal, surrounding a personified Roma, succinctly describes his program: *Renovatio imperii romanorum*. The obverse of the seal bears an image of Charlemagne that is surrounded by Otto's name as legend. It was Otto III who nominated the first German pope, Gregory V (996–99). Gregory V was succeeded by Gerbert of Aurillac, a Frenchman, at one time archbishop of Reims and elected archbishop of Ravenna. Gerbert selected the papal name Sylvester II, barely disguising the reference to Constantine and Sylvester I. It is noteworthy that Otto III and his advisors, especially Leo of Vercelli, refused to renew the privilege of Otto I for the papacy, the *Ottonianum* of 962, and rejected the Donation of Constantine as well because, they argued, crucial passages were based on forgeries. The rejection did not imply, however, an intention to diminish ecclesiastical rights. Otto III in fact bestowed on Saint Peter, that is, Pope Sylvester II, a major part of the Pentapolis which had been promised in the *Ottonianum*, and he stressed that he did so voluntarily, without any obligation on his part. A special bond existed between Otto III and the church. As P. E. Schramm notes, Otto expanded the imperial title with the additional designations *servus Jesu Christi* and *servus apostolorum* in connection with his pilgrimage to Gniezno. His close ties not only to Saint Adalbert, martyred in 997 by the Prussians, but also to Nilus and to the hermits in the marshes of Ravenna are further unmistakable evidence for Otto's deep piety. But all of Otto's bold dreams and plans for the *renovatio imperii* came to nought when he died of a fever in Paterno near Rome, at twenty-one years of age and without an heir. In accordance with his wishes he was buried in the palace at Aachen.

2. The Successors of the Ottonians

A renewed Roman uprising, which Otto III had countered with armed force shortly before his death, spread to the north and transformed all of Italy into a sea of rebellion. Margrave Arduin of Ivrea succeeded in having himself crowned king of Italy in 1002. But Henry II (1002–24), who was eventually elected king by the secular and ecclesiastical magnates of Germany largely because of his relationship with the Ottonians (he was Henry III of Bavaria and great-grandson of Henry I), managed to isolate Arduin and to have himself crowned at Pavia in 1004. The imperial coronation in Rome by Pope Benedict VIII (d. 1024), a Tusculan (the family had expelled their rivals, the Crescentians, in 1012), did not take place until ten years later. Still, even repeated Italian uprisings had not succeeded in preventing or even seriously threatening the ties between the German kingship and the Roman imperial dignity that had developed since the time of Otto's coronation in 962. Italy, split into different power blocs, stood in need of an emperor, just as the kings of Germany were confronted by the necessity to strengthen their authority over and against the dukes.

Nonetheless, the accession of Henry II brought a clear change with regard to Italy. The king abandoned the imposing plans of Otto III and cut back the extent of German involvement in Italian politics, reducing it to a level roughly equal to that of the reign of Otto I. Henry's attitude represented a conscious change of course. Once again this is illustrated by the legend of his seal, *Renovatio regni Francorum,* for it replaced, after all, that of Otto III: *Renovatio imperii Romanorum.* Accordingly, Henry II did not aspire to personal rule in Rome, which he left to the Crescentians, and after 1012 to the Tusculans. He did, however, introduce a special Italian coronation at Pavia, mentioned earlier, once he had destroyed the power base of his rival, Arduin of Ivrea. He deemed such steps sufficient for a *Renovatio regni Francorum,* a concept that for Henry II implied measures to secure German influence in bordering territories, such as Burgundy and Lombardy, as well as in the East, and furthermore, a strengthening of royal power within Germany. The coronation of Pavia confirmed his influence on the church of northern Italy and secured for him as well the strategic Alpine passes; there was no reason, therefore, to hasten to Rome for the imperial anointing and coronation.

Henry II, who at one point in his youth had been destined to become a cleric, showed himself an extraordinary friend and strong supporter of monastic reform throughout his life. Due to his support, the southern German/Bavarian reform, linked especially with the names Godehard of Niederaltaich and Bishop Wolfgang of Regensburg, expanded into all of Germany and even into Italy. While still duke of Bavaria, Henry had entrusted Godehard with the reform of the abbeys of Niederaltaich and Tegernsee. After renewing observances in the monastery of Hersfeld, Godehard became bishop of Hildesheim (1022–38). The Lotharingian reformers also owed much to Henry's support. He sent Abbot Immo of Gorze to Prüm and Reichenau. Henry II particularly admired Richard of Saint Vanne, Verdun, and Poppo of Stablò. He supported their efforts as generously as he did those of William of Dijon. In a royal privilege Henry II confirmed the liberty and the property of William's own foundation, Fruttuaria, although William had founded his monastery in close association with Arduin of Ivrea, Henry's rival for the crown of Pavia. In 1020

Henry asked Poppo to reform the abbey of Stablò-Malmédy, and in 1023 Saint Maximin at Trier. Although Cluny did not directly influence the German monastic reform in this period, Henry was also on excellent terms with Abbot Odilo of Cluny. In 1007 he founded the bishopric of Bamberg, his favorite foundation which he richly endowed and where he was buried. Bamberg held Henry's memory in high honor and obtained his canonization in 1146. As early as the second half of the eleventh century, legends that idealized Henry had begun to circulate; his marriage to Kunigund, for example, was thought of and widely described as chaste.

Contemporaries as well as historians were so impressed by Henry's personal piety that they often failed to notice that it was precisely this pious king who purposefully developed the Ottonian state-church system that was to become such a stumbling block during the investiture controversy. It was also Henry II who instituted the systematic utilization of the *servitium regale* of monasteries and cathedral chapters for government purposes. Much more so than did his predecessors, he translated royal sovereignty over the church into reality. Like them, he convened and then presided at ecclesiastical synods; like them, he accepted the proprietary church system as a matter of course and readily disposed of monastic property by redistributing it as grants not only to bishoprics but also to vassals. As under his predecessors, the palace chapel continued to be an important educational and formative center for the German episcopacy.

What was new, however, was more economic utilization of the cathedral chapters, going beyond the now customary and well-defined *servitium regale* of the abbeys. For the first time, episcopal towns predominated and thus replaced the old royal *palatia* on the itinerary of the king and his entourage. As Josef Fleckenstein emphasizes in a discussion with Bruno Heusinger, such a change was possible only because Henry II also dominated the church politically far more than the Ottonians had done. Not only did Henry nominate and depose abbots, he also unwaveringly insisted that his own candidates for episcopal sees be accepted, whatever the cost. Even armed resistance was no obstacle for Henry. The archdiocese of Trier is an example. In 1008 Henry had rejected the election of his brother-in-law Adalbero and nominated in his place his court chaplain, Megingoz, as archbishop of Trier. The result was years of feud with the relatives of his spouse, Kunigund of Luxembourg.

Henry did not act merely on a whim. His aim was to gain acceptance of the principle that is expressed by the insertion of the formula "*salvo tamen regis sive imperatoris consensu*" (saving the royal or imperial consent) into the confirmation of privileges for episcopal churches when their charters granted free episcopal elections. The events surrounding the elections in Magdeburg bear this out. The cathedral there, referring to the right of free episcopal elections, had elected the provost Waltherd as new bishop in 1004, although Henry II had sent his chaplain Wigbert to Magdeburg. Wigbert was supposed to induce the chapter of canons to elect Henry's chaplain Tagino. When this failed, Henry requested Waltherd's presence at court, and then persuaded him to renounce the archbishopric in favor of Tagino. After Tagino's death in 1012, the cathedral canons of Magdeburg tried once again to assert effectively their right to free elections and elected Waltherd once more. As before, Waltherd was called before the king, who recognized him eventually as archbishop, but not before Henry had obtained new elections, which proceeded on the basis of a royal nomination of Waltherd as candidate. At least formally, therefore, Henry insisted on reserving for himself the initiative in episcopal elections. A few months later Waltherd died. This time Henry simply rejected the Magdeburg election out of hand, without any negotiation, and appointed the court chaplain Gero as the new archbishop of Magdeburg. The candidate of the Magdeburg chapter, Dietrich, became a royal chaplain in the *palatium* of Grone. Similarly, Henry reserved for himself the initiative in episcopal elections in 1012 at Cambrai, in 1013 at Bremen, and in 1023 at Halberstadt. These sensational elections, however, only constitute the proverbial exceptions. Royal episcopal nominations usually proceeded smoothly. The nominations for Magdeburg deserve to be mentioned chiefly because they illustrate that it was actually Henry II who fully realized the Ottonian principle of the royal disposition of bishoprics.

In the same context two further aspects of the ecclesiastical program of Henry II deserve comment. The first is the role of the king as member of cathedral chapters. Otto III had already been a canon at the chapel of Saint Mary in the Palace of Aachen, which he had splendidly endowed, and very likely also at the cathedral of Hildesheim under his friend and teacher Bernward. Nevertheless, we owe the institution of the king's membership as canon in cathedral chapters to Henry II rather than to Otto III. Henry had himself adopted as canon by several chapters: Bamberg, Strasbourg, Magdeburg, Paderborn, and Hildesheim. In Bamberg he was adopted together with the empress. No other institution exemplifies with equal vividness the intimate relationship between church and monarchy, ecclesiastical sovereignty and ecclesiastical reform. The second aspect of Henry's ecclesiastical program worthy of a brief comment is the relationship between the palace or court chapel and the most important churches in the realm. The palace chapel, which since Carolingian times had not been included in the diocesan organization but had been chiefly responsible for worship services at the ruler's court, also served as chancery with the arch-chancellor as its head. From the time of Otto I the palace chapel evolved into a "school" for future bishops. The chaplains, who were usually members of the most eminent noble families and the closest collaborators of the king, simultaneously were canons in one or another of the cathedral chapters. According to Fleckenstein, toward the end of the reign of Otto III the court chapel was represented through canons who were also royal chaplains in about half of the more important episcopal churches of Germany. Henry II further strengthened these tendencies. The more important German churches therefore were in constant contact with the royal palace chapel: the churches adopted court chaplains as canons of their own chapters; court chaplains were nominated to episcopal sees following completion of service in the palace chapel; and the king maintained a direct link between himself and certain favored cathedral chapters by accepting a canonry.

3. The First Salians

With the death of Emperor Henry II in 1024, the Liudolfing line of male descent came to an end. For the second time within a short period, therefore, the principle of royal election could fully assert itself. Only two candidates for the kingship are mentioned—cousins, both named Conrad, and descendents of Henry I in the female line. The older Conrad was elected in Franconia, across from Oppenheim on the Rhine, and was crowned by the archbishop of Mainz, some disagreements notwithstanding. The coronation ceremony followed in detail the example provided by Henry II. Conrad II was the first of the Salian line of kings. This change of dynasty is most noteworthy for the ease with which it was accomplished. It was accepted by the members of the palace chapel and the chancery, and it had little effect on foreign and internal policies. There were some changes, however, especially in the attitude of Conrad and his successors to the ministerials of Germany, who had risen from unfree servants to the lower ranks of the nobility. The Salian kings also differed from their predecessors in their attitude toward the growing towns and to the subvassals of Italy, the *valvassores*. Economic and demographic circumstances had changed, and to some extent Salian politics reflected these changes. Still, the most important political features continued without interruption. To underscore this continuity scholars frequently cite Conrad's purported response to the citizens of Pavia when they tore down the royal palace at Pavia after the death of Henry II, claiming that "the kingship had died with him." At Constance, Conrad announced that empire and kingship continue even after the death of a king, just as a ship remains after the death of its captain (*si rex periit, regnum remansit, sicut navis remanet, cuius gubernator cadit*). This statement, preserved by Wipo, illuminates the essential element of Conrad's reign: continuity. Theodor Schieffer describes the reign most succinctly as a new beginning in 1002 and practically seamless continuity in 1024.

Before we turn to the reign of Henry III, the son and heir of Conrad II, however, we must briefly examine the relationship between Conrad II and the church. Maybe there were differences, after all, between the sainted Henry II and Conrad II, who was described by Rodulf Glaber as more or less inspired by the devil. One might be inclined to dismiss accusations levied against Conrad, assuming that they can ultimately all be traced to Conrad's marriage to Gisela, a marriage that did not meet full canonical requirements. However, even Conrad's loyal biographer Wipo did not always side with his hero when it came to the church. Perhaps, therefore, criticism was justified, and Conrad's behavior did contribute to the later disagreements between *regnum* and *sacerdotium*, for by the time of Conrad II monastic renewal had already begun to merge into reform of the church at large.

Conrad II adhered closely to the policies of his predecessor, Henry II, who had paved the way for a stable and unchallenged theocratic regime. At Conrad's anointing and coronation Archbishop Aribo of Mainz referred to the king as the representative of Christ, and contemporaries accepted the king's sovereignty over the church as a natural consequence of the royal *ministerium* imposed by God. Conrad for his part did not hesitate to intervene decisively in internal ecclesiastical affairs and pointedly expressed his wishes at synods which he convened and attended. Thus he succeeded, for example, in gaining acceptance of a compromise solution to an old dispute between Bishop Godehard of Hildesheim and Aribo of Mainz over the possession of the abbey of Gandersheim. Conrad quashed the matrimonial proceedings against the count of Hammerstein, a matter that had long troubled Henry, the pope, and the bishops. The bishops had no choice but to acquiesce. Conrad himself also dealt with liturgical problems and was, moreover, responsible for the transfer of the bishopric of Zeitz to Naumburg. Like Henry II, Conrad II balanced dominion over the church with responsibility for its well-being. He did indeed dispose of abbeys and bishoprics, but he also provided for reform. Under Conrad's guidance, the Lotharingian reform gained widespread influence in Germany. Like his predecessor, Conrad energetically supported Abbot Poppo of Stablò-Malmédy. A short time after his accession, he asked Poppo to reform his own dynastic foundation, Limburg, and later entrusted Poppo or his disciples with the abbeys of Echternach, Saint Ghislain, Hersfeld, Weissenburg, and Saint Gall as well as with the monastery Waulsort and Hastiere, which belonged to the bishopric of Metz and, unlike the others, was not a royal proprietary abbey. Partly as a consequence of the royal example, both clergy and laity, either as founders or as proprietary bishops, entrusted the Lotharingian abbot with the reform of additional monasteries. Poppo's influence in Germany eventually far exceeded that of his teacher, Richard of Saint Vanne. Poppo's severe, ascetic piety and his uncompromising insistence on absolute obedience and denial of self-will, even for men whom he himself had raised to abbacies, were not welcome everywhere; nor were they always comprehensible. Poppo also believed that it was the duty of a monk to experience vicariously and incessantly the sufferings of Christ, and therefore he considered any kind of levity inappropriate. Famous are the sketches of Ekkehard IV of Saint Gall, pupil of Notker. Ekkehard describes life at the abbey of Saint Gall before it came under the rule of Poppo without making any effort to disguise the enmity he and his fellow monks felt toward the foreign abbot. He conceived of the Lotharingians—Galls as he called them—as schismatics who destroyed the unity of the church by forming an association of monasteries. Most German abbeys—repeatedly reformed within a short period of time—did not see why their own customs should not be as appropriate for their style of piety as were those of the Lotharingians or of the Cluniacs. Resistance could be strong, and therefore, as Theodor Schieffer explains, "Conrad's actions can only be understood in light of his sincere sympathy for the particular habits of Poppo and for the new and strict forms of organization which went beyond the individual monastery." Conrad pursued similar policies with the palace chapel and the nomination to bishoprics. He appointed reformers but never hesitated to exploit the bishoprics economically, just as his predecessor had done. Conrad became a canon at Worms and Speyer, his favorite sees, and thus expanded the list of cathedrals where the king was a member of the chapter. The romanesque cathedral of Speyer, Conrad's foundation, remains to this day an awe-inspiring artistic memorial to his rule.

Already certain contemporaries, however, were unwilling to overlook some of the negative aspects of Conrad's theocratic rule. Three issues in particular provoked periodic criticism: (1) Conrad's marriage to Gisela, because it did not fully satisfy canonical requirements; (2) the distribution of bishoprics, abbeys, and church property in return for financial and territorial concessions; and (3) his actions against the archbishops Aribert of Milan and Burchard of Lyons. The second and third issues attracted the most attention, and they are also responsible for some negative evaluations of Conrad by historians. Aribert of Milan (1018–45), leader of the imperial party of the Italian episcopate and a great favorite of Emperor Conrad, rebelled against him when Conrad took the side of the lower vassals, the *valvassores,* who had risen against the church of Milan. Aribert, who was supported in his rebellion by the episcopate of Lombardy, closed the gates of the city of Milan to the emperor. Conrad's adjudication of the conflict, the *Constitutio feudorum* of 1037, greatly altered feudal law in favor of the *valvassores.* When Aribert refused to submit, the emperor acted in anger. He deposed the archbishop on his own without waiting for a synodal decision. Thus politics formed the background to the Aribert affair. Although we know very little about the events in the Burgundian city of Lyons, political factors are once again implicated. Even so, by this time informed opinion was set against Conrad's actions, which conflicted with canon law, though they were subsequently affirmed by Pope John XIX (1024–32) as well as by a synod. Conrad's son and successor, Henry III, was willing to come to a compromise with Aribert, who reappeared at the German court shortly after Conrad's death in 1039.

The discordant note that brought Conrad's reign to a close is proof that the emperor did not keep pace with the evolution of the ecclesiastical reform that began to spread and become more general, notwithstanding his efforts on behalf of the very same reform. Conrad, in contrast to his son, apparently lacked appreciation and understanding of the new and subtle variations that arose within this movement. This evaluation is borne out by Conrad's episcopal and abbatial appointments, in which he is reproached with simony. The weightiest condemnation in this context is probably the speech that Rodulf Glaber, Conrad's most hostile critic, attributed to Henry III. Henry supposedly said that he felt grave concern for the salvation of his father's soul, since his father had committed simony during his lifetime. ("Nam et pater meus, de cuius animae periculo valde pertimesco, eandem damnabilem avariciam in vita nimis exercuit.") Wipo, Conrad's biographer who usually speaks of him in very positive terms, reported that in 1025 a cleric named Ulric had paid a large sum of money to the king and queen in return for the bishopric of Basel. Later Conrad had promised and vowed in the future not to accept money for a bishopric or an abbey, "a vow which he very nearly kept." There are a few other statements by contemporaries accusing Conrad of simony which historians often adopted word for word without further examination. Simony, simply defined as the sale and purchase of clerical offices, estates, or functions, had been condemned from the earliest days of Christianity as a sin against the Holy Spirit. Conrad himself was opposed to simony and had the synod of Tribur of 1036 condemn it. The resulting legislation reflects the connotation the term was given in Conrad's lifetime. The synodal decrees prohibited the sale of holy oil, of baptisms, and of funerals, and the acquisition of altars by the clergy. The concept of simony was narrowly defined and there was no mention of demands made by Conrad in return for investiture with bishoprics and abbeys. As in other respects, Conrad merely followed the precedent set by Henry II. The payments claimed fell into the context of the *servitium regale,* which the kings had long required of the church. The *servitium regale* can in no way be compared with the sums of money that were changing hands in the trade of bishoprics or abbeys in the south of France. Thus while no one in Conrad's lifetime would have identified his appointments with the sale of ecclesiastical office, a more subtle and sophisticated interpretation of the concept of simony which evolved in the mid-eleventh century, when Conrad's actions were still widely remembered, is responsible for their subsequent condemnation (T. Schieffer). The deeds of Henry II, historically more distant, emerged unscathed from this reinterpretation, and so the image of a saint was falsely juxtaposed with the image of his successor as a ruler lacking in piety and overly preoccupied with secular concerns.

When Emperor Conrad II died in June 1039, his son, Henry III, had already been king of Germany for ten years. The crown of Burgundy had also been his since the autumn of 1038. Furthermore, he had been duke of Bavaria since 1027, and duke of Swabia and duke of Burgundy since 1038. Henry III (d. 1056) was to become a truly great emperor, although his reign was burdened by serious wars, especially in the East, as well as by insurrections and famines in Germany. More than Otto I or Otto III, Henry III symbolizes theocratic rule, the guidance of church and state as a single entity by the divinely elected, anointed emperor described by many as *vicarius Christi* or *vicarius Dei:* ". . . all were agreed that the king, who ruled on earth, typified the Saviour, who ruled in Heaven" (Tellenbach, trans. Bennett). Deeply felt piety and an exacting interpretation of his duties were combined in the person of Henry with a proud consciousness of the fullness of his power and the sanctity of his high office as representative of God in the secular as well as the ecclesiastical realm. Despite his sincere Christian humility, it seems never to have occurred to Henry to renounce any of the rights acquired by his predecessors. He strove to strengthen royal authority and to expand it where and whenever possible, emphasizing the sacrality of his office and the majesty of the crown. It is this which lends his reign its most distinguishing feature. In Henry III religious and political motives were closely intertwined with an exalted understanding of his *ministerium*. All of these sentiments came to the fore in his peace proclamations. Against the backdrop of the largely French movement of the Peace and Truce of God (probably most enthusiastically supported by Abbot Odilo of Cluny, Abbot Richard of Saint Vanne, and Bruno of Toul), Henry chose to accomplish the royal task of preserving peace and justice in a particularly solemn and public manner. At the synod of Constance (1043) he proclaimed a Peace edict and, addressing the crowd from the altar of the cathedral, granted a pardon to his enemies and asked all those present to do the same for their enemies. Soon thereafter Henry granted similar amnesty at Trier, and in 1044 on the battlefield of Menfö, where he had won a victory over Hungarian rebels. This victory enabled Henry to reinstate Peter Orseoli, the legitimate successor, to the Hungarian throne, probably on the occasion of a similar peace manifestation between Peter and the Hungarians. Once more, in 1047 in Rome, and then presumably in connection with his imperial coronation, Henry pronounced a pardon for his enemies, excepting only Godfrey of Lotharingia, who had repeatedly rebelled against the emperor.

As indicated earlier, Henry, unlike his father, brought a refined sensitivity and empathy to ecclesiastical reform. His perception of simony— now with at once broadened and very specific connotations unsuspected in his father's day—was in harmony with that of his reformers. Simony and nonobservance of the rule of celibacy for priests (nicolaitism) were considered the root of all evil, and Henry took pains to preclude there falling even the shadow of suspicion on his nomination of bishops and abbots. This is not to imply, though, that bishoprics and abbeys faced fewer demands than in the past under the concept of *servitium regis,* although Henry pointedly differentiated between bishoprics and monasteries. With the exceptions of Fulda and Saint Ghislain, no monastery was endowed with counties or comital rights, and surprisingly often Henry confirmed charters with free abbatial elections and permitted these to take place. Now as before, however, actual bestowal of the dignity on the abbot-elect continued to rest with the emperor. Henry renewed and strengthened the immediate dependence of the abbeys on the empire (*Reichsunmittelbarkeit*) and in doing so avoided the alienation of monastic appurtenances and of the monasteries themselves, especially to episcopal churches. Whenever possible he rescinded grants of this kind made either by himself or by his predecessors. Henry stipulated that certain monasteries were under the protection and dominion of the Empire and therefore inalienable even by king or emperor. Although even under Henry III this protection could not always be implemented, Henry was obviously strongly influenced by the Cluniac conception of liberty. Liberty in the Middle Ages could only be conceived of in the context of lordship, which was an ideological reference point. For Cluny, such association derived from Saint Peter's dominion over the abbey and corresponded to royal or imperial dominion over the German imperial abbeys. Assuming a hierarchy of earthly power with the consecrated ruler at its head, imperial protection and lordship equalled the highest degree of freedom attainable on earth, while at the same time providing the greatest possible subjection to God, in the sense of Augustine's *libera servitus*. Side by side with imperial protection stood papal protection, which early in the reform might lead to a monastery's enjoying protection through both royal and papal privilege.

Henry III, like his predecessors, relied during his reign primarily on the episcopate of Germany, Burgundy, and Italy for administrative assistance and advice. More than half of the bishops had served in the court chapel, which maintained its full importance as an instrument of government. Not only Germans were members, but also Italians, such as Anselm of Besate, and Burgundians. Several among them simultaneously held canonries in German cathedral chapters. In this fashion the king maintained uninterrupted contact with the bishoprics of the Empire, even if a bishop had by chance not served in the palace chapel before his elevation to the see. Henry also furthered the development of the royal canonicate as a means to express the special relationship he had established with his most favored cathedrals. It is characteristic of the king that he joined the chapters of Bamberg and Cologne as a canon together with Pope Leo IX, the former Bishop Bruno of Toul. Fleckenstein points out that many of Henry's chaplains were honored with *vitae* after their deaths and that the image of sainthood reflected in the hagiographical writings accorded with the ideas so recently introduced by the reform. One might conclude, therefore, that Henry preferred to surround himself with chaplains who in their lifetimes were already beholden to the just emerging ideals of religious renewal. Such a judgment, however, should be subject to extreme caution. As Paul Fridolin Kehr notes, Henry by no means gathered only saints in his palace chapel. One of his chaplains, for example, was the highly controversial Anno, whom Henry named successor to Archbishop Hermann as chancellor for Italy in 1056. The infamous Nitker of Freising was also a member of the royal chapel. More typically, Henry appointed candidates who measured up to ecclesiastical standards and he rejected immediately, for example, the son of a priest. In Metz, Toul, and Verdun (Lotharingia), as well as in Lyons (Burgundy), Henry deliberately appointed reformers to bishoprics who fell in with the sentiments of these regions, making sure, at the same time, that their ecclesiastical objectives did not slight imperial interests. A case in point is that of Bishop Wazo of Liège.

As in all his pursuits, Henry managed skillfully to further royal interests and church reform at the same time. His firmly controlled episcopal nominations offer a clear example. There were generally three ways to elevate a bishop to a vacant see in the reign of Henry III. (1) The king could nominate the new bishop himself and then request consent from the clergy and people of the respective diocese; such consent was expressed through acclamation. (2) The king could ask advisors to suggest a suitable candidate. (3) The respective cathedral chapter could propose a candidate. Under items (2) and (3), imperial consent prior to election was mandatory. Election was succeeded by investiture through the king and, finally, consecration by the metropolitan bishop assisted by at least two other bishops. No one took exception to Henry's investiture of the future bishop or abbot with the new office and its appurtenances by means of the symbolic transfer of the crosier or abbatial staff. Nor were objections raised when Henry, in typical accentuation of the sacrality of his actions, added to the crosier the episcopal ring, which stood for the mystical marriage of the bishop to his church, his bride. Henry was apparently the first ruler to include the ring. The invested abbot or bishop then swore an oath of fealty to the emperor.

The fealty oath was ordinarily as much taken for granted as was its equivalent, the investiture. Voices began to be heard in some monastic circles, however, rejecting the oath as incompatible with the monastic calling. The earliest example known is that of William of Volpiano, abbot of Saint Bénigne at Dijon, founder of Fruttuaria and disciple of Majolus and Odilo of Cluny. In a play on his nickname, *Wilhelmus supra regulam*, Kassius Hallinger describes him as a "super-Cluniac" (*Überkluniazenser*). When William was to be ordained a deacon in the monastery of Saint Mary at Locedia, and was routinely asked to swear an oath of fealty to Bishop Leo of Vercelli, his diocesan, he refused. His *Vita* reports— presumably from a later point of view—that William thought of the oath as simony because it constituted a return for the ordination by the bishop. According to canon law, the ordination had to be bestowed free of charge. During the reign of Henry III a similar dispute arose over the nomination of Halinard, also abbot of Saint Bénigne at Dijon, as archbishop of Lyons. Halinard had been elected by the clergy of the city with the consent of the laity. Several years earlier, Halinard had rejected such an election, since, he explained, the episcopal dignity could not be harmonized with his position as monk. Now, in 1046, Halinard asked Pope

Gregory VI for advice. The pope commanded him to submit to the wishes expressed by the clergy and people of Lyons. In August of that year the city then sent a delegation of neighboring bishops and clergy from Lyons to Henry, who happened to be staying at Speyer. The ambassadors asked the king to invest Halinard without requiring the oath of fealty for the bishopric (*honor episcopii*). They argued that the Gospels as well as the Rule of Saint Benedict prohibited monks from taking an oath. The German bishops in the royal entourage, especially Bishop Sigebert of Speyer and Archbishop Hugh of Besançon, chancellor for Burgundy and a close friend of Henry, argued that the oath of the new archbishop was absolutely essential, whereas Dietrich of Metz, Bruno of Toul (later Pope Leo IX), and Richard of Verdun, that is, all the Lotharingians, warmly supported Halinard's request. The king relented. Just before Henry left for Italy, Halinard was consecrated without the oath by Archbishop Besançon in the presence of the king.

The narrative in the more or less contemporary chronicle *Sancti Benigni Divionensis* implies that Henry acceded only reluctantly to Halinard's wish. Soon, however, Henry was to show a growing sympathy for the special dilemma the swearing of oaths could pose for ecclesiastics. In an imperial edict, dated Rimini, 3 April 1047, Henry absolved all clerics and monks from the judicial oath (*iusiurandum calumpnie*) and stipulated that a representative could take it instead. Nor does Henry seem to have held a grudge against Halinard, if the report is trustworthy that Halinard's election to the papal office by the Romans came to nought because Halinard declined the high dignity, and not because of any objections by the king. Halinard's refusal to take an oath undoubtedly rested primarily on his beliefs about his monastic obligations. But once this has been admitted, it would not do to underestimate the significance of his resistance to royal demands. Hartmut Hoffmann points out that Halinard had been a pupil of William of Volpiano and thus could not have been blind to the political consequences of an apolitical action. According to the chronicle *Sancti Benigni*, the refusal to take an oath had the purpose of allowing Halinard to remain aloof from secular affairs. This can only be a reference to the *servitium regale*, expected of an archbishop of Lyons. Consciously or not, such an attitude came close to a rejection of the Ottonian-Salian state-church system, whatever may have been the effective reasons for Halinard's rejection of the customary interweaving of secular and spiritual competencies.

No other ruler gave the quasi-priestly aspects of the imperial dignity as much emphasis as did Henry III. This is not to say that the purely secular aspects were treated as less important. The secular sphere demonstrates the limits of authority even of a Henry III. Kehr cautioned: "Care should be taken not to overestimate the power and might of the kings of Germany; in the final analysis everything depended on their ability to play off one entrenched party against the other, new families against old ones; foreigners against local nobles, in a period when kings were unable to prevent the newcomers from quickly taking root in the alien environment, becoming in the process just as dangerous a threat to the kingship as the earlier enemies." As far as possible Henry III followed the example of his father, whose personnel he kept on, just as Conrad II in his time had followed the example of Henry II. He tried to keep the might of the dukes in check by appointing nobles from other regions to the ducal office whenever a family dynasty died out. The situation in Saxony and Lotharingia was especially dangerous. He kept the Billungs and the Saxons under control by relying prominently on Margrave Ekkehard of Meissen, who had loyally conducted campaigns in Bohemia and Hungary. When Ekkehard died in 1046, Henry increased his reliance on Saxon counts palatine. His expansion of the *palatium* at Goslar created an additional counterweight. There he founded the famous Chapter of Saints Simon and Jude, the saints of the day of his birth. In the north, the able, ambitious, but intensely loyal Archbishop Adalbert of Bremen kept Billung influence in check. Henry elevated two of Adalbert's brothers, Frederick and Theti, to the position of Saxon counts palatine. Frequent campaigns against Bohemia, which the king brought under permanent control, and against Hungary, which he could subdue only temporarily, resulted in Henry's most enduring achievement: the protection of Austria, Carinthia, and Styria from the Hungarian threat. In Poland Henry resumed the politics of Otto III.

Lotharingia might well be described as the Achilles' heel of Henry's policies. Henry refused to grant more than the Upper Lotharingia to the warlike and extremely able Duke Godfrey the Bearded, because he wished to avoid too large a concentration of power in the latter's hands. Duke Gozelo the Elder had died in 1044, leaving Upper Lotharingia to Godfrey and Lower Lotharingia to his younger brother Gozelo, who, however, died in 1046. At the diet of the same year, Henry gave the duchy of Lower Lotharingia to Frederick of the Lützeburg family. Frederick was a brother of Duke Henry of Bavaria, whom Henry III had appointed to the Bavarian duchy in 1042 following his own renunciation of this dignity. Between 1044 and 1046 the king had already enfeoffed the bishopric of Utrecht with several counties of Lower Lotharingia with the intention of breaking the power of Godfrey the Bearded and his allies there. Henry could hardly have been surprised by their insurrection when his decision went against Godfrey in 1046 upon the death of Gozelo. Godfrey was defeated and deposed, but the former duke knew how to create for himself a new power basis: he married Beatrice, the widow of the murdered Margrave Boniface of Tuscany. In 1055 Henry III set out on his second Italian expedition to counter this new threat. Kehr has convincingly shown the skill with which the emperor successfully broke the might of the house of Canossa and thus Godfrey. Godfrey was forced to flee to Lotharingia. His wife, Beatrice, and her daughter, Mathilda, had to accompany Henry on his return north. When Godfrey made his submission to the emperor, probably at the end of June 1056, nobody would have predicted that "the vanquished Godfrey would defeat his imperial conqueror by surviving him" (Kehr).

Henry's Italian policies have always been the focus of particular interest by historians, and more specifically his relationship to the papacy, which due to Henry's intervention had been liberated from its excessive involvement with the local Roman nobility. This feat created a reinvigorated, universalist papacy that in turn became the guiding principle of church reform, until then nourished and led by a host of disparate forces. For juridical reasons Henry had never recognized the deposition of Archbishop Aribert of Milan. But he nonetheless heeded the political implications of Aribert's uprising against his father, Emperor Conrad II. Aribert and his ally, Margrave Boniface of Tuscany, pillars of imperial authority in Italy, lost their former influence. Henry ceased to rely exclusively on the great lords of Italy and instead made contact also with the monastic-eremitical reformers around Peter Damian, prior of Fonte Avellana, and Abbot Guido of Pomposa. Furthermore, Henry, like his father, was sympathetic toward new economic and social developments that were leading to structural changes in society. On the occasion of his second Italian expedition Henry granted privileges to several cities—at the expense, however, of the house of Canossa, margraves of Tuscany.

Henry did not disdain making use also of earlier means to strengthen royal government in Italy. Following the pattern set by Otto III and Henry II, his nominations to Italian bishoprics increasingly gave preference to German clergy, primarily from the court chapel. He probably considered Aquileia, Ravenna, and Ferrara of particular importance because they were intended to counterbalance Milan. German bishops elsewhere in Italian sees were Gregory of Vercelli and Walter of Verona. A Bavarian became bishop of Benevento. Kehr tries to show that the selection of German bishops, like that of their Italian colleagues, served in the first instance to secure imperial rule, and thus he assigns them no more than an administrative function. German clerics, because they were strangers in an alien land, were especially dependent on imperial support. It is also true that the bishops, appointed by Henry after consultation with the Italians, formed a valuable link to the German court and helped to reinforce the ties created by the permanent and traveling royal *missi* whom Henry used to govern Italy in an orderly manner. But this was not the sole purpose of Henry's episcopal nominations. As usual, he combined political and religious intentions. Indeed, he controlled the Italian imperial church with a firm hand but used this control to shape the church in accordance with the reforming ideals of his time. Abbot Lambert of Sant'Apollinare of Classe at Ravenna, a monastery reformed by Peter Damian and maintaining close ties to him, arrived at the palace of Bodfeld, accompanied by a messenger sent by Abbot Guido of Pomposa. They had made the long journey to present a complaint against Archbishop Widger of Ravenna. Henry had appointed Widger two years earlier but did not hesitate to depose him in response to the complaints raised by the Italian prelates. For unknown reasons Pope Gregory VI had never consecrated Widger, but the reason given for Henry's deposition of the archbishop of Ravenna was that Widger had celebrated mass in episcopal robes he had not yet been entitled to.

Henry's first Italian expedition in 1046—he obviously did not consider the imperial coronation urgent—brought the deposition and banishment of Pope Gregory VI together with that of both his rivals, Benedict IX and Sylvester III, pronounced at two synods in Sutri and Rome, which were convened shortly before Henry's imperial coronation on Christmas 1046. The details behind these stirring events are still controversial. Important sources, such as synodal minutes, are lost. An uprising, of unknown cause, in the fall of 1044 caused the expulsion from Rome of Pope Benedict IX (elected in 1032), a member of the Tusculan family. Subsequently, in January 1045, the bishop of Sabina was elected to the papal office. He enjoyed the support of a lateral branch of the Crescentian family, and chose the papal name of Sylvester III. Already in the spring of 1045, however, supporters of Benedict expelled Sylvester. But Benedict IX, a figure surrounded by scandalous rumors, including a tale of his intention to marry, no longer felt safe in Rome in his position as pope. After negotiations, he agreed to resign in favor of his godfather, the priest John Gratian, who was a canon of San Giovanni fuori Porta Latina. John Gratian was a relative of the Tusculans and possibly of a family that was to enjoy increasing prominence in city politics and was eventually given the name Pierleoni. Gratian became pope under the name Gregory VI, once Benedict IX had received "severance pay," an indemnity paid by either Gregory or his supporters.

As far as we know, no discussions were held about conditions in Rome before Henry left for Italy. The purpose of the expedition was twofold— the imperial coronation and pursuit of channels of communication with Italian reformers. The first indication of concern about Roman problems is perhaps a decree forbidding simony, promulgated by the synod of Pavia which Henry celebrated in the fall. The minutes of the synod unfortunately are lost. We do know, however, that Henry subsequently met with Gregory VI at Piacenza and that the pope was received with all due reverence. Once again we know nothing about the discussions between pope and king. The next reliable piece of information pertains to the synod held on 20 December 1046 at Sutri, a small town just north of Rome. The assembly discussed and adjudicated not only Gregory but also popes Benedict IX and Sylvester III. Gregory and Sylvester were deposed, although the latter had long renounced his claim to the chair of Saint Peter. A Roman synod held three days later also deposed Benedict IX and elected, as well as consecrated, a new pope, the court chaplain and bishop Suidger of Bamberg, who adopted the papal name Clement II. On Christmas day 1046 Clement celebrated the imperial coronation of Henry and his spouse, Agnes. On this occasion Henry also obtained the patrician dignity from the Romans, which permitted him to participate in future papal elections. This particular imperial right had not been claimed since the Ottonian age.

Henry's actions were widely welcomed and supported. No one seems to have doubted that money had played a part in the election of Gregory VI, who thus became guilty of simony, his links to the reformers notwithstanding. Peter Damian, elated at first by the pontificate of Gregory VI, wrote in a letter to Pope Clement II, in which he also reproached the pope for having failed to fulfill the expectations of the reformers with regard to the bishops of Fano and Osimo, that Henry's action had brought the apostolic see from darkness into light. Abbot Odilo of Cluny, too, was on Henry's side, as Gerd Tellenbach is able to show against the arguments of Borino. A few isolated critics, the unknown author of the treatise *De ordinando pontifice* and Bishop Wazo of Liège, who had already reproached Henry for the deposition of Archbishop Widger of Ravenna, did not advance opinions about Gregory's guilt or innocence. They merely pointed out that Henry was not qualified to depose the pope because the pope could not be judged by anyone except a general synod. It is possible, too, that Gregory resigned the office himself, under pressure. The contradictory sources only agree that after his deposition Gregory went into exile in Germany, accompanied by Hildebrand, who was later to become Gregory VII.

It is sometimes argued, especially by Kehr, that Henry intended to in-
corporate the papacy into the "imperial state church system" to secure
his ecclesiastical sovereignty. If this indeed was Henry's purpose, he could
be said to have had an uncharacteristic quick change of heart, namely in
1048, after the deaths in quick succession of the first two German popes,
Clement II (9 October 1047) and Damasus II (9 August 1048), when he
nominated Bruno of Toul to the papacy. Roman emissaries, presumably
with Henry's support, had proposed the bishop as a candidate. The probable truth, here as in other decisions, is that Henry's political and religious objectives were closely interwoven. Between 1039 and 1046 Henry
all but ignored Roman affairs, but once he was forced to intervene in
Rome, his actions were in perfect keeping with those of a theocratic ruler
entrusted with the well-being of the church at large. It is clear that the
emperor intended to stamp out simony in Rome and to initiate reforms,
but can we fault him for seeking, as Kempf expresses it, not only to protect but also to direct and lead this reform which was bound to affect the
church as a whole?

Bibliography for Chapter 2

Social Structure

Beech, George T. *A Rural Society in Medieval France. The Gâtine of Poitou in the
    Eleventh and Twelfth Centuries.* Baltimore, 1964.
Bloch, Marc. *Feudal Society.* Translated by L. A. Manyon. 2 vols. Chicago, 1964.
Bosl, Karl. *Die Grundlagen der modernen Gesellschaft im Mittelalter.* 2 vols.
    Stuttgart, 1972.
———. "Herrscher und Beherrschte im deutschen Reich des 10.–11. Jahrhun-
    derts." In *Frühformen der Gesellschaft im mittelalterlichen Europa.* Munich,
    1964.
Bullough, Donald A. "Urban Change in Early Medieval Italy: The Example of
    Pavia." *Papers of the British School at Rome* 34 (1966):82–130.
Cowdrey, H. E. J. [Herbert Edward John]. "Anselm of Besate and Some North-
    Italian Scholars of the Eleventh Century." *Journal of Ecclesiastical History* 23
    (1972):115–24.
Duby, George. *La Société aux XIe et XIIe siècles dans la région mâconnaise.* 2
    vols. Paris, 1953.
———. *The Three Orders: Feudal Society Imagined.* Translated by Arthur Gold-
    hammer. Chicago and London, 1980.
Ennen, Edith. *Die europäische Stadt im Mittelalter.* 2d ed. Göttingen, 1975.
Fasoli, Gina. *Dalla "civitas" al comune nell'Italia settentrionale.* Bologna, 1969.
Ganshof, François Louis. *Feudalism.* Translated by Philip Grierson. New York,
    1957.

Goody, Jack. *The Development of the Family and Marriage in Europe.* Cambridge, 1983.

Herlihy, David. "Land, Family and Women in Continental Europe, 701–1200." *Traditio* 18 (1962):89–120. The conclusions by now need revision but the methodology is still important.

———. *Medieval Households.* Cambridge, Mass., and London, 1985.

Keller, Hagen. "Die Entstehung der italienischen Stadtkommunen als Problem der Sozialgeschichte." *Frühmittelalterliche Studien* 10 (1976):169–211.

Leyser, Karl. "The German Aristocracy from the Ninth to the Early Twelfth Century." *Past and Present* 41 (1968):25–53.

Maurer, Helmut. *Konstanz als ottonischer Bischofssitz: Zum Selbstverständnis geistlichen Fürstentums im zehnten Jahrhundert.* Göttingen, 1973.

Schwineköper, Berent. *Königtum und Städte bis zum Ende des Investiturstreits: Die Politik der Ottonen und Salier gegenüber den werdenden Städten im östlichen Sachsen und in Nordthüringen.* Sigmaringen, 1977.

Tellenbach, Gerd. "From the Carolingian Imperial Nobility to the German Estate of Imperial Princes." In *The Medieval Nobility: Studies on the Ruling Classes of France and Germany from the Sixth to the Twelfth Century,* edited and translated by Timothy Reuter. Amsterdam, 1978.

Violante, Cinzio. "I vescovi dell'Italia centro-settentrionale e lo sviluppo dell'economia monetaria." In *Vescovi e diocesi in Italia nel Medioevo (sec. IX–XIII),* 193–217. Atti del II convegno di storia della chiesa in Italia. Italia sacra, no. 5. Padua, 1964.

———. "Quelque caractéristiques des structures familiales en Lombardie, Emilie et Toscanie aux XIe et XIIe siècles." In *Famille et parenté dans l'occident médiéval,* 87–125. Collection de l'Ecole Française de Rome, no. 30. Rome, 1977.

———. "Pievi e parrocchie dalla fine del X all'inizio del XIII secolo." In *Le istituzioni ecclesiastiche della societas christiana' dei secoli XI–XII. Diocesi, pievi e parrocchie.* Miscellanea del Centro di studi medioevali, vol. 8. Milan, 1977.

———. *La società milanese nell'età precommunale.* Rome, 1981.

German Kingship

Baaken, Gerhard. "Königtum, Burgen und Königsfreie." In *Vorträge und Forschungen* herausgegeben vom Konstanzer Arbeitskreis für mittelalterliche Geschichte 6:9–95. Sigmaringen, 1961.

Bloch, Marc. *The Royal Touch: Sacred Monarchy and Scrofula in England and France.* Translated by J. E. Anderson. London, 1973.

Bosl, Karl. *Die Reichsministerialität der Salier und Staufer.* MGH Schriften 10. Stuttgart, 1950–51.

Brühl, Carlrichard. *Fodrum, gistum, servitium regis.* 2 vols. Cologne and Graz, 1968.

Fleckenstein, Josef. *Die Hofkapelle der deutschen Könige.* Vol. 2, *Die Hofkapelle im Rahmen der ottonisch-salischen Reichskirche.* MGH Schriften 16. Stuttgart, 1966.

———. "Problematik und Gestalt der ottonisch-salischen Reichskirche." In *Reich und Kirche vor dem Investiturstreit: Vorträge beim wissenschaftlichen*

Kolloquium aus Anlass des achtzigsten Geburtstags von Gerd Tellenbach, edited by Karl Schmid, 83–98. Sigmaringen, 1985.

Folz, Robert. *The Concept of Empire in Western Europe from the Fifth to the Fourteenth Centuries.* London, 1969.

Ganahl, Karl Hans. *Studien zur Geschichte des kirchlichen Verfassungsrechts im 10. und 11. Jahrhundert.* Innsbruck and Vienna, 1935.

Grundmann, Herbert. "Freiheit als religiöses, politisches und persönliches Postulat im Mittelalter." *HZ* 183 (1957):23–53.

Heusinger, Bruno. "Servitium regis in der deutschen Kaiserzeit." *Archiv für Urkundenforschung* 8 (1923):26–159.

Hlawitschka, Eduard. "Die Thronkandidaturen von 1002 und 1024: Gründeten sie im Verwandtenanspruch oder in Vorstellungen von freier Wahl?" In *Reich und Kirche vor dem Investiturstreit,* edited by Karl Schmid, 49–64. Sigmaringen, 1985.

Keller, Hagen. "Grundlagen ottonischer Königsherrschaft." In *Reich und Kirche vor dem Investiturstreit,* edited by Karl Schmid, 17–34. Sigmaringen, 1985.

Leyser, Karl. *Medieval Germany and Its Neighbours, 900–1250.* London, 1982. Collected papers.

———. *The Ascent of Latin Europe.* Oxford, 1985.

Mayer, Theodor. "The Historical Foundations of the German Constitution." In *Medieval Germany,* 1–33.

———. "The State of the Dukes of Zähringen." In *Medieval Germany,* 175–202.

———. *Fürsten und Staat.* Weimar, 1950. Collected papers.

———, ed. *Das Königtum: Seine geistigen und rechtlichen Grundlagen.* Vorträge und Forschungen herausgegeben vom Konstanzer Arbeitskreis für mittelalterliche Geschichte, vol. 3. Lindau and Constance, 1956. The papers by E. Ewig, O. Höfler, W. Schlesinger, R. Buchner, H. Büttner, T. Mayer, H. Beumann, F. Kempf, M. Hellmann, and O. Brunner have lost nothing of their importance.

Mitteis, Heinrich. "Feudalism and the German Constitution." In *Medieval Germany,* 235–80.

Müller-Mertens, Eckhard. *Regnum Teutonicum. Aufkommen und Verbreitung der deutschen Reichs- und Königsauffassung im frühen Mittelalter.* 2d ed. Vienna, 1970.

Pahncke, Hans. *Geschichte der Bischöfe Italiens deutscher Nation von 951–1264.* Vol. 1, *951–1004.* Vaduz, 1913.

Prinz, Friedrich. *Klerus und Krieg im frühen Mittelalter: Untersuchungen zur Rolle der Kirche beim Aufbau der Königsherrschaft.* Stuttgart, 1971.

Reuter, Timothy. "The 'Imperial Church System' of the Ottonian and Salian Rulers: A Reconsideration." *Journal of Ecclesiastical History* 33 (1982):347–74.

———, ed. and trans. *The Medieval Nobility: Studies on the Ruling Classes of France and Germany from the Sixth to the Twelfth Century.* Amsterdam, 1978. A very important collection of papers that are nowhere else available in English.

Santifaller, Leo. *Zur Geschichte des ottonisch-salischen Reichskirchensystems.* Akademie der Wissenschaften, Vienna. Philosophisch-historische Klasse. *Sitzungsberichte,* vol. 229 Erste Abhandlung. 1954.

Sauerländer, Willibald. "Cluny und Speyer." In *Investiturstreit und Reichsverfassung*, 9–31.

Schmeidler, Bernhard. "Franconia's Place in the Structure of Mediaeval Germany." In *Medieval Germany*, 71–93.

Schmidt, Roderich. "Königsumritt und Huldigung in ottonisch-salischer Zeit." In *Vorträge und Forschungen* herausgegeben vom Konstanzer Arbeitskreis für mittelalterliche Geschichte 6:97–233. Sigmaringen, 1961.

Schmitt, Ursula. *Villa regalis Ulm und Kloster Reichenau. Untersuchungen zur Pfalzfunktion des Reichsklostergutes in Alemannien (9.–12 Jahrhundert).* Göttingen, 1974.

Tellenbach, Gerd. *Königtum und Stämme in der Werdezeit des deutschen Reichs.* Weimar, 1939.

———. "Die abendländische Kirche des zehnten und elften Jahrhunderts im Ganzen der Kirchengeschichte." In *Aus Kirche und Reich: Studien zu Theologie, Politik und Recht im Mittelalter. Festschrift für Friedrich Kempf.* Edited by Hubert Mordek, 125–30. Sigmaringen, 1983.

Ullmann, Walter. "Reflections upon the Medieval Empire." *Transactions of the Royal Historical Society,* 5th ser., 14 (1964):89–108.

Werner, Karl Ferdinand. "Das hochmittelalterliche Imperium im politischen Bewusstsein Frankreichs (10.–12. Jahrhundert). *HZ* 200 (1965):1–60.

Wollasch, Joachim. "Der Einfluss des Mönchtums auf Reich und Kirche vor dem Investiturstreit." In *Reich und Kirche vor dem Investiturstreit: Vorträge beim wissenschaftlichen Kolloquium aus Anlass des achtzigsten Geburtstags von Gerd Tellenbach,* edited by Karl Schmid, 35–48. Sigmaringen, 1985.

The Ottonians

Anton, Hans Hubert. *Der sogenannte Traktat "De ordinando pontifice": Ein Rechtsgutachten in Zusammenhang mit der Synode von Sutri.* Bonn, 1982.

Bloch, Herbert. "Der Autor der 'Graphia aurea urbis Romae.'" *DA* 40 (1984): 55–175.

Erdmann, Carl. "Der Heidenkrieg in der Liturgie und die Kaiserkrönung Ottos I." *MIÖG* 46 (1932).

Fichtenau, Heinrich. "Vom Ansehen des Papsttums im zehnten Jahrhundert." In *Aus Kirche und Reich: Studien zu Theologie, Politik und Recht im Mittelalter. Festschrift für Friedrich Kempf.* Edited by Hubert Mordek, 117–24.

Franke, Wilhelm. *Romuald von Camaldoli und seine Reformtätigkeit zur Zeit Ottos III.* Berlin, 1913.

Goez, Werner. "Imperator advocatus Romanae ecclesiae." In *Aus Kirche und Reich: Studien zu Theologie, Politik und Recht im Mittelalter. Festschrift für Friedrich Kempf.* Edited by Hubert Mordek, 315–28.

Hamilton, Bernard. *Monastic Reform, Catharism and the Crusades (900–1300).* London, 1979. Pt. 1: 5–216, contains important papers on the church in Rome, including its relationship with the East.

Hoffmann, Hartmut. "Zur Geschichte Ottos des Grossen." *DA* 28 (1972): 42–73.

Holtzmann, Robert. *Otto der Grosse.* Berlin, 1936.

Keller, Hagen. "Das Kaisertum Ottos d. Gr. im Verständnis seiner Zeit." *DA* 20 (1964):325–88.

———. "Grundlagen ottonischer Königsherrschaft." In *Reich und Kirche vor dem Investiturstreit,* edited by Karl Schmid, 17–34.

Leyser, Karl. *Rule and Conflict in an Early Medieval Society.* Bloomington, Ind., 1979.

———. "Ottonian Government." *EHR* 96 (1981):721–53.

Lintzel, Martin. *Die Kaiserpolitik Ottos d. Gr.* Munich, 1943.

Löwe, Heinrich. "Kaisertum und Abendland in ottonischer und frühsalischer Zeit." *HZ* 196 (1963):529–62.

Mitteilungen des Instituts für Österreichische Geschichtsforschung. Ergänzungsband 20, *Festschrift zur Jahrtausendfeier der Kaiserkrönung Ottos des Grossen.* Vienna, 1962.

Morghen, Raffaele. "Otto III. servus apostolorum." In *I problemi dell'Europa postcarolingia.* Miscellanea del Centro di studi medioevali 2. Milan, 1955.

Ohnsorge, Werner. *Das Zweikaiserproblem.* Hildesheim, 1947.

Rentschler, M. *Liudprand von Cremona: Eine Studie zum ost-westlichen Kulturgefälle im Mittelalter.* Frankfurt am Main, 1981.

Schieffer, Theodor. "Heinrich II. und Konrad II.: Die Umprägung des Geschichtsbildes durch die Kirchenreform des elften Jahrhunderts." *DA* 8 (1950):384–437.

Schramm, Percy Ernst. *Kaiser, Rom und Renovatio: Studien und Texte zur Geschichte des Römischen Erneuerungsgedankens vom Ende des karolingischen Reiches bis zum Investiturstreit.* 2 vols. Leipzig and Berlin, 1929.

Uhrlirz, Mathilde. "Otto III. und das Papsttum." *HZ* 162 (1940):258–68.

Vollrath, Hanna. "Kaisertum und Patriziat." *ZKG* 85 (1974):11–44.

Henry III

Anton, Hans Hubert. "Bonifaz von Canossa, Markgraf von Tuszien, und die Italienpolitik der frühen Salier." *HZ* 214 (1972):529–56.

Borino, Giovanni Battista. "L'Elezione e la deposizione di Gregorio VI." *Archivio della R. Società Romana di Storia Patria* 39 (1916).

Boshof, Egon. "Das Reich in der Krise." *HZ* 228 (1979):265–87.

Bulst-Thiele, Marie Luise. *Kaiserin Agnes.* Leipzig, 1933.

Cowdrey, H. E. J. "Archbishop Aribert II of Milan." *History* 51 (1966):1–15.

Erdmann, Carl. "Der ungesalbte König." *DA* 2 (1938):311–40.

Fuhrmann, Horst. "Studien zur Geschichte mittelalterlicher Patriarchate, 3. Teil (Schluss)." *ZRG Kan. Abt.* 41 (1955):95–183.

Gaudemet, Jean. "Note sur le symbolisme médiéval: Le mariage de l'évêque." *L'Année canonique* 22 (1978):71–80.

Glaeske, Günter. *Die Erzbischöfe von Hamburg-Bremen als Reichsfürsten.* Hildesheim, 1962.

Hoffmann, Hartmut. *Gottesfriede und Treuga Dei.* MGH Schriften, vol. 20. Stuttgart, 1964.

———. "Von Cluny zum Investiturstreit." *Archiv für Kulturgeschichte* 45 (1963):165–203. Reprinted with important additions in *Cluny: Beiträge zu*

Gestalt und Wirkung der cluniazensischen Reform, edited by Helmut Richter, 319– 70. Darmstadt, 1975.

Johnson, Edgar N. "Adalbert of Hamburg-Bremen." *Speculum* 9 (1934) : 147–79.

Kehr, Paul Fridolin. "Vier Kapitel aus der Geschichte Kaiser Heinrichs III." *Abhandlungen der Preussischen Akademie der Wissenschaften Berlin.* Philosophisch-historische Klasse. 1931.

Ladner, Gerhart Burian. *Theologie und Politik vor dem Investiturstreit.* Baden near Vienna, 1936.

Poole, Reginald Lane. "Benedict IX and Gregory VI." In *Studies in Chronology and History.* Oxford, 1934.

Schmidt, Paul Gerhard. "Heinrich III: Das Bild des Herrschers in der Literatur seiner Zeit." *DA* 39 (1983) : 582–90.

Schnith, Karl. "Recht und Friede: Zum Königsgedanken im Umkreis Heinrich III." *Historisches Jahrbuch* 81 (1962) : 22–57.

Tellenbach, Gerd. *Church, State and Christian Society at the Time of the Investiture Contest.* Translated by R. F. Bennett. Oxford, 1970.

Violante, Cinzio. "Aspetti della politica italiana di Enrico III prima della sua discesa in Italia (1039–1046)." *Rivista storica italiana* 64 (1952) : 157–76, and 293–314. Chapter 2 of Violante, *La Pataria.*

———. *La Pataria Milanese e la Riforma ecclesiastica, I: Le premesse (1045– 1057).* Milan, 1955.

Zimmermann, Harald. *Papstabsetzungen des Mittelalters.* Graz, 1968.

CHAPTER 3

Reform and Rome

1. Monastic Renewal and Reform of the Church at Large

With the intervention of Emperor Henry III in 1046 at Sutri and in Rome, church reform began to take hold in the Eternal City. Because of the extremely brief reigns of the first two German popes, Clement II and Damasus II, only their names, harking back to namesakes in the ancient church, indicate a connection with reform efforts. In fact, Damasus ruled for no more than twenty-three days from Rome, for he had had to battle once more against the Tusculan pope, Benedict IX. Neither Damasus nor Clement had the opportunity to identify with his new dignity and new environment. Their former dioceses continued to be the primary focus of concern, and as was customary at the time, they continued to administer the bishoprics. The first imperial nominee to experience a longer pontificate was the Lotharingian Bishop Bruno of Toul (since 1026), who was enthroned in 1049 with the name of Leo IX (1049–54). It was Pope Leo IX, therefore, who accomplished the first significant breakthroughs on behalf of the early reform in Rome. By the time of his pontificate, renewal of religious life had become a matter of the deepest concern for many monks and for members of the clergy and the laity. With the ascent of Leo IX, the pope became the leader of the eleventh-century reform movement.

The origins of the reform are still hotly debated. Are they rooted in the monastic renewal associated with Cluny or in the reform associated with Gorze? Did they come from Lotharingian centers of legal study? Are they primarily, if not exclusively, due to the revolutionary genius of Gregory VII, inspired perhaps by Cardinal Humbert of Silva Candida? To answer these questions, it is essential to begin with the recognition that the Gregorian reform ideology evolved gradually and that we cannot single out any one event, or any one individual if we are to discover the wellsprings of that reform.

There can be no question that the same roots nourished both monastic and church reform and that the monastic reforms prepared the way for the reform of the church at large. This movement is best described as an expansion and deepening of monastic concern for religious renewal that eventually was shared by ever larger groups both within the church and among the laity. We would do well, though, to recall Kassius Hallinger's admonition that "connecting links are not to be confused with equal signs." Reform connotes renewal and return to an original, earlier condition perceived to have been both perfect and pristine. For the monastic reform, this original, perfect condition was represented by the state of monastic life created, at least in theory, by Benedict of Aniane. For the ecclesiastical reform, the ideal was a return to the primitive church and the conditions associated with it. Chronologically, the "primitive" church was never precisely defined. The reformers harkened back to the church that seemed to them to issue from the pages of the correspondence of Pope Gregory the Great (590–604) and the ancient canonical collections, or collections assumed to be ancient. Both branches of the reform, ecclesiastical and monastic, were expressions of the contemporary spirituality, whereby church and world were but different aspects of a single unified Christian entity. Laymen, priests, and monks had been assigned specific functions, but all pursued a single purpose: the fullest possible realization of the Kingdom of God in the here and now.

Since the publication of Ernst Sackur's impressive volumes on Cluny and the Cluniacs, and particularly of Gerd Tellenbach's influential work, the monastic ideal of withdrawal from the world is cited by those who hold that monastic renewal and ecclesiastical reform were separate and fundamentally different movements. Tellenbach, discussing the medieval concept of a hierarchical world order "which linked all things together, but also classified and ranked them," sketches the traits of what he calls the monastic hierarchy. To him, monasticism, and especially eremitism, represent the noblest rank attainable on earth. The ideal of monasticism—flight from the world—permits the full flowering of the monastic hierarchy without ever coming in conflict with or even impinging on the theocratic hierarchy with the anointed ruler at its head. This is not to say, however, that monastic reform extended no further than the walls of the monastery. Certainly, neither Cluny nor Gorze could have prospered as they did without the support of their founders. Had not the laity shared monastic ideals, Duke William of Aquitaine would probably not have insisted on the unusual charter that he granted to his foundation Cluny, near Mâcon in Burgundy. According to the charter's provisions, Cluny was to be subject only to Saint Peter, and no earthly power was to have the right to interfere. William's action has been interpreted as a protest against the feudal divisions in French society, but this interpretation is groundless. Surely, William's reasons lay in the very natural desire to protect his monastery from economic as well as spiritual decline, which could easily have been brought about if his descendants, as proprietary lords, should, for example, have appointed a lay abbot, or alienated monastic property. Bishops as proprietary lords often differed very little from noble proprietors. Thus it was an appropriate and logical follow-through to the intentions of the founder when in the course of the tenth and early eleventh centuries Cluny attained, through several papal privileges, complete exemption from its diocesan, the bishop of Mâcon. Since the pope, Cluny's protector and lord, resided in distant Rome, and furthermore, since neither French kings nor German emperors were able to exercise their theoretical sovereignty within the border region of Burgundy, Cluny eventually achieved a "quasi-sovereignty" (Hoffmann), which made it, in effect, an island of independence in Burgundy. It was not, however, the privilege of exemption—and therefore not papal protection—that transformed Cluny into a model of ecclesiastical *libertas:* this transformation is solely the achievement of Cluny's great and saintly abbots and their stern monastic spirituality which, given the abbey's independence, could blossom without hindrance. Joachim Wollasch's study on the foundation of Bourg-Dieu illustrates most clearly why the subjection of a monastery to the Holy See meant very little by itself. Bourg-Dieu, a monastery in Déols, was founded in 917 with a foundation charter that agreed verbatim in every relevant aspect with the foundation charter of 909 for Cluny. Bourg-Dieu, however, never attained a position that could be even remotely compared with the singular standing of Cluny. Cluny's later abbots, in the spirit of its founder, continued efforts to preclude the potential detrimental effects of the proprietary church system on the monastic sphere. The abbey secured its continuous and direct influence on monasteries it had reformed by appointing priors who were subject to the abbot of Cluny. All monasteries directly affiliated with Cluny sent their novices to the Burgundian abbey to make profession there.

The abbots of Cluny saw their foremost task in the preservation of the strict monastic life espoused by the Rule of Saint Benedict. This is not to say, however, that they turned away from the world. Some historians even believe that Cluniac monks organized the reconquista of Spain by French knights in the first half of the eleventh century. Others inappropriately link Cluny's presumed advocacy of the *Pax* and *Treuga dei* (Peace and Truce of God) movement with the warlike aspects of the Peace efforts.

But both of these arguments are as remote from the historical reality as is the belief that Cluniacs disdained any involvement with the world. For the first half of the eleventh century we know no more than that Cluny, like other churches and monasteries, benefited from the efforts of the *Pax* movement to restrict the constant private wars of the nobility. In a letter of September 1016 addressed to the bishops of Burgundy, Aquitaine, and Provence, as well as certain counts of the region, Pope Benedict VIII asked for the protection of Cluny, which was then subject to hostilities by feudal lords from the surrounding territories. The only other item extant about Cluny and the *Pax* and *Treuga* pertains to a council celebrated in the 930s at the earliest, but possibly already promulgating the younger form of the Peace, the *Treuga dei* (Hoffmann). All we know is that Abbot Odilo attended this synod. Thus, claims that Cluny at the time of Saint Odilo was prominently engaged in furthering the Peace and Truce of God are obviously exaggerated. The evidence is even weaker in support of claims that the Cluniacs were involved in the Spanish campaigns. Carl Erdmann pointed out long ago that a letter of Odilo is our only evidence for Cluny's interest in the reconquista. In it the abbot mentioned his many prayers for the liberation of Spain from the infidels!

The legend of the warlike spirit of Cluny can probably be attributed to Bishop Adalbero of Laon (d. 1030). In a famous satire, addressed to the French king, Robert the Pious, Adalbero describes in one section how "King Odilo of Cluny" lined up his monks to fight the Muslims. Adalbero complains that the monks had turned into warrior knights although clergy were to refrain from all secular occupations. Clergy, and Adalbero includes the Cluniacs among them, were to devote their lives to the service of God alone. Erdmann correctly emphasizes that the Cluniacs never engaged in warfare. Hoffmann seems to agree. He points out that Adalbero cannot possibly have had the council of Anse in mind, for he died in 1030, while the council, which is difficult to date, met in the early 1030s. Adalbero's narrative, taken as a whole, suggests that the bishop excoriated the interference of monks in the day-to-day events of secular life, something he apparently resented as an inversion of the social order.

Contemporary sources make abundantly clear that monks from Cluny and elsewhere did not simply banish the laity from their range of vision in order to devote themselves to contemplation and prayer without distraction. There is no need to underline here once again that the same monks who were renowned for their asceticism and sanctity were everywhere among the most highly esteemed advisors of kings, bishops, and nobles, who entrusted them with the reform of monasteries, or that the greatest among them bore the mark of missionary zeal. They believed monasti-

cism to be the most perfect embodiment of the Christian ideal but did not
deny that laymen, too, could lead a life pleasing to God, as we know, for
example, from the *Vita Geraldi* written for a layman by Abbot Odo of
Cluny, or, later, from the correspondence of Gregory VII. Erdmann
points out that "it is a specific characteristic of western monasticism that
an ascetic life for its own sake was deemed unsatisfactory. While always
adhering in principle to the ideal of flight from the world, western monasticism again and again made its influence felt in the secular world, raising
its voice so as to affect the church at large. . . . The revival of asceticism
essentially portended nothing other than a renewal of religious ideals."
The tension between flight from the world and openness to the world is
found not only among the Cluniacs but also among the Lotharingian
monks with their more eremitical inclinations. Strictly speaking, such a
tension is incompatible with the monastic vocation, but was so characteristic of monasticism in the High Middle Ages that even the great Italian
hermits fell under its spell. Under Romuald and Saint Peter Damian a
type of monastery came into being that combined the essential features of
both cenobitic and anchoritic monasticism. The effects of monastic renewal were far from being restricted to the monastic sphere. Nor were
they intended to be; reformation of the world as a whole was the aim.
The influence on kings, the nobility, and the common man was both re-
markably lively and very productive.

A central link between monastic reform and the renewal of Christian
life in general was the reform of the regular canons. Research in this field
still shows many lacunae, but preliminary results indicate that this offshoot of the reform transplanted the ideals of renewal from the monastery to the chapters of the secular clergy. By way of the pulpit, the
unlearned laity, too, became directly acquainted with the causes and aims
of the reform and was touched by spiritual renewal. In the best of all
worlds, the life of the cathedral clergy was to be the equivalent of the life
of the reformed monks. It was to be adapted to a stricter version of the
Aachen rule for canons of 816, obliging them to a life in common. At the
Lateran synod of 1059, Hildebrand especially pressed for a prohibition—
eventually accepted by the assembly—of private property for canons, as
had been permitted under the Aachen rules. Later reforming popes continued to support such efforts, but it must not be forgotten that the reform of regular canons had been initiated by the bishops of France and
Italy. The papacy merely continued what they had begun. The most famous new foundations of houses of regular canons, Saint Ruf at Avignon,
San Frediano at Lucca, and Sante Lorenzo at Olux (diocese Turin), date
to the first half of the eleventh century. The reformation of cathedral

chapters proceeded apace, especially toward the end of the century and in the early twelfth century. Since the days of Gerard of Brogne the adherents of reform had targeted their criticism on priests, and reform of the regular canons is one aspect of wider efforts by the reformers to raise the level of morals, piety, and learning among the clergy. In pursuit of such aims proprietary lords of churches, be they kings, nobles, or bishops, were wont to appoint to episcopal sees monks who were zealous and experienced reformers. In this fashion monks would propagate their monastic convictions in priestly circles and among the laity as well. Odilo of Cluny, Poppo of Stablò-Malmédy, and Richard of Saint Vanne indeed refused episcopal nominations, but they were exceptions confirming the rule that during the eleventh century monks penetrated the ranks of the secular clergy.

There is yet another significant point of contact between monastic reform and the secular world. Abbeys frequently became proprietors of churches and chapels that had been in the hands of laymen or perhaps bishops. This turnover of proprietorship created another forum for acquainting the general public with at least those aspects of monastic reform that touched upon the lives of all Christians. Since the beginnings of monastic renewal in the post-Carolingian period, laity, bishops, and clergy tended to transfer proprietary churches and monasteries to reformed—or even unreformed—monks as donations. In Germany, where the great abbeys pertained to the Empire and were under the protection of the king, this was at first an infrequent occurrence. But it is with only slight exaggeration when Albert Hauck writes of this period that direction of the church devolved from the episcopacy to the monastic order. The diocese of Verdun is an apt illustration. Half of its parish churches were under the care of monasteries "preaching monastic spirituality from the pulpit and demanding it in the confessional." In later years the relations between bishops and monasteries were frequently under serious strain. Cluny's disputes with the bishops of Mâcon, which led to Cluny's successful pursuit of exemption, were only the beginning. Bishops were gradually discovering that they had lost not only much influence in their sees but also income to the reformed monasteries. To remedy the situation, Gregory VII decreed at the Roman council of 1078 that monasteries could accept church fees only with the approval of the diocesan bishop. Hugh of Die, Gregory's legate, soon promulgated a general prohibition forbidding monasteries to accept donations of proprietary churches unless they had obtained episcopal permission. In the ninth and tenth centuries, and even the first half of the eleventh century, the situation had been very different. Bishops friendly toward the reform generally supported the acquisition of churches by monasteries, sometimes hoping to augment their own influence in this fashion. Charters throw light on the motivation behind such donations to the monks. Like other gifts to the church, they were made by men acutely conscious of the burden of sin they had accumulated in the course of a lifetime. In fear of eternal damnation, they hoped the prayers of the ascetic and chaste monks would help them to prevail amidst the horrors of the Last Judgment. Up to the mid-eleventh century, however, there is no sign, for example, that Cluny sought to obtain churches and monasteries for reasons of rejection of the proprietary church system and the concomitant lay influence on the church (Tellenbach).

2. Pope Leo IX, His Collaborators, and Reforms at the Curia

Contacts between monastery and world were strikingly many and varied. It might seem superfluous to underline this cardinal fact, but the relationship between monastic reform and renewal of the church at large is still debated and only poorly understood. Following the breakthrough by Emperor Henry III in Rome, church reform progressed rapidly and reached a watershed with the pontificate of Leo IX. The future pontiff arrived in Rome in pilgrim's dress. His biographer reports that he had insisted on election by the clergy and people of Rome before accepting the nomination, that is, an election in harmony with the canon law. Paul Schmid's well-known work shows persuasively that Leo IX shared understanding of the concept of "canonical election" with his contemporaries: the voluntary acclamation of a designated candidate. Many of those who entered the Eternal City together with Leo are later found in the vanguard of reform: Hildebrand (later Pope Gregory VII), fresh from spending some two years north of the Alps as companion of the exiled Gregory VI; the monk Humbert from the monastery of Moyenmoutier (diocese Toul); and the Archdeacon Frederick of Liège, a brother of the Duke Godfrey the Bearded, who had rebelled so often against Emperor Henry III. Frederick was later to become abbot of Montecassino and eventually Pope Stephen IX. Hugh the White from the abbey of Remiremont (diocese Toul), later a cardinal-priest, also came to Rome at this time. Another influential person in the entourage of Leo IX was Archbishop Halinard of Lyons. Halinard was one of Leo's closest collaborators and spent as much time as possible in his company, although he did not stay permanently at the curia.

When the new pope and his entourage of monks and clergy crossed the Alps into Italy, they brought along concepts and ideology honed in their native Lotharingia, a border area between France and Germany. Like Burgundy, Lotharingia had earlier attracted attention. Its bishops and abbots displayed unusual attitudes toward the kings of France and Germany. Furthermore, the study of canon law enjoyed particular favor in the region. Thus the conclusion seems attractive that church reform had been imported from the "Lotharingian law schools." But does this necessarily imply that the Italians looked upon these ideas as alien? Despite some recent revisions, the consensus is still that the last Tusculan popes were hardly zealous reformers. And yet, even in the darkest of times they upheld papal ideology as it had evolved at least since the time of Leo I (440–61). Witness the arenas of the papal chancery and synodal decisions, such as those of the 1022 council of Pavia. At the urging of the pope this assembly renewed the ancient prohibition on clerical marriage and decreed that the sons of unfree clergy were to remain in their fathers' status. It is true that these decrees were issued in order to protect ecclesiastical and monastic property and not to raise ecclesiastical morals, but the reference to ancient canon law and the requirement of celibacy may suffice to prove a point. The earliest demands of the reformers were precisely celibacy and the abolition of simony.

The writings of Peter Damian prove that the chief concerns of the Lotharingians were far from being considered innovative in Italy. Damian, the fervent disciple of Romuald, was born in Ravenna and eventually became prior of Fonte Avellana. Indefatigable in his pursuit of reform, he considered simony and clerical marriage the most serious abuses crying out for remedy. The long-sought support came at first from Emperor Henry III, but then also from Pope Leo IX, to whom Damian had dedicated his *Liber Gomorrhianus* shortly after his arrival in Rome. Leo's synods leave no doubt that he shared the views of Peter Damian on moral laxity among the clergy, the primary focus of reform in Rome. Damian and the Lotharingians were also in full agreement on another issue, which was to be of great significance for reform of the church at large: papal primacy. Damian's views had developed long before Leo assumed the papal mantle. Monsignor John J. Ryan has shown conclusively that Damian was more than an excellent rhetorician—he had also studied canon law extensively. Like many of his contemporaries, Damian literally regarded the authentic decrees of the fathers as *sacri canones*, the sacred pronouncements of popes, councils, and church fathers inspired by the Holy Spirit. Abbot Siegfried of Gorze took the same position in his letter of 1043 to Poppo of Stablò-Malmédy, in which he equates canons with the divine law ("constat et indubitanter verum est canonicam auctoritatem dei esse legem").

Peter Damian was convinced that it was impossible for the laws of God to contradict each other, and harmonization of seemingly contradictory passages was one of his main concerns. In 1049, in his *Liber Gomorrhianus* he excluded two canons he found lacking in authenticity. They were, he wrote, of dubious origin, and their prescriptions were unclear. For Damian, all councils, even if not ecumenical, and all papal decretals—because the pope is the successor of Saint Peter—represent legal sources of universal validity. Elsewhere, he further declared that a canon is no longer valid when it contradicts papal decretals ("si decretis Romanorum pontificum non concordat"). This straightforward principle served Damian as the touchstone for the authenticity of any canon, whatever its origin (Ryan). Differing from Cardinals Atto and Humbert of Silva Candida, Damian thus did not presuppose positive papal confirmation of a canon. Instead, he was in agreement with the *Decretum* of Burchard of Worms, a canonical collection he frequently used. Reasoning from this principle of concordance Damian came to declare anyone a heretic who did not agree with the Roman church ("haereticus esse constat, qui Romanae ecclesiae non concordat"). Slightly altered, this sentence is frequently attributed to Ambrose of Milan ("haereticum esse constat, qui Romanae ecclesiae non concordat") and is found in very similar form in the *dictatus papae* of Gregory VII: "Quod catholicus non habeatur, qui non concordat Romanae ecclesiae." It should be noted, however, that according to Peter Damian, disobedience turns into heresy only if it is maintained pertinaciously and with inner conviction, that is, if it corresponds to *contumacia*. As a final corollary of the concordance requirement, Damian defined as a heretic "anyone wishing to deprive the Roman church of the privilege she alone has received from Christ." This ringing declaration of the divine foundation of the Catholic church and of the primacy of the Roman church, but as textually transmitted by the *Decretum Gelasianum*, was also the basis for one of the sentences of the *dictatus papae*. The Apostle Peter, the pope, and the Roman church were, for Damian, one and the same, and the obedience owed to the pontiff thus became absolute.

During the Gregorian reform obedience to papal commands was raised to the level of dogma, as Yves Congar and Othmar Hageneder stress. Congar holds that the "Ambrose" statement constitutes the main theme of the Gregorians, a view shared by Horst Fuhrmann. The theme of the Gregorian reform, then, was a principle of Peter Damian even before the synod of Sutri of 1046. Although historians have paid scant attention to Damian's views until recently, his contemporaries were very much aware of them. Hildebrand, later Gregory VII, certainly had good reason for turning to Peter Damian once again in 1059 and repeating the earlier request that he compile a canon law collection from excerpts of papal letters and from the papal histories that "specifically concerned the authority of the Holy See."

Damian certainly had no need to await instruction in canon law from the Lotharingian companions of Leo IX. The once-convincing thesis that church reform was an import from Lotharingia is no longer tenable. Even before Leo's accession, the prior of Fonte Avellana had come across definitions of papal primacy in canon law, the *Decretum* of Burchard of Worms and the *Dionysiana*, as well as in the register and the *Vita* of Pope Gregory the Great, that reflected his sentiments on the incomparably exalted position of the papacy. He then used these formulations in his works as legal undergirding for his convictions. In contrast to Humbert of Silva Candida, Peter Damian used Pseudo-Isidorian texts only rarely, and when he did so, it was probably indirectly through works that had incorporated the False Decretals. While there were indeed several currents among the reformers, there is no hint of disagreement about papal primacy. The reformers all felt a great urgency to reform the papacy: in accordance with the *decreta patrum* the papacy had to be at the head of ecclesiastical reform. Damian declared in a letter of mid-1045 to Cardinal Stephen that the entire world would certainly long continue in its sins, unless the Holy See were to find itself once again in the state of grace. Little wonder that Peter Damian joyously welcomed Henry's intervention at Sutri in the autumn of 1046.

The pontificate of Leo IX was the first fruitful result of the imperial intervention, since both of his German predecessors, Clement II and Damasus II, reigned only very briefly. Leo IX faced three major problems: realization of church reform, protection of the papal states from Norman attacks, and resolution of disputes with Byzantium. His extensive journeys through Italy, France, and Germany, even through Hungary, are the most obvious feature distinguishing Leo's pontificate from that of his predecessors as well as his successors. He convened numerous synods and supported the *Pax* and *Treuga dei* movement in France. At least north of the Alps, the papacy had been venerated more or less in the abstract. Under Leo IX, almost overnight, the papacy became a living and ever-present reality for all Christians.

On the reform front, Leo IX fought most vehemently against clerical marriage and simony. But enforcing celibacy was a difficult task. The issue touched primarily on the lives of the lower-ranked clergy; a married bishop was an exception, even in Italy. The pontiff also furthered the cause of canonical elections with his own entry into Rome, and the great synod of Reims celebrated in October 1049. "Free canonical election," in the parlance of Leo and his contemporaries, meant acclamation of a designated candidate by clergy and people of the new diocese. Leo IX had insisted on just such an "election" by the clergy and people of Rome when he accepted the designation as pope just before Christmas 1048 from a Roman delegation staying at the imperial court. Leo's wishes coincided with those of the chapter of Magdeburg cathedral that had created so many difficulties at the time of Henry II. The concurrence shows that it would not do simply to dismiss Leo's conditional acceptance of the nomination as mere form, at the same time, however, it has to be kept in mind that Leo did not reject the imperial right to designations, but these had to be in harmony with the wishes of the diocese or abbey.

Soon after Leo arrived in Rome he attacked nicolaitism—the marriage or concubinage of priests—and simony. In April 1049 he already held his first synod in the Lateran palace. Following solemn reconfirmation of the decrees of the first four ecumenical councils and the demand for obedience to all papal decretals, the council immediately launched proceedings against bishops accused of simony. Anyone unable to prove his innocence was deposed without further ado. All consecrations by simonists were declared invalid. At this stage the Lateran basilica erupted in tumult. Priests and deacons, with the support of some bishops, declared that such a nullification would cause the cessation of divine services. Eventually Leo had to content himself with a repetition of the decree of the synod of January 1047, held by Clement II and Emperor Henry III. The canon imposed forty days of penance on all who had knowingly allowed themselves to be ordained or consecrated by a simonist. Such clerics were permitted, however, to retain their offices. Peter Damian and Bonizo of Sutri rounded out this report by adding that Leo further stipulated that all wives and concubines of priests in Rome and its vicinity were to be declared unfree and to become the property of the Roman Church. The canons of the synod of Mainz held in the same year contain similar decisions, whereas the extant decrees of the synod of Reims include only canons from the reformers' program against simony and for canonical elections. Damian's statement, that Leo reordained bishops who had been ordained by simonists, is to be taken at face value according to Louis Saltet, John T. Gilchrist, and Friedrich Kempf. If Leo indeed "repeated" such ordinations, it follows that he must have looked upon simoniacal ordinations as being without substance whatsoever. Such uncompromising strictness was later to be propagated by the first two books of the *Libri tres adversus simoniacos* by Humbert of Silva Candida and was perhaps also shared to some extent by Pope Gregory VII, as the autumn synod of 1078 indicates. The term *simony* is derived from Simon Magus of the Acts of the Apostles, who offered money to Saint Peter to impart the Holy Spirit (8:9–24). But from the fourth century on, the connotations of simony went beyond the attempted purchase of spiritual power described in Acts. Simony meant, first, the purchase or sale of ecclesiastical offices, estates, and sacraments, even if money changed hands in the guise of fees or gifts (*munus a manu*); second, their acquisition through service or favors (*munus ab obsequio*); and third, their acquisition through intercession (*munus a lingua*). The tripartite division derives from Pope Gregory the Great and was frequently cited in the course of eleventh-century reform. *Simoniaca haeresis* as a concept was older still, but here, too, the definition used during the reform was that given by Gregory I.

Historically, the dispute over the validity of simoniacal ordinations is part of the debate on the efficacy of sacraments conferred by unworthy priests. In alignment with Augustine, orthodox Catholic teaching today accepts the validity of such sacraments. In the eleventh century this attitude had its foremost proponent in Peter Damian. It was especially Damian's *Liber gratissimus* that provided firm theological foundations for orthodox arguments. The treatise was based on the work of Auxilius (c. 870–920), a contemporary defender of the ordinations conveyed by Pope Formosus (891–96), and focused on the question of the validity of ordinations conferred without charge by simonists. Damian argued that a priest thus ordained could not be reordained, nor was he a heretic who had to be received anew into the church. Damian not only rejected reordination but also did not regard the simonist himself, albeit guilty of *simoniaca haeresis,* as a heretic, in the strict sense of the word. In Damian's view, the efficacy of a sacrament did not depend on the personal worthiness of the priest who conferred it but was mediated by the Holy Spirit immanent in the sacrament.

Humbert of Silva Candida vehemently disagreed. In the first two books of the *Libri tres adversus simoniacos,* written in 1057/58, he pronounced the nullity of simoniacal ordinations and the necessity for "(re)ordinations." He reserved his most violent rhetorical attacks for Auxilius' arguments, the same arguments Peter Damian had relied on earlier, in favor of the ordinations and consecrations (at the time, these terms were not distinguished) of the unfortunate Pope Formosus. The very word *reordination* evoked horror in Cardinal Humbert. Since a simonist did not actually purchase but only seemingly purchased the Holy Spirit, he did not possess it and could not pass it on in his ordinations. To Humbert, every ordination conferred by a simonist was nothing but an empty formality without the least significance. Thus it is only logical for Humbert to deny that Leo conferred reordinations. In the eyes of Humbert, the laying on of hands practiced by the pope constituted the first effective ordination. "Humbert perceived an indissoluble bond between the ultimate truth revealed in the sacrament and its temporal effect, mediated by the human priest. . . . Even baptism performed by a heretic was to Humbert no more than an imperfect sacrament" (Ladner). Humbert's views in turn gave rise to the logical conclusion that priests as human beings were beyond the faults of ordinary men and had left behind the sins of the world at their ordination. Moreover, it seemed proper that, just as the priests' sacraments belonged to the realm of the spirit and of the intellect, so then did the priests as human beings. Notwithstanding the then undisputed preeminence of the spiritual over the secular sphere, Humbert's deductions were unusual. Augustine had already accepted the impossibility of realizing here on earth a church that is spiritually pure, and it is not surprising that Humbert's ideas, as expressed in the *Libri tres,* found barely an echo among his contemporaries. Victory was to be with the sacramental theology of Peter Damian.

At the time of Leo IX the theoretical disputations between Peter Damian and Humbert of Silva Candida still lay in the future, although Leo's activities in harmony with Humbert's ideas surely were one of the impulses leading to the dispute. Attracting less attention than Leo's vigorous persecution of simony and nicolaitism, but in the long run at least as influential, were the administrative changes in the Roman ecclesiastical bureaucracy during his pontificate, which made possible a papal policy independent of Roman noble families and their supporters. The most important change, the rise of the college of cardinals, had its origins in his pontificate. For centuries, the cardinal-bishops of the suburbicarian sees and the cardinal-priests and deacons of the title churches had shared liturgical functions at the basilica of the Lateran and at certain other Roman churches. Under Leo and his successors these liturgical functions quickly receded into the background. Instead, the cardinals became increasingly active in papal government and were to be found among the foremost collaborators of the popes. When the election decree of 1059 was issued under Pope Nicholas II, the political leadership role of the cardinal-bishops was already prominent. The other two ranks of the later college of cardinals, the cardinal-priests and cardinal-deacons, evolved in the same direction, but they were not immediately considered the equals of cardinal-bishops. In short, the later college of cardinals was no more than adumbrated in Leo's reign.

The pontificates of Urban II (1088–99) and Paschal II (1099–118) were particularly significant for subsequent developments regarding the cardinals. Both popes sought out the cardinals as allies in their fight against the anti-pope Wibert-Clement III and his successors and were thus obliged to make concessions. Leo IX himself apparently nominated only Humbert of Moyenmoutier as cardinal-bishop of Silva Candida in 1050. Bonizo's references to Azelin of Sutri, who had come from Compiègne, are unclear. Nevertheless, Leo IX did not name any new suburbicarian bishop besides Humbert. Given these circumstances, we may tentatively conclude that the cardinal-bishoprics were already in the hands of worthy ecclesiastics who supported the efforts of Leo IX to renew the church. The next pope to fill a vacant suburbicarian see was Victor II (1055–57). He raised the Italian monk Boniface to the cardinal-bishopric of Albano. Pope Stephen IX (1057–58) elevated Peter Damian to the cardinal-bishopric of Ostia. By this time the cardinal-bishops were proving themselves loyal assistants of the popes. Exceptions were John of Velletri and Rainerius of Palestrina, also abbot of the monastery of Saints Cosmae et Damiani. After the death of Stephen IX in 1058, the Romans elected John (anti-)Pope Benedict X. Rainerius supported John-Benedict, and thus both were eliminated from the ranks of the reformers. In about 1060, therefore, all of the suburbicarian bishops were to be counted among the supporters of the reform, an astonishing feat, considering that the lands surrounding the sees of Albano, Palestrina, Velletri, Sutri, and Tusculum were in the hands of the feudal nobility, as Tilmann Schmidt points out. The reformers had broken the hold of these families on the papacy. According to one of the *vitae* of Leo IX, the pope is said to have decided at the April synod of 1050 in Rome to lead a campaign against Tusculum in order to break the resistance of the former Pope Benedict IX and his supporters who were entrenched there. Anti-pope Benedict X (1058–59) had supporters in Tusculum as well and fled there when he was driven from Rome.

We know little in this period about the cardinal-priests of the Roman titular churches. Only rarely can we say with certainty whether or not a priest named in the sources was an adherent of the Roman reformers. But there are some exceptions. Hugh Candidus from the monastery of Remiremont, who had been among Leo's original companions, became cardinal-priest of the church of San Clemente during his pontificate. Also, three title churches in Trastevere, San Grisogono, Santa Cecilia, and Santa Maria, were in the hands of reformers. For San Grisogono, Pope Victor II consecrated Frederick of Lotharingia cardinal-priest. Earlier, Frederick had been chancellor of the Roman church and abbot of Montecassino and eventually was to succeed Victor II as Pope Stephen IX. At

Santa Cecilia, Desiderius of Montecassino was cardinal, and Cardinal-
Priest John of Santa Maria was likewise an adherent of the reformed papacy. The latter held the title at the time of Pope Alexander II (1061–73)
and became cardinal-bishop of Tusculum in 1073.

Although we are relatively well informed about the evolution of the
role of the cardinals, we have almost no information about the *sacrum
palatium Lateranense,* the central papal administrative offices. There are
a few references to individual papal officials, and these are carefully analyzed in the studies of Paul Fridolin Kehr, Karl Jordan, and Reinhard Elze.
The *sacrum palatium Lateranense*—the name is derived from the Donation of Constantine—was the center of what is generally known as the
Papal States, which owed their theoretical foundation to the same forgery.
The former chief administrators were the *iudices de clero* or *ordinarii,* also
called judges palatine, and two especially prominent dignitaries, apparently members of the most powerful Roman noble families, the *ves-
tararius* (administrator of the papal treasury and wardrobe) and the
vicedominus (supervisor of the Lateran palace). As far as we know, the
titles bore little relationship to the offices they designated. These were of
far greater importance than we are initially led to assume. The *vicedominus,* who during the first half of the eleventh century was also archdeacon of the Roman church, represented the pope in his absence from
Rome and had jurisdiction over the clergy of Rome's regional divisions.
During vacancies, the *vicedominus* became one of the administrators of
the papacy in a role the cardinals fully assumed after the middle of the
eleventh century. At the turn of the eleventh century several new initiatives are discernible in the papal administration that apparently relate
to the *Renovatio imperii* of the Ottonians. Some of these changes at the
Lateran, such as institution of the office of chancellor, were modeled after
innovations at the royal court. Karl Jordan argues that the sources indicate a desire on the part of the Tusculan popes to strengthen the ecclesiastical administration, for which their alliance with the German
emperors would provide the necessary backing. In an administrative context, therefore, Leo IX had not broken with the past. Had not the Deacon
Peter, who was simultaneously liberarian and chancellor, continued in
office until his death in 1050? Institutional changes, such as the formation
of the curia and the chapel, had to await the pontificates of Urban II and
Paschal II.

The papal chancery is somewhat better understood than the *sacrum
palatium Lateranense.* Leo introduced several novelties into papal privileges. These documents either reconfirmed or granted for the first time
special and permanent rights to individuals and to corporations such as

monasteries. The changes, some of which grew out of such external pressures as Leo's long, extensive journeys, set a pattern that was followed for many centuries. During Leo's five-and-one-half year pontificate, he spent no more than about half a year in Rome. One conspicuous result was that papyrus almost ceased to be used; another, that the old curial script, in exclusive use until the end of the tenth century, was now replaced by the minuscule script. North of the Alps it would have been impossible to obtain papyrus, a material that was becoming rare about this time. The Roman notaries of the *scrinium,* who alone were skilled in curial script, would accompany the pontiff only infrequently, and so he was forced to rely on non-Roman scribes who wrote in Caroline minuscule. The circumstances were similar under Victor II, who was also often in the entourage of Emperor Henry III. The replacement of the Roman *scriniarii* was certainly not intentional, for under Stephen IX and his successors, up to Pope Calixtus II (1119–24), the curial script reappeared and was used side by side with the minuscule until it disappeared for good after 1123. Of greater interest are textual and formulaic changes in the privileges themselves which were introduced through initiatives of the curia "and very likely of the pope himself" (Santifaller). These changes are witness to the self-confidence of a foreign pope, Leo IX, and his advisors who did not hesitate to break with old customs in chancery style. The rota was introduced into the eschatocol, the last lines of a privilege following upon the body of the text. The rota, a double circle surrounding a cross, replaced a simple cross. One other notable change is the transformation of the old *Bene Valete* of the popes into a monogram, a change with antecedents in imperial documents.

3. The Papacy and the Normans

Although the concerns of church reform took Leo frequently north of the Alps and into amicable collaboration with Emperor Henry III, the situation in southern Italy must have worried him at least as much as did reform in the north. Indeed, though the Saracens had been repelled early in the eleventh century, the Byzantines had once again increased their foothold there and were not willing to relinquish their ancient claims to Apulia, Calabria, and Sicily, having tenaciously defended them against the occidental emperors for many centuries. By the second decade of the eleventh century at the latest, southern Italy had to contend with new arrivals, the Normans. Thus along the southern borders of the Papal States, Lombards, Byzantines, Saracens, and Normans fought for dominance in ever new and shifting patterns of alliance. At the request of Prince

Waimar V of Salerno, an ally of the Normans, Emperor Conrad II, Waimar's feudal lord, enfeoffed one of the Norman leaders with the county of Aversa in a ceremony repeated by Henry III for the latter's successor. Montecassino, like San Vincenzo al Volturno an imperial abbey at the time, had appealed to Henry III for help against the Normans, and in 1047 (?) the emperor invested Drogo, one of the twelve warlike sons of Tankred of Hauteville (Normandy) with the area of and around Melfi, which Drogo had conquered. These enfeoffments, which probably included the use of a flag as a symbol for the investiture, as Josef Deér argues convincingly, represent the first legal recognition of the adventurers from Normandy. Henry III, during his Italian expedition of 1047, had also reinstated Pandulf IV as prince of Capua and had thus forced Waimar to give up Capua and the title *dux Apuliae et Calabriae* which Waimar had used before the emperor's arrival. Conditions in southern Italy must have appeared relatively stable when Henry returned to Germany, and the hopes of Pope Leo IX to enforce papal claims in the region with imperial backing do not appear unreasonable. In 1050 Leo appointed Humbert of Moyenmoutier archbishop of Sicily, which was at the time in the hands of the Saracens and still to be conquered. After the Roman synod of April of the same year, Leo traveled to the south to accept, both on his own behalf and on behalf of the emperor, new submissions by southern Italian counts and princes. The pontiff's activities fell under an imperial-papal condominate, an arrangement for the joint support of church reform and the political interests of the emperor. The loyalty oaths demanded on the occasion also took account of the security needs of the papacy.

Alas, relations between Rome and the Normans soon took a turn for the worse as it became obvious that the Normans were not willing to content themselves with their past conquests. In 1051, in response to an appeal by the citizens of Benevento for papal aid against a Norman siege, Leo IX took over the city on behalf of the Empire and the papacy. Two imperial vassals, Waimar of Salerno and Count Drogo, were murdered one after the other. The situation was so threatening that Leo concluded an alliance with Argyros, the *dux et princeps Italiae* appointed by Constantinople. Argyros, though a son of Meles of Bari who had fought against the Byzantines in the early eleventh century and was eventually forced to flee to the German court, enjoyed the full support and confidence of Emperor Constantine IX Monomachos. Leo thus expected the alliance to engender Byzantine aid against the Norman robber barons. His boldest dream was a triple alliance between both emperors and the papacy, designed to expel the Normans from Italy once and for all. Leo visited Henry in 1052 in an attempt to elicit the dispatch of a German army. The negotiations at Worms resulted in the conclusion of an agreement that is difficult to interpret. Henry III transferred Benevento to the pope *vicariationis gratia*. In return, Leo renounced some uncertain rights in the bishopric of Bamberg, in the abbey of Fulda, and in some other monasteries. Because of opposition by the chancellor, Bishop Gebhard of Eichstätt, however, Henry did not provide the pope with the requested army, and Leo, who felt the urgency of an immediate return, arrived back in Rome with only a small private troop he had hired himself. In June 1053 a united Norman army confronted Leo and his troops at Civitate. The Normans are said to have offered to recognize Leo as feudal lord if he would abandon the Byzantine alliance. But negotiations were unsuccessful and the battle was joined. It ended in the wholesale slaughter of Leo's army and his capture by the Normans. Leo was treated most honorably, however, and released about six months later. It is said that the pope never ceased to mourn his troops, who were soon to be revered as saints. Leo himself died within a year, on 19 April 1054.

Leo's death spared him from learning of the disastrous failure of the embassy he had dispatched to Constantinople under Humbert of Silva Candida, who was arguably Leo's closest collaborator. The purpose had been to reorganize the alliance with Byzantium after the catastrophe of Civitate. Humbert's travel companions were Frederick of Lotharingia, chancellor of the Roman church, and Peter of Amalfi. Emperor Constantine IX was a peace-loving prince, and it was unlikely that he would obstruct a renewal of the alliance. The masterful Patriarch Michael Caerularius (1043–58) was another matter. His anti-Latin measures in Constantinople and hostile anti-Roman propaganda had worked successfully against the imperial southern Italian policies and Constantine's support of Argyros. Cardinal Humbert was never a man to tread softly. In replies, which he may have formulated on behalf of Pope Leo IX, Humbert insisted uncompromisingly on papal primatial rights and papal claims to southern Italy based on the Donation of Constantine. No agreement was possible. Dramatically stormy scenes finally came to an end when Humbert, before his departure, deposited a bull of excommunication of the patriarch and his supporters on the altar of Hagia Sophia. The fateful day was 16 July 1054, long after the death of Leo IX. Humbert and his entourage left without having accomplished anything. At a synod held the same month, Caerularius in his turn excommunicated the Roman legates, designating them legates of Argyros. These events in the summer of 1054 initiated the schism between the Roman and Greek churches.

After drawn-out negotiations, Emperor Henry III designated his chancellor Gebhard of Eichstätt as Leo's successor in 1055. Gebhard adopted the papal name Victor II. An agreement with Byzantium naturally was out of the question, but papal plans for southern Italy initially stayed the course. During Henry's successful Italian campaign against Godfrey of Lotharingia, who had married the widow of Margrave Boniface of Tuscany, the emperor entrusted Pope Victor II with the administration of the duchy of Spoleto and the marquisate of Fermo. The Normans, however, proved unwilling to compromise in any way, their military conquests continued. In the autumn of 1056 Victor thus had to turn to the emperor with a request for military aid, just as Leo IX had been obliged to do before him. This at least is what the so-called *Annales Romani* record. Other sources claim that Victor concluded a peace treaty. Both claims are probably correct, for unexpectedly the emperor died during Victor's stay in Germany. On his deathbed, Henry III entrusted his son and heir, Henry IV, who was less than six years old at the time, as well as the Empire to the care of the pope. Under the circumstances, campaign plans for southern Italy had to be shelved. Victor II succeeded in securing the succession for Henry IV and the regency for the Empress Agnes, but a few months after his return to Italy the pontiff also died without having solved the Norman question. This was also to be the fate of his successor, Frederick of Lotharingia, who ascended the throne as Pope Stephen IX. His experiences as abbot of Montecassino induced him to return to the anti-Norman policies of Pope Leo IX. It was primarily due to Hildebrand that the curia completely reversed its policies toward the Normans under Pope Nicholas II (1059–61). Taking up once again the policies of Emperor Henry III, Nicholas legitimized Norman conquests in southern Italy when at the council of Melfi in August 1059 he invested Robert Guiscard and Richard of Capua with the Italian territories they had conquered and received them as vassals of the Roman church. Robert Guiscard was enfeoffed with present as well as future possessions, which were at the time in the hands of the Byzantines (driven from Italy with the loss of Bari in 1071) and the Saracens (conquest of Messina 1061, of Palermo 1072).

Robert's oath of fealty is preserved in the canonical collection of Cardinal Deusdedit. He promised as duke of Apulia and Calabria by the grace of God and Saint Peter, and with the aid of both, as future duke of Sicily, that he would henceforth be a vassal of the Roman church and of his lord, Pope Nicholas. With the usual formulae of loyalty oaths, Robert Guiscard promised to protect the pope. Another phrase must have appeared of yet greater import: he promised to aid the pope in regaining and preserving regalia and lands of Saint Peter as well as in maintaining him in the papal office. Guiscard also renounced future attacks on papal territories unless requested by the pope or his successors. Furthermore, he swore to pay faithfully a feudal census of twelve *denarii* a year for each yoke of oxen on his lands and to transfer all churches with appurtenances to the pope, with himself as the churches' advocate. He would never swear fealty to anyone except with a provision in favor of the Roman church. In the event that Pope Nicholas or his successor were to die before he did, Robert Guiscard promised to support and aid the "better" cardinals and the Roman clergy and laity in the election and consecration of a new pontiff.

Historians do not agree on the importance of the transformation of the Roman church into the feudal suzerain of secular princes, particularly when that transformation is seen in the framework of the papal-imperial relationship that was marked by rapid shifts during the minority of Henry IV (until 1065). The influential studies of Kehr and Jordan contrast with the work of Augustin Fliche, who rates the event as one of minor importance. Jordan perceives in the actions of Nicholas, set in motion by Hildebrand-Gregory VII, a challenge to the German king, with the papacy usurping generally acknowledged royal rights. To some extent one cannot but agree with Jordan. More recent research, however, particularly by Deér, illuminates the remarkable, heretofore unsuspected complexity of the problem. Any number of traditions could have been cited in support of the feudal policies of the papacy, had the popes wished for theoretical and legal justification. But they did not. They put purely practical considerations first. The Roman reformers were in urgent need of military assistance. Several other concerns might also have combined to induce the papacy to emphasize anew the prerogative of the popes to act as feudal suzerains. Old imperial privileges for the papacy, the *Constitutum Constantini,* and the condominate of emperor and pope at the time of Leo IX and Henry III, might have been adduced as precedents for papal rights in territories designated *terra S. Petri* beyond the frontiers of the Papal States. The popes of the reform period were familiar with the Donation of Constantine and made various use of it. The break with Constantinople obviated any restraint in using the purported Donation as evidence for the legality of territorial claims, should the pope have considered it expedient. The hypothesis that practical difficulties of the papacy were behind the ceremony of Melfi seems closer to the truth than the argument that purely theoretical, hierocratic principles transformed the papacy into a feudal suzerain, principles that were ultimately derived from Saint Peter's power to loosen and to bind and from the preeminence of the spiritual over the temporal. Precedents for investiture by the Roman church were also available from the history of the papacy, but they would have needed reinterpretation. Any feudal payments to Rome, for example, would have had to have been put into the guise of a feudal census, as Hildebrand was to do during his pontificate.

Whatever may have persuaded the reformed papacy to give in to Norman demands and to enfeoff them with a large portion of southern Italy, it was not the papal intention to detract from the rights of the western emperor. The first investitures under Nicholas II and Alexander II occurred during the minority of Henry IV; but in 1073, when Gregory VII accepted the oath of fealty of Richard of Capua, even he does not seem to have objected to a simultaneous second oath to the German king, provided it contained a clause of exception in favor of the papacy. To conclude, during the minority of Henry IV the balance of power in southern Italy had significantly shifted in favor of the papacy, but an emperor who was allied with the papacy might very well have been able to reassert his old rights in amicable cooperation with the popes.

Already in the lifetime of Nicholas II, there were disruptions in the papal-Norman alliance. The Normans did not feel in the least obliged to hold to their promise of desisting from attacks on territories under papal dominion. These difficulties persisted under Pope Alexander II as well as under Gregory VII (1073–85). Gregory excommunicated Robert Guiscard from 1073 to 1079 and did not reinvest him with his fief until 1080. It must be said, however, that the Normans fulfilled as much as possible their positive obligations: payment of a census and military assistance. Already in 1059, Richard of Capua and Robert Guiscard provided knights, which permitted Pope Nicholas II to campaign against the count of Galeria, who supported the anti-pope Benedict X. It was Norman troops, too, who made the enthronement of Alexander II possible; and last but not least, it was Robert Guiscard and his men who freed Gregory VII from the Castello of Sant'Angelo where he had fled after Henry IV entered Rome in 1084. Guiscard then accompanied Gregory to Salerno. The pope died there on 25 May 1085.

4. The Papacy and Germany During the Minority of Henry IV

The shift in the balance of power, noted for southern Italy in the relationship among emperor, pope, and Normans, also occurred in the context of the relationship between papacy and German court under the successors of Pope Victor II, the last pope to be nominated by Henry III. The political instability during the regency of the Empress Agnes was such that the reformed papacy felt constrained to look for reliable sources of support other than the very pious regent, who, influenced by a coterie of advisors, proved incapable of sustained policy. The papacy turned to Godfrey of Lotharingia, husband of the Countess Beatrice of Tuscany. Godfrey had become reconciled with Henry III shortly before the emperor's death and may be considered to some extent as a representative of imperial interests in Italy. Three days after the reformers in Rome learned of the death of Victor II on 23 June 1057 at Arezzo, they elected Godfrey's brother Frederick to the papacy and enthroned him as Pope Stephen IX. Frederick, a former deacon from Liège and at the time of his election abbot of Montecassino and cardinal-priest of San Grisogono, had come to Italy in the entourage of Pope Leo IX. Stephen's Norman policies and his nomination of Peter Damian as cardinal-bishop of Ostia indicate congruence of his concerns with those of Leo. The election of Stephen was the first since 1046 to have taken place initially without the participation of the German king. A post-facto confirmation was soon obtained, however, probably as early as the end of August 1057, when Bishop Anselm of Lucca was sent on an embassy to Germany. Later events establish that Frederick's electors had no intention of whittling away royal rights. Instead, the hasty election, and thus the failure to consult the German court, was above all an attempt to protect the papacy from the Roman nobility.

In the autumn of 1057, Pope Stephen IX sent Anselm of Lucca to Germany once more, this time in the company of the Subdeacon Hildebrand. Nothing is known about their negotiations at the German court, although the Norman question may have been on their agenda. Around Christmas, Stephen fell seriously ill, and by March 1058 his condition had worsened to such an extent that, with foreboding, the pope made certain arrangements in case he should die during a planned visit to Florence. Before his departure from Rome on 24 March, an assembly of Roman clergy and laymen had to promise Stephen under oath that when he died they would defer election of a successor until Hildebrand's return from Germany. The sources give no reason for the papal request. A few days later, on 29 March, Pope Stephen died at Florence. The Romans, however, reneged on their sworn promise and on 5 April hastily elected one of their own as pope, Cardinal-Bishop John of Velletri, a member of reforming circles. It is most telling that John adopted the papal name of Benedict X. But the Romans erred in thinking that their precipitate action would overwhelm the curia. Traditionally, the pontifical consecration was a prerogative of the cardinal-bishop of Ostia. But Peter Damian, who held that rank, refused to recognize Benedict X and fled to Florence, the territory of the duke of Lotharingia, where all the other cardinals except John of

Velletri/Benedict X and one of his supporters had already assembled. In the meantime, Hildebrand had joined them.

What the quick election of Stephen IX in 1057 had forestalled, had now occurred: the Roman nobility was once again in command of the papal office. Nothing short of armed force would suffice to reverse this fact. Most likely it was Hildebrand who, having just returned from Germany and being fully aware that no military aid could be expected from there, turned to Duke Godfrey for such assistance and arranged for election of a candidate trusted and supported by the duke. With the participation of Godfrey of Lotharingia, the cardinals agreed on the election of Bishop Gerard of Florence, a Burgundian by birth, and they sent emissaries to the German court, which had been ignored by the Romans during the election of Benedict. The legates appeared on Pentecost 1058 at the diet of Augsburg (7–15 June), and at the request of the "Romans," the young king solemnly designated Gerard of Florence pope. Benedict X was repudiated and Godfrey of Lotharingia was charged with conducting Gerard to Rome. It is probable that Gerard's official election was delayed until the king had given his consent and that it took place at Siena on 6 December 1058, Saint Nicholas's day. Godfrey's troops then conducted the future pope to the Eternal City, accompanied not only by the duke and the cardinals but also by the German chancellor for Italy, Wibert of Ravenna. Benedict X, who had just been excommunicated at a synod held at Sutri, fled the city, and Nicholas II, as Gerard now called himself, was enthroned in Saint Peter's basilica on 24 January 1059. Together with Stephen IX, his predecessor, and Alexander II (1061–73), his successor, Nicholas II is counted among the "Lotharingian-Tuscan" popes, champions of church reform in Rome and in the church at large, who relied for primary support on the house of Lotharingia and on the countess of Canossa, and on the Normans to a lesser extent.

Contemporary sources now more than earlier reveal new attitudes and a pronounced militancy among the reformers. Peter Damian's prediction of 1045 that the reform would come into its own once the papacy had been renewed was being fulfilled. A survey of what had already been accomplished must have enhanced the self-confidence of the reformers and spurred their sense of mission. Papal policies in southern Italy reflected the shift of power in favor of the papacy and the detriment of the Empire. The famous papal election decree of April 1059, discussed below, testified to a rather similar shift with regard to papal elections. Nevertheless, it would be erroneous to equate Roman developments for which the election decree and other events seem to have paved the way, with the carefully planned phases of a program for church reform.

An inquiry into the wellsprings of the reform is in effect an inquiry into the origin of the movement to exclude lay influence from the church. It is this aspect of reform which led to the violent confrontation between *regnum* and *sacerdotium*, that is, the investiture struggle. Nothing prevented the papal and the imperial power from cooperating harmoniously in the fight against simony and clerical marriage (nicolaitism), but such cooperation became impossible once the struggle shifted to an attack on lay influence in the church. Within the framework of the proprietary church system, which had led to the development of the Ottonian-Salian state church under the German kings, lay influence translated primarily into influence on the appointments to bishoprics and abbeys and on the right to dispose of ecclesiastical properties. To begin with, however, the problem appeared in a more general guise. To the best of our knowledge, Wazo (d. 1048), nominated by Henry III to the bishopric of Liège, was the first to point out to Emperor Henry III the fundamental qualitative difference between royal and sacerdotal consecrations; the one would entail death, but the other was a means of God to impart eternal life. For this reason, Wazo said, sacerdotal anointing was as superior to royal anointing as life was to death. Wazo's biographer, Anselm, recorded this conversation between bishop and emperor without explaining the background. It took place on the occasion of a diet at which Wazo had been requested to appear. But regardless of the background, Wazo's remark contains a strong hint that priests belong to a higher order than kings, whose claims to sacrality Wazo appears to reject.

Wazo is otherwise known for his strict application of canonical precepts to all aspects of life, not unlike Peter Damian and Abbot Siegfried of Gorze. When Henry III, for example, consulted him about a papal candidate after the death of Pope Clement II, Wazo criticized Henry's actions at the synod of Sutri of 1046 by pointing out that in accordance with the canons nobody could judge the pope. Still earlier, at Henry's diet held before the king's departure on his first Italian expedition in 1046, Wazo proclaimed unhesitatingly that the king had no right to permit a synod to judge Archbishop Widger of Ravenna. The pope alone could make such a decision. Wazo purportedly buttressed this statement with the remark that the king could only adjudicate secular wrongdoing of bishops, because the bishops owed fealty to the king, but obedience only to the pope. Wazo was apparently familiar with Gelasian doctrine on the relationship between the church and the monarchy. The famous epistle of Pope Gelasius I (492–96) of the year 494, addressed to Emperor Anastasius, had played a prominent role in late-Carolingian debates and had not been entirely forgotten in the tenth century. The same is true for the ancient ecclesiastical canons regulating episcopal elections. Wazo of Liège was one of the first to apply the Gelasian concept to Henry III, and he also reproached the king on the basis of such canons for his interventions in ecclesiastical affairs. Furthermore, the bishop reminded the king of the separation between the spiritual office of bishop and the secular appurtenances of the bishopric. Contemporaries were familiar with this concept; ordinarily, however, only simonists referred to it, trying to justify whatever disbursements they had made by claiming that such payments pertained only to the temporalities of the see with which they had been invested. Wazo was even less of an innovator when he rejected the legality of the deposition of Pope Gregory VI by Henry's synod. Few canons were as well known as the stipulation that a pope could not be judged by anyone. The decree was quoted for the first time in the early sixth century at the time of Pope Symmachus, and attributed to a synod of the very early fourth century before the reign of Constantine. It surfaced both at the time of Charlemagne and of Otto the Great, when these rulers intervened in Rome. Thus it is hardly surprising that Wazo of Liège was not the only person to recall the canon when Henry had Gregory VI and both his predecessors deposed. An anonymous Lotharingian or Frenchman, the *Auctor Gallicus*, sharply criticizes Henry's action at Sutri in a partially preserved treatise, *De ordinando pontifice* (perhaps late 1047, early 1048). The emperor is there described as an *imperator nequissimus* who had not hesitated to depose someone whom he was not entitled to elect, and who had elected someone whom he was not entitled to depose. No earthly judge, but God alone, can call on the pope to account for his deeds, even if a pope has been uncanonically promoted. It is sacrilege, he writes, to attack a priest of God, be he worthy or not. The emperor is subject to the bishops. Possibly the most remarkable passages of the treatise refer to the author's views on papal elections. According to the *Auctor*, the agreement of all bishops was mandatory in an election, whereas none of the bishops of France had participated in the promotion of Pope Clement II.

At the time, Wazo and the *Auctor Gallicus* were individual voices who recalled ancient canon law so forcefully that it was to lead to criticism of Henry's interventions in ecclesiastical affairs, that is, to criticism of theocratic kingship. Ancient canon law was at times represented by the False, or Pseudo-Isidorian, Decretals, a collection of generally spurious papal briefs that appeared around the mid-ninth century from Clement I until Gregory II. Very likely originating from the archdiocese of Reims, they had the purpose of protecting suffragan bishops from their ecclesiastical superior, the metropolitan or archbishop. During the investiture period, however, they were used among other collections as a quarry for statements supporting the papal primacy. Approximately ten years after the statements by Wazo and the *Auctor Gallicus,* most likely during the year 1058, Cardinal Humbert of Silva Candida wrote the third of his *Libri tres adversus simoniacos.* Following a different route from that of Wazo and the *Auctor Gallicus,* he reached the conclusion that the conditions in the church of his day did not meet canonical requirements. In the first two books of the *Libri,* Humbert unhesitatingly proclaims simony a heresy in the sense of dogmatic deviation, and he stresses therefore that heretics, who, by definition, are outside of the church, cannot confer effective ordinations or perform the sacraments. A simonist cannot pass on what was not in his possession, irrespective of whether he conferred ordinations free of charge or not.

In his third book Humbert approaches simony from a completely different angle. Going beyond the condemnation of simony as a fundamental evil that dishonors the church, the cardinal now searches for its causes. Unlike Abbot Abbo of Fleury (988—97), who had branded simony as an evil within the church and blamed in particular the bishops, Humbert relates simony primarily to lay influence in the church. From top to bottom, from the highest to the lowest order, he sees trade in ecclesiastical goods flourishing. Primarily, however, it was emperors, kings, princes, judges, and just about anyone with some kind of secular power, who engaged in this shameful trade. Never mind that they had been entrusted with the defense of the church. All of them therefore carried the sword in vain. They neglected their proper tasks, only to devote themselves body and soul to the acquisition of ecclesiastical property. Even then they were not content. They would preside at synods and use their worldly power to have the councils arrange everything in accordance with their wishes. These laymen were the first to influence episcopal elections, notwithstanding that the canons—Humbert cites here Celestine and Leo I—permitted them only to consent to the wishes of clergy and people. The canonical election sequence had been turned upside down, and the last had become the first. Bishops elected in this manner, that is, first nominated by secular rulers, then acclaimed by clergy and people, and finally consecrated by the metropolitan, could not be counted among the bishops since their elections had been uncanonical. For, Humbert argues, with ring and staff the candidate is invested with all of his priestly authority, in short, with the episcopal office. Since the restoration of the Empire under the Ottonians, secular princes had been selling *ecclesiastica,* disguising it under the term *investitura*. Even lay women—a pointed reference to the Empress Agnes—would invest those with ring and crosier who had gained their favor through *favor,* worldly *obsequium,* or money.

Humbert blames these conditions on the negligence of the priests and clergy, who did not protest and even supported the princes. Humbert recalls that he himself had been present when princes of this world invested bishops and abbots with ring and crosier and the attending archbishops had not dared object. The great magnates had no rights in the church, except to obey and to protect it. The church did not belong to them and could not be administered by them. The priests constituted the soul through which the Holy Spirit sanctified the church at large. The laity was forbidden from coming into contact with even the outer reaches of the ecclesiastical sphere, and their sacrilegious deeds had turned them into thieves and murderers of the *Pauperes Christi,* whose property they would seize. These laymen did not deserve to be treated like ordinary undisciplined Christians in the bosom of the church. They deserved to be dealt with as heretics. They had broken laws that had been written and sealed by the finger of God, and thus they had mocked the Holy Spirit and effectively removed themselves from the church. Metropolitans who consecrated bishops nominated by such laymen shared their guilt.

In this third book of the *Libri,* then, Humbert switches strategy and instead of attacking simony now attacks the participation of the laity in the election process for ecclesiastical office. This intervention in internal ecclesiastical affairs rendered laymen—Humbert specifically includes here emperors and kings—heretics who had forfeited their membership in the community of the faithful. He labels their investiture with ring and crosier a mere pretext for engaging in simony without restraint. Although he stresses simony linked to ecclesiastical elections, he condemns all lay intervention in ecclesiastical matters. The concept of simony had ceased to evolve in the Middle Ages after Gregory I and remained very vaguely defined. "According to canon law, simony came into play whenever any kind of payment and gifts changed hands in return for the transfer of an ecclesiastical office" (Meier-Welcker). Humbert goes a step further when he extends the concept to cover lay intervention or participation even when no de facto simony occurred. To the cardinal, lay intervention was symbolized by investiture with ring and crosier. He condemns lay investiture first because it was a pretext for simony (i.e., lay intervention), and second because ring and crosier were sacramental symbols. Throughout the *Libri tres adversus simoniacos* the issue of investiture is secondary and is referred to only for the purpose of clinching Humbert's chief argument against simony, that is, lay intervention in episcopal and abbatial elections. No one reading the *Libri Tres* without preconceived ideas would suspect that the briefly sketched incidents linked to simony would later become the chief concern of the reform. One must agree with Albert Hauck against Anton Michel and Henning Hoesch that the treatise of Cardinal Humbert of Silva Candida does not constitute a blueprint for reform. But the work is nevertheless of the greatest interest to historians, for on the basis of ancient canon law, it puts forth demands for a radical reordering of the relationship between church and monarchy. What is mere conjecture for the writings of Wazo of Liège, and only somewhat clearer in the treatise of the *Auctor Gallicus,* is forcefully enunciated in Humbert's work: lay influence in the church contradicts the divine law; emperors and kings, too, are laymen and are therefore subject to the church and owe her obedience. Cardinal Humbert was surely one of the most influential and esteemed collaborators of Pope Leo IX and probably continued to exert his influence after the death of this pope in 1054. Unfortunately, however, studies by earlier scholars—especially by Anton Michel, who attributed to Humbert numerous anonymously transmitted tracts dealing with the investiture conflict—tended to overemphasize the role of Humbert to such an extent that no one could be faulted for assuming that Humbert was single-handedly responsible for both church reform and the investiture conflict. Today, however, only a few of Michel's attributions are still accepted as probable. Our picture of the investiture controversy as reflected in the sources is undergoing constant change and correction because it is no longer necessary to interpret everything in the light of Humbert's radical views.

Close examination of the dates and language of the sources attributed to Humbert reveals that several could not possibly be by him. For example, the first Gregorian canonical collection (Fournier), in *Seventy-Four Titles* or the collection *Diversorum patrum sententiae,* could not date from Humbert's lifetime. Humbert died in 1061, and the *Diversorum patrum sententiae* were not used until 1076. John Gilchrist's critical edition of the compilation confirms this conclusion. Furthermore, in tone as well as substance, two extremely significant policy declarations, usually, albeit incorrectly, designated fragments *De sancta romana ecclesia,* and most likely written in the context of Humbert's legation of 1054 to Constantinople, correlate better with the ideas of Pope Leo IX than those of Humbert (Ryan). Also, the papal election decree of 1059 is certainly not exclusively a result of Cardinal Humbert's influence on the April synod of 1059, for its text—attributed by Michel and H. Hoesch to Humbert—reveals clear analogies to the language and the thought of Peter Damian.

All of this, however, does not negate the fact that the cardinal of Silva Candida was a radical and most zealous supporter of church reform. His *Libri tres adversus simoniacos* prove this sufficiently. Unless extant sources deceive us, no one else in the Rome of the late 1050s attacked the contemporary political order with equal vehemence, although Humbert, too, had once gratefully praised Henry's intervention at Sutri. In fact, Humbert's later opposition to the royal appointment and nomination of bishops and abbots—a tradition based on the sacrality of kingship and evolved in analogy to the proprietary church system chiefly applicable to minor churches—was so unusual that his writings found no echo at first. He probably did not publicize them; it is certain that the practices criticized by Humbert continued to flourish during the pontificates of Stephen IX, Nicholas II, and Alexander II, as well as into the early years of the reign of Gregory VII.

Humbert's discussion, in the first two books, of simony and the invalidity of simoniacal ordination and consecration merges almost imperceptibly "in the third book . . . into a discussion of the more general problem of lay disposition of churches (even when simony is not an issue)" (R. Schieffer). Humbert's arguments parallel the later legislative developments countering lay investiture, but this fact does not suffice "to draw conclusions as to the causality of historical effects" (idem). Today, only a single Florentine manuscript preserves Humbert's work in nearly complete form; the first book and excerpts from the second and third book of the *Libri tres adversus simoniacos* are also found in a codex in the archive of the Cathedral Chapter of Vich. The rarity of allusions to Humbert's work in the later pamphlet (*libelli*) literature confirms the limitation of his influence. Humbert's attack on lay influence in the church, and especially on the royal nomination of bishops, was, for the moment, to remain only a theory.

The papal election decree compiled and promulgated by the Roman synod of April 1059 under Pope Nicholas II in Rome had very different antecedents. The *narratio* is emphatic in pointing out that the decree should be interpreted in its historical setting: the nomination and election of Nicholas at Florence and Siena. The synodal *acta* of 1059 do not represent a first step toward the realization of the ideas of Cardinal Humbert and are most definitely not the initial skirmish of the investiture struggle, as has been argued occasionally in the past. The decree does not oppose imperial influence on papal elections. It does, however, reflect more clearly than other sources the experiences of the first years of church reform in Rome with all their attendant problems. According to contemporaries, by ruling out simony the decree was to prevent a repetition of the

events that had occurred at the death of Stephen IX. Simony in papal elections would be avoided by assigning only a very limited role to the
Romans, for, the decree explains, they usually voted on the basis of blood
relationship or of payments. Thus simony is once again the primary tar-
get of the decree; simony would prevent church reform. The decree may
also have been intended to legitimize the election of Nicholas II after the
fact, but it is future elections that are stressed. By the spring of 1059 Pope
Nicholas II was generally recognized, although Benedict X was still entrenched in a fortress of the nobility near Rome. Furthermore, the unusual circumstances of his election paled in significance when compared
with the introduction of the firm hierarchical principle for future papal
elections and the limiting of the electorate. Above all, the pope himself
should be truly worthy of his high office, and simonists must be excluded
at all cost. In a letter to Archbishop Henry of Ravenna about the double
election of Nicholas and Benedict, Peter Damian describes Benedict X
as precisely that—a simonist. Benedict had become a simonist because
he had been enthroned in the middle of the night, by force of arms,
notwithstanding the protests, the resistance, and the anathema of the
cardinal-bishops who had been present. Damian's important letter to
the archbishop is further proof of the elasticity of the concept "simony,"
the focal point for reforming efforts. It is also evidence for the special
position Peter Damian ascribed to cardinal-bishops. In another letter
written two years earlier, after Damian himself had been elevated to the
rank of cardinal-bishop of Ostia, he already upholds the special status of
cardinal-bishops. His ideas were mirrored in the papal election decree
of 1059.

In analogy to episcopal elections, where according to canon law metropolitans played the crucial role, the decree determined that as quasi metropolitans the cardinal-bishops were to debate papal elections in the first
instance, subsequently admitting the other cardinals to their deliberations. The remaining clergy and the laity were to give their consent once
the election had been determined. The crucial role in papal elections thus
belonged to the cardinal-bishops. If possible they were to elect the future
pope from among the clergy of the Roman church, but if necessary a
member of another church could be elected. Should it be impossible to
hold elections free of simony in Rome, the cardinal-bishops could proceed with the election at another place of their choice, together with
pious clergy and laymen, even if these were few in number. If wars or
rebellion should prevent the customary enthronement of the pope-elect in
Rome, then the elect would enjoy full papal rights to govern the church
even without this ceremony.

One paragraph of the decree refers to the rights of Henry IV in the papal elections, "presently king and with the help of God emperor-to-be."
The new regulation was not to affect them in any way. According to H.-G.
Krause, these rights were not only honorary but were also real, albeit un-
written, customary imperial rights rooted in the concept of theocratic
government. The papal election decree subjects these rights "like the election rights of the Romans . . . to the hierarchical principle" (Kempf, *The
Church in the Age of Feudalism*). The very fact of a conciliar regulation
of papal elections subjects imperial rights to a higher authority, to ecclesiastical law. Pope and council together determined the future shape of
the election process, specifying that existing imperial rights—unfortunately not described—were to be preserved. In *Disceptatio synodalis,*
composed in October 1062 to terminate the schism of Cadalus, Peter
Damian describes these customary rights as having been inherited by
Henry IV from his father, Henry III, and thus he defines them not only as
hereditary but also as very far-reaching under certain circumstances.
"Just as the German king is not made emperor automatically, though he
alone can become emperor, but requires coronation by the pope, so his
right to participate in the papal election, vested in his person as emperor,
is subject each time to reconfirmation by the pope, as had been the case
for Henry IV in 1059" (Krause). Only the claim, therefore, to this imperial prerogative was hereditary and, like a privilege, could be forfeited
through misuse. In the *Disceptatio synodalis* Damian cites several reasons for the failure to observe the prerogative at the time of the election of
Alexander II to support his claim that the omission did not affect the validity of the election: the youth of the king, the events in Rome (making
an election urgent), and the disagreements between the royal court and
the papal see. The new-found spiritual and moral strength of the reformed papacy may be construed as the cause of the transformed relationship between *regnum* and *sacerdotium*. Among the key evidence is
the election decree of 1059, which subjected the imperial prerogative of
participation in papal election to ecclesiastical authority without either
abrogating or diminishing it.

At the time of the synod of April 1059 the city of Rome was in the
hands of the reformers, but the pope still required military aid, for Godfrey
had returned to his own territories without completely subjugating the
Tusculans. With Desiderius of Montecassino and Hildebrand acting as
intermediaries, the pope turned to the Normans. In August, at the council
of Melfi, Nicholas received the feudal homage of the Norman prince
Robert Guiscard and most likely of Richard of Aversa as well. As mentioned earlier, this occasion revealed a similar shift in papal-royal rela-

tions as did the election decree. One of the obligations the Normans swore to fulfill was support of the "better cardinals" in case of disputed elections. Accordingly, they campaigned against the Roman opposition and handed over Benedict X to Nicholas, who had him deposed, probably at a synod of Rome held in the spring of 1060. Now Nicholas II and the reformers were free to turn their full attention to church reform.

Decrees that severely punished clerical marriage (nicolaitism) and simony in particular were transmitted as summaries or excerpts in papal letters to the faithful in all corners of Europe. One of the canons of the synod of 1059 ordered the faithful to boycott masses celebrated by married priests or by priests who were known to live with women. The text also contained a prohibition on the celebration of mass by such priests and on their holding of church benefices until their cases had been decided by the papacy. Furthermore, all priests were to lead lives in common at their churches of ordination, that is, to become canons regular. They were no longer permitted to own private property. At the same time, laymen were ordered by the council of 1059 to return tithes and other donations to the bishops. Another passage of the encyclical prohibited clergy or priests from obtaining a church from a layman, either with or without payment. This has sometimes been interpreted as a prohibition of lay investiture and as a summary of conciliar discussions on the topic. However, the continuation of customary royal nominations to bishoprics into the pontificate of Gregory VII is evidence to the contrary. The decree of 1059 can only have had reference to the investiture of priests with minor churches within the framework of the proprietary church system, a custom lamented in the past and now for the first time formally prohibited at a papal synod.

The decrees against nicolaitism seem to have stirred up much more unrest in 1059, especially because they sought to rely on the help of the population in enforcing celibacy. Popular enmity against married or simoniacal priests erupted in tumultuous uprisings. In Milan, the unrest helped create the Pataria—the name is perhaps derived from the rag market of the city—a popular movement led by Ariald of Carimate and Landulf Cotta but embracing chiefly the lower social classes. The attack on the traditional order by the Pataria combined sociopolitical with ecclesiastical aims. In a first insurrection in May 1057 the Pataria had used arms to force priests to renounce their concubines. In the autumn of 1057, Pope Stephen IX sent Hildebrand, a sympathizer of the Pataria, together with Bishop Anselm of Lucca to the German court, to ask the legates also to visit Milan. Stephen probably wanted more information on the Pataria, which was fast becoming a true revolutionary movement.

Perhaps in late 1059, Pope Nicholas II sent Peter Damian and Anselm on a peace mission to the city. They had the task of resolving the dispute between the Pataria and Archbishop Wido of Milan. Anselm of Lucca was the scion of a well-known Milanese noble family and acquainted with the archbishop. Only on the issue of church reform did Anselm's concerns overlap those of the Pataria, and Landulf's *Historia Mediolanensis* is in error when it reports that Anselm was connected with the movement. Landulf's motive may have been spite because Anselm, a son of the church of Milan, supported the efforts of Cardinal Peter Damian to bring the proud church of Milan to acknowledge papal primacy—a church that had defended its independence and the Ambrosian tradition for centuries. Damian's report of the embassy addressed to the Archdeacon Hildebrand indicates that this objective was achieved and that the cardinal was then in a position to obtain a hearing as arbiter. Damian's investigation—Anselm's role if any must have been negligible—revealed that almost the entire clergy of Milan were simonists since they all had paid the customary fee when they took up their offices. The complaints of the Pataria were justified, it seemed. Peter Damian was primarily interested in fostering intra-city harmony, and still more in the recognition of the Roman primacy by the higher Milanese clergy. He therefore imposed only a small penance on the respective clergy and immediately readmitted to the church without reordination clergy who had obeyed the decrees against nicolaitism and who were sufficiently educated. Archbishop Wido merely had to promise to intervene against simony and nicolaitism as far as possible. He participated in the next synod of Rome, perhaps in 1060.

Pope Nicholas II died on 20 July 1061. Just before his death a break had occurred in relations between the German court and Rome. Nothing is known about the underlying issues. The sources mention disputes between the pope and Archbishop Anno of Cologne, but again, no reason or explanation is given. All that is certain, however, is that the German court condemned the decrees (*statuta* without further identification) of Pope Nicholas II at an assembly whose composition is still debated. Apparently the court broke off relations with Rome and refused to receive Cardinal Stephen of San Grisogono, a friend of Peter Damian as well as of Hildebrand. Against this background Bishop Anselm of Lucca, due to the influence of Hildebrand, was elected pope. As an imperial bishopric, Lucca was, after Florence, a center of influence of Duke Godfrey of Lotharingia. Although the sources do not spell it out, one may assume that the Lotharingian connection is one reason why the choice fell upon Anselm. Furthermore, ever since September 1056 when Emperor Henry III had invested him with the bishopric of Lucca, Anselm had been in close contact with the Roman reformers. The popes had frequently employed him as ambassador, especially to Germany, and at first had sent him with more experienced legates such as Hildebrand or Peter Damian. Anselm does not appear to have had any connection to Godfrey before his elevation to the bishopric, but their subsequent collaboration was amicable.

It is very likely that Anselm was well known at the German court. He had first visited there shortly after his ordination, when he accompanied his archbishop, Wido of Milan, in September 1056. Members of his family, traceable from the ninth to the thirteenth century in Milan and vicinity, served as royal *missi,* and Anselm's descent from northern Italian imperial loyalists can hardly have been a secret in Germany. In his *Disceptatio synodalis,* composed to obtain the recognition of Anselm-Alexander by the king, Damian described Anselm as "almost a confidant of the king." The remark is sometimes misconstrued and interpreted to mean that Anselm had been a royal chaplain before his election to the bishopric of Lucca. This is incorrect (T. Schmidt), but Anselm was nevertheless so well known in Germany that his election has to be seen as a conciliatory move at a time of serious tension between the court and Rome. The reformers may well have hoped that, like Pope Stephen IX's election, Anselm's election would receive post-facto German consent. Hildebrand, after first negotiating unsuccessfully with the Romans, probably traveled to Lucca to urge Anselm to accept the candidacy. The election proper by the cardinals in Rome presumably then followed, as did consent by acclamation from the remaining clergy and the Roman people. At least in the formal sense, therefore, the election procedure observed the pattern set by the papal election decree—with the difference that "the people" were represented by only a small party friendly to the cardinals, and the king did not participate. The election occurred on 30 September 1061, but the enthronement, scheduled for the same day, was delayed into the middle of the night. From the first, the cardinals had taken the precaution of calling in Richard of Capua with a troop of knights. Hostile Romans nevertheless succeeded in blocking the route to the basilica San Pietro in Vincoli for the new pope and his entourage until after nightfall.

The Romans had learned from past experience and were unwilling to accept a fait accompli. Unfortunately, we have no information about the content of Hildebrand's negotiations with them. It seems, however, that they sent a legation to the German court requesting the designation of a pope, once the cardinals had decided to go against the wishes of the Romans and to elect Anselm-Alexander. In 1046 the Romans had granted Emperor Henry III the patrician dignity, and their emissaries now delivered the insignia of this office, a green mantle and circlet for the forehead, to Henry IV. In agreement with the bishops of Lombardy and the chancellor for Italy, Wibert of Ravenna, the leaders of the delegation, Count Girard of Galeria, and the abbot of the Roman monastery San Gregorio in Clivo Scauri, suggested Bishop Cadalus of Parma as the new pope. Accordingly Cadalus was formally designated by the diet that had assembled at Basel at the end of October 1061. Barely four weeks after the election and enthronement of Alexander II in Rome, therefore, the Romans and the German court designated a second pope without the participation of the cardinals. In the spring of 1062, at the head of an army, Cadalus approached Rome, where Bishop Benzo of Alba and his Roman allies had prepared to welcome him. But because Alexander had also armed his supporters and was able to maintain himself in Rome, Godfrey of Lotharingia had enough time to mediate. Godfrey obtained from both popes the promise to withdraw to their old bishoprics, Lucca and Parma, respectively, and to await there the decision of a diet, which was eventually called for Augsburg at the end of October 1062. Damian composed the important *Disceptatio synodalis* for this occasion. His hopes were fulfilled in the end, although the diet of Augsburg only agreed to a compromise and dispatched Bishop Burchard of Halberstadt to Rome to investigate the circumstances of Alexander's election. In the meantime, however, the pope who was already enthroned, Alexander II, was to return to the Holy See.

The final decision in favor of Pope Alexander II was rendered at the synod of Mantua, which met in 1064 on the suggestion of Peter Damian, a fact that Hildebrand found unforgivable. By this time, Cadalus of Parma, whose second attempt to fight his way into Rome had also failed, found little support either at the German court or in Rome, except from Archbishop Wibert of Ravenna. Cadalus continued to see himself as the legal pope for the rest of his life (d. 1072), but he remained an insignificant figure in the overall context. From among his electors at Basel the Empress Agnes had been the first to withdraw recognition and switch to support Alexander II. Evidently, the schism of Cadalus was not an act of defiance on the part of the German king against the reformed papacy. Local Roman and Lombard policies were primarily responsible for the setting up of an anti-pope, but the Cadalus coalition, united only in opposition to Alexander II, quickly disintegrated under the pressure of events. The authority of Alexander II remained unchallenged after the council of Mantua.

Bibliography for Chapter 3

General

Anton, Hans Hubert. *Der sogenannte Traktat "De ordinando pontifice": Ein Rechtsgutachten in Zusammenhang mit der Synode von Sutri.* Bonn, 1982.

Capitani, Ovidio. *Immunità vescovili ed ecclesiologia in età "pregroriana" e "gregoriana": L'avvio alle "restaurazione."* Spoleto, 1966.

————. "Imperatori e monasteri in Italia centro-settentrionale." In *Il monachesimo e la riforma ecclesiastica (1049–1122)*, 423–89. Atti della quarta settimana internazionale di studi, Mendola. Miscellanea del centro di studi medioevali 6. Milan, 1971.

Fliche, Augustin. *La Réforme Grégorienne.* 3 vols. Paris, 1924. Still indispensable despite an occasional apologetic flavor. For this chapter see esp. vol. 1, *La formation des idées grégoriennes.*

Fuhrmann, Horst. "Konstantinische Schenkung und abendländisches Kaisertum." *DA* 22 (1966): 143–78.

Goez, Werner. "Reformpapsttum, Adel und monastische Erneuerung in der Toscana." In *Investiturstreit und Reichsverfassung*, 205–39.

Hauck, Albert. *Kirchengeschichte Deutschlands* 3:665–752. Berlin, 1958.

Hoerschelmann, Ernst. *Bischof Wazo von Lüttich und seine Bedeutung für den Beginn des Investiturstreites.* Düsseldorf, 1955.

Kempf, Friedrich. *The Church in the Age of Feudalism*, 351–66.

Krause, Hans-Georg. "Das Constitutum Constantini im Schisma von 1054." In *Aus Kirche und Reich. Festschrift für Friedrich Kempf.* Edited by Hubert Mordek, 131–58. Sigmaringen, 1983.

Ladner, Gerhart Buridan. *The Idea of Reform: Its Impact on Christian Thought and Action in the Age of the Fathers.* Cambridge, Mass., 1959.

————. *Theologie und Politik vor dem Investiturstreit.* Baden near Vienna, 1936.

Laudage, Johannes. *Priesterbild und Reformpapsttum im 11. Jahrhundert.* Beihefte zum Archiv für Kulturgeschichte 22. Cologne and Vienna, 1985.

Scharnagl, Anton. *Der Begriff der Investitur in den Quellen und der Literatur des Investiturstreits.* Stuttgart, 1908.

Schmid, Karl. "Adel und Reform in Schwaben." In *Investiturstreit und Reichsverfassung*, 295–319.

Schmid, Paul. *Der Begriff der kanonischen Wahl in den Anfängen des Investiturstreits.* Stuttgart, 1926.

Tellenbach, Gerd. *Church, State and Christian Society at the Time of the Investiture Contest.* Translated by R. F. Bennett. Oxford, 1970.

————. "Il monachesimo riformato ed i laici nei sec. XI e XII." In *I laici nella 'Societas Christiani' dei secoli XI e XII*, 118–42. Miscellanea del Centro di studi medioevali, vol. 5. Milan, 1968. Reprinted in a German translation in *Cluny*, edited by Helmut Richter (see below, under "Cluny and the Reform").

Ullmann, Walter. *The Growth of Papal Government in the Middle Ages: A Study in the Relation of Clerical to Lay Power.* 3rd ed. London, 1970. A controversial approach that is generally not accepted.

Wollasch, Joachim. "Reform und Adel in Burgund." In *Investiturstreit und Reichs-verfassung,* 277–39.

———. "Kaiser und Könige als Brüder der Mönche: Zum Herrscherbild in liturgischen Handschriften des 9. bis 11. Jahrhunderts." *DA* 40 (1984): 1–20.

Cluny and the Reform

See also the bibliography for Chapter 1. An excellent introduction to recent work is the volume in the series Wege der Forschung: *Cluny, Beiträge zu Gestalt und Wirkung der Cluniazensischen Reform,* edited by Helmut Richter, Wege der Forschung, no. 241 (Darmstadt 1975). It reprints in German articles by Hourlier, Smith, Talbot, Theodor Schieffer, Hallinger, Tellenbach, Violante, Leclercq, Hoffmann, and Conant; the selected bibliography contains 241 publications, many from the 1960s.

Cowdrey, Herbert Eduard John. *The Cluniacs and the Gregorian Reform.* Oxford, 1970.

Fornasari, Giuseppe. "Fondazioni Cluniacensi non dipendenti da S. Benedetto di Polirone nelle regioni Venete: Un primo sondaggio." *Italia Benedettina* 8:89–103. Cesena, 1985.

Tellenbach, Gerd, ed. *Neue Forschungen über Cluny und die Cluniacenser.* Freiburg/Br. 1959. Particularly important in this essay collection are contributions by Diener, Mager, and Wollasch.

Peter Damian

Capitani, Ovidio. "San Pier Damiani e l'istituto eremitico." In *L'Eremitismo in occidente nei secoli XI e XII,* 122–63. Miscellanea del Centro di studi medioevali, vol. 4. Milan, 1965.

Convegno Internazionale di Studi Damianei. Studi Gregoriani, vol. 10. Vatican City, 1972. With contributions by Lucchesi, Palazzini, Savioli, Pierucci, Capitani, Hamilton, Reindel, Grégoire, and Werner.

Dressler, Friedrich. *Petrus Damiani, Leben und Werk.* Studia Anselmiana, vol. 34. Rome, 1954.

Kempf, Friedrich. "Pier Damiani und das Papstwahldekret von 1059." *Archivum Historiae Pontificiae* 2 (1964):73–89.

Leclercq, Jean. *S. Pierre Damien, érmite et homme d'Eglise.* Rome, 1960.

Löwe, Heinz. "Petrus Damiani, ein italienischer Reformer am Vorabend des Investiturstreits." In *Geschichte in Wissenschaft und Unterricht* 6 (1955): 65–79.

Meyvaert, Paul. "Alberic of Monte Cassino or St. Peter Damian?" *Revue bénédictine* 67 (1957):175–81.

Reindel, Kurt. "Petrus Damiani und seine Korrespondenten." *Studi Gregoriani* 10 (1975):205–19. Especially useful because it characterizes Damian's correspondence: some of his letters were never sent.

———. "Neue Literatur zu Petrus Damiani." *DA* 32 (1976):405–44.

Ryan, John J. *Saint Peter Damiani and His Canonical Sources: A Preliminary Study in the Antecedents of the Gregorian Reform.* Pontifical Institute of Mediaeval Studies. Studies and Texts, vol. 2. Toronto, 1956. An excellent study, illuminating not only Damian but the characteristics of the reform generally.

Vollrath, Hanna. "Kaisertum und Patriziat in den Anfängen des Investiturstreits." *ZKG* 85 (1974):11–44, deals with the *Disceptatio synodalis*.

Woody, Kennerly M. "Sagena piscatoris: Peter Damiani and the Papal Election Decree of 1059." *Viator* 1 (1970):33–54.

Humbert of Silva Candida

Halfmann, Hermann. *Cardinal Humbert, sein Leben und seine Werke mit besonderer Berücksichtigung seines Traktates: Libri tres adversus simoniacos.* Göttingen, 1882.

Hoesch, Henning. *Die kanonischen Quellen im Werk Humberts von Moyenmoutier: Ein Beitrag zur Geschichte der gregorianischen Reform.* Cologne, 1970. Includes a discussion of Michel's studies. In connection with Hoesch's book, see also John F. Gilchrist, "Cardinal Humbert of Silva-Candida, the Canon Law and Ecclesiastical Reform in the Eleventh Century," *ZRG Kan. Abt.* 58 (1972):338–49.

Michel, Anton. "Die folgenschweren Ideen des Kardinals Humbert und ihr Einfluss auf Gregory VII." *Studi Gregoriani* 1 (1947):65–92.

———. *Die Sentenzen des Kardinals Humbert: das erste Rechtsbuch der päpstlichen Reform.* MGH 7. Stuttgart, 1943.

Robinson, Elaine G. "Humberti Cardinalis Libri Tres Adversus Simoniacos: A Critical Edition with an Introductory Essay and Notes." Ph.D. diss., Princeton University, 1972.

Ryan, John Joseph. "Cardinal Humbert of Silva Candida and Auxilius: The 'Anonymous Adversary' of Liber I adversus simoniacos." *Mediaeval Studies* 9 (1947):151–61.

———. "Cardinal Humbert De s. Romana ecclesia: Relics of Roman-Byzantine Relations 1053/54." *Mediaeval Studies* 20 (1958):206–38.

The Regular Canons

Dereine, Charles. "Chanoines." *Dictionnaire d'Histoire et de Géographie Ecclésiastiques* 12 (1953):375–405.

———. "L'elaboration du statut canonique des chanoines réguliers spécialement sous Urbain II." *Revue d'Histoire Ecclésiastique* 46 (1951):534–65.

Fonseca, C. D. "Le canoniche regolari riformate nell'Italia nord-occidentale." In *Monasteri in alta Italia dopo le invasioni saracene e magiare*, 335–82. XXXII Congresso storico subalpino. Turin, 1966.

Fuhrmann, Horst. "Papst Urban II. und der Stand der Regularkanoniker." Bayerische Akademie der Wissenschaften, Munich. Philosophisch-historische Klasse. *Sitzungsberichte*, 3–44. 1984. Includes an extensive bibliography.

Schmidt, Tilmann. "Die Kanonikerreform in Rom und Papst Alexander II. (1061–1073)." *Studi Gregoriani* 9 (1972):201–21.

La Vita Comune del clero nei secoli XI e XII. Miscellanea del Centro di studi medioevali, vol. 3. 2 vols. Milan, 1962.

Weinfurter, Stefan. "Neuere Forschung zu den Regularkanonikern im deutschen Reich des 11. und 12. Jahrhunderts." *HZ* 224 (1977):379–97.

Canon Law

Autenrieth, Johanne. "Bernold von Konstanz und die erweiterte 74-Titelsammlung." *DA* 14 (1958):375–94.

Fournier, Paul, and Gabriel LeBras. *Histoire des collections canoniques en occident dépuis les Fausses Décrétales jusqu'au Décret de Gratien.* 2 vols. Paris 1931, 1932. Fundamental and indispensable introduction.

Fuhrmann, Horst. *Einfluss und Verbreitung der pseudoisidorischen Fälschungen.* 3 vols. *MGH*, Schriften vol. 24, parts 1–3. Stuttgart 1972, 1973, 1974. In vol. 2 the collections from the Decretum of Burchard up to Gratian's Decretum are analyzed with respect to Pseudo-Isidore with extensive bibliographical annotations.

———. "Pseudoisidor im Kloster Cluny." *Proceedings, Second International Congress of Medieval Canon Law,* 17–22. Monumenta Iuris Canonici, series C: Subsidia 1. Vatican City, 1965.

———. "Pseudoisidor in Rom vom Ende der Karolingerzeit bis zum Reformpapsttum, eine Skizze." *ZKG* 78 (1967):15–66.

———. "Über den Reformgeist der 74-Titel-Sammlung (Diuersorum patrum sententiae)." In *Festschrift für Hermann Heimpel zum 70. Geburtstag* 2:1101–20. Göttingen, 1972.

Gilchrist, John T., ed. *Diuersorum patrum sententie siue Collectio in LXXIV titulos digesta* [*The Sentences of Various Fathers or the Collection compiled in Seventy-Four Titles*]. Monumenta Iuris Canonici. Ser. B, Corpus collectionum 1. Vatican City, 1973.

———. *The Collection in Seventy-Four Titles* (with a translation of the collection into English). A Canon Law Manual of the Gregorian Reform. Mediaeval Sources in Translation. Toronto, 1980.

College of Cardinals

Hüls, Rudolf. *Kardinäle, Klerus und Kirchen Roms, 1049–1130.* Bibliothek des Deutschen Historischen Instituts Rom vol. 48. Tübingen, 1977. With a comprehensive bibliography. Particularly important: Hans-Walter Klewitz, "Die Entstehung des Kardinalkollegiums," *ZRG Kan. Abt.* 25 (1936):115–221 (the paper has been reprinted in Klewitz, *Reformpapsttum und Kardinalkolleg,* 11–134 [Darmstadt, 1957]; and Stephan Kuttner, "Cardinalis: The History of a Canonical Concept," *Traditio* 3 [1945]:129–214).

Maleczek, Werner. *Papst und Kardinalskolleg von 1191 bis 1216.* Vienna, 1984. The origin of the consistory is often placed into the late eleventh century. This meticulous examination of the sources illuminates the collaboration of pope and cardinals during the twelfth century, dating the consistory to the late twelfth century.

See also below under "The Papacy."

The Normans

Buisson, Ludwig. "Formen normannischer Staatsbildung, 9. bis 11. Jahrhundert." In *Studien zum mittelalterlichen Lehnswesen,* edited by Theodor Mayer, 95–184. Vorträge und Forschungen herausgegeben vom Konstanzer Arbeitskreis für mittelalterliche Geschichte, vol. 5. Sigmaringen, 1960.

Cahen, Claude. *Le régime féodal de l'Italie normande.* Paris, 1940.

Deér, Josef. *Papsttum und Normannen: Untersuchungen zu ihren lehnsrechtlichen und kirchenpolitischen Beziehungen.* Cologne, 1972. Particularly important, with detailed bibliography.

Falkenhausen, Vera von. *Untersuchungen über die byzantinische Herrschaft in Süditalien vom 9. bis ins 11. Jahrhundert.* Wiesbaden, 1967.

Heinemann, Lothar von. *Geschichte der Normannen in Unteritalien und Sicilien.* Vol. 1. Leipzig, 1894.

Herde, Peter. "Das Papsttum und die griechische Kirche in Süditalien vom 11. bis zum 13. Jahrhundert." *DA* 26 (1970):1–46.

Hoffmann, Hartmut. "Die Anfänge der Normannen in Süditalien." *Quellen und Forschungen in italienischen Archiven und Bibliotheken* 49 (1969):59–144.

Jordan, Karl. "Das Eindringen des Lehnswesens in die römische Kurie." *Archiv für Urkundenforschung* 12 (1932):13–110.

Kehr, Paul Fridolin. "Die Belehnungen der süditalienischen Normannenfürsten durch die Päpste." *Preussische Akademie der Wissenschaften.* Philosophisch-historische Klasse. *Abhandlungen.* Berlin, 1934.

Le Patourel, John. *The Norman Empire.* Oxford, 1976.

Loud, G. A. "How 'Norman' Was the Norman Conquest of Southern Italy?" *Nottingham Medieval Studies* 25 (1981):13–34.

Morton, Catherine. "Pope Alexander II and the Norman Conquest." *Latomus: Revue d'études latines* 34 (1975):362–82.

Vehse, Otto. "Benevent als Territorium des Kirchenstaats bis zum Beginn der avignonesischen Epoche." *Quellen und Forschungen aus italienischen Archiven und Bibliotheken* 22 (1930–31):87–160.

See also the bibliography for Chapter 1.

Milan and the Pataria

Cowdrey, H. E. J. "Archbishop Aribert II of Milan." *History* 51 (1966):1–15.

Keller, Hagen. "Pataria und Stadtverfassung, Stadtgemeinde und Reform: Mailand im 'Investiturstreit.'" In *Investiturstreit und Reichsverfassung,* 321–50.

Miccoli, Giovanni. "Per la storia della Pataria milanese." *Bullettino del Istituto storico italiano per il Medio Evo* 70 (1958):43–123. Reprinted in Miccoli, *Chiesa gregoriana,* 101–67. Rome, 1966.

Violante, Cinzio. *La Pataria Milanese e la Riforma ecclesiastica, I: Le premesse (1045–1057).* Rome, 1955.

———. *La società milanese nell'età precommunale.* Rome, 1981.

Werner, Ernst. *Pauperes Christi, Studien zu sozialreligiösen Bewegungen im Zeitalter des Reformpapsttums.* Leipzig, 1956.

See also the bibliography for Chapter 2.

The Papacy

Blumenthal, Uta-Renate. "Ein neuer Text für das Reimser Konzil Leos IX. (1049)?" *DA* 32 (1976):23−48.

Brucker, Pierre. *L'Alsace et l'Eglise au temps du pape Saint Léon IX.* 2 vols. Strasburg and Paris, 1889.

Congar, Yves. "Der Platz des Papsttums in der Kirchenfrömmigkeit der Reformer des 11. Jahrhunderts." In *Sentire Ecclesiam, Festschrift Hugo Rahner,* edited by Jean Daniélou and Herbert Vorgrimler, 196−217. Freiburg, 1961.

Goez, Werner. "Papa qui et episcopus. Zum Selbstverständnis des Reformpapsttums im 11. Jahrhundert." *Archivum Historiae Pontificiae* 8 (1970):27−59.

Hägermann, Dieter. "Zur Vorgeschichte des Pontifikats von Nikolaus II." *ZKG* 81 (1970):352−61.

Herrmann, Klaus-Jürgen. *Das Tuskulanerpapsttum (1012−1046).* Päpste und Papsttum, vol. 4. Stuttgart, 1973.

Krause, Hans-Georg. "Über den Verfasser der Vita Leonis IX papae." *DA* 32 (1976):49−85.

Schmidt, Tilmann. *Alexander II. und die römische Reformgruppe seiner Zeit.* Päpste und Papsttum, vol. 11. Stuttgart, 1977.

Tritz, Heinrich. "Die hagiographischen Quellen zur Geschichte Papst Leos IX." *Studi Gregoriani* 4 (1952):191−353.

Wollasch, Joachim. "Die Wahl des Papstes Nikolaus II." In *Adel und Kirche, Gerd Tellenbach zum 65. Geburtstag,* 205−20. Freiburg/Br., 1968.

The Papal Election Decree of 1059

Hägermann, Dieter. "Untersuchungen zum Papstwahldekret von 1059." *ZRG Kan. Abt.* 56 (1970):157−93.

Jasper, Detlev. *Das Papstwahldekret von 1059: Überlieferung und Textgestalt.* Beiträge zur Geschichte und Quellenkunde des Mittelalters, edited by Horst Fuhrmann, 12. Sigmaringen, 1986. Fundamental. Clarifies the transmission of the original and forged election decree as well as the history of the councils of 1060 and 1061. Detailed bibliography.

Krause, Hans-Georg. *Das Papstwahldekret von 1059 und seine Rolle im Investiturstreit.* Studi Gregoriani, vol. 7. Rome, 1960. Provides the historical context.

Scheffer-Boichorst, Paul. *Die Neuordnung der Papstwahl durch Nikolaus II.* Leipzig, 1879.

Woody, Kennerly M. "Sagena piscatoris: Peter Damiani and the papal election decree of 1059." *Viator* 1 (1970):33−54.

The Papal Chancery

Bresslau, Harry. *Handbuch der Urkundenlehre für Deutschland und Italien.* Edited by Hans-Walter Klewitz. 2 vols. Leipzig, 1912, 1931.

Fichtenau, Heinrich. "Arenga, Spätantike und Mittelalter im Spiegel von Urkundenformeln." *MIÖG* Ergänzungsband 18. Vienna, 1957.

Katterbach, Bruno, and Wilhelm M. Peitz. "Die Unterschriften der Päpste und

Kardinäle in den 'Bullae maiores' vom 11. bis 14. Jahrhundert." *Miscellanea F. Ehrle 4. Studi e Testi,* 40. Vatican City, 1924.

Kehr, Paul Fridolin. *Scrinium und Palatium. MIÖG* Ergänzungsband 6. Vienna, 1901.

Rabikauskas, Paul. *Die römische Kuriale in der päpstlichen Kanzlei.* Miscellanea Historiae Pontificiae, vol. 20. Rome, 1958.

Santifaller, Leo. *Saggio di un elenco dei funzionarii, impiegati e scrittori della cancelleria pontificia dall'inizio all'anno 1099. Bullettino dell'Istituto storico italiano per il Medio Evo 56—57.* Rome, 1940.

The Papal Administration

Elze, Reinhard. "Das 'sacrum palatium Lateranense' im 10. und 11. Jahrhundert." *Studi Gregoriani* 4 (1952): 27—54.

Jordan, Karl. "Die päpstliche Verwaltung im Zeitalter Gregors VII." *Studi Gregoriani* 1 (1947): 111—35. As excellent as brief.

Santifaller, Leo. "Über die Neugestaltung der äusseren Form der Papstprivilegien unter Leo IX." In *Festschrift Hermann Wiesflecker,* 29—38. Graz, 1973.

Sydow, Jürgen. "Cluny und die Anfänge der Apostolischen Kammer." *Studien zur Geschichte des Benediktiner Ordens* 63 (1951) 45—66.

———. "Untersuchungen zur kurialen Verwaltungsgeschichte im Zeitalter des Reformpapsttums." *DA* 11 (1954—55): 18—73.

Simony

Gilchrist, John T. "'Simoniaca haeresis' and the Problem of Orders from Leo IX to Gratian." *Proceedings, Second International Congress of Medieval Canon Law,* 209—35. Vatican City, 1965. Includes a detailed bibliography.

Hirsch, Ferdinand. "Die Auffassung der simonistischen und schismatischen Weihen im elften Jahrhundert, besonders bei Kardinal Deusdedit." *Archiv für katholisches Kirchenrecht* 87 (1907): 25—70.

Meier-Welcker, Hans. "Die Simonie im frühen Mittelalter." *ZKG* 64 (1952—53): 61—93.

Saltet, Louis. *Les réordinations: étude sur le sacrement de l'ordre.* Paris, 1907.

CHAPTER 4

Henry IV and Gregory VII

1. The Minority of Henry IV, 1056–1065

The regency of Empress Agnes gave rise to complications in relations between the German court and the reformed papacy which led to a partial forfeiture of imperial influence in Rome. Empress Agnes also created problems in Germany, where her erratic leadership and skewed policies turned many a friend of the crown into a foe. In appointing candidates to the imperial bishoprics, Agnes followed as far as possible the pattern established by Henry III. Several of her nominees, among them Archbishop Siegfried of Mainz, formerly abbot of Fulda, later aligned themselves with the opposition to Henry IV, and in this respect the empress has been criticized unfairly. The revolutionary reordering of loyalties in the Saxony of the 1070s could at that time hardly have been predicted. Far more worrisome from the beginning of her regency had been her policies toward the German dukes and other members of the aristocracy. She gave up the duchy of Bavaria by bestowing it on the powerful Saxon Count Otto of Northeim. She also strengthened the position of Rudolf of Rheinfelden in the southwest of the Empire, the same Rudolf whom the opposition to Henry IV elected king in 1077, and entrusted him with the duchy of Swabia and the administration of Burgundy. Rudolf, moreover, managed to marry Agnes's daughter Matilda (sister of Henry IV), whom he perhaps abducted. Although Matilda died a short time later, the now very influential southern German prince continued to claim the position of son-in-law to Henry III, no doubt to emphasize his proximity to the throne. Empress Agnes gave the duchy of Carinthia to Berthold of Zähringen, probably as replacement for Bavaria reputedly promised to him by Henry III. Later Berthold, too, was among the enemies of Henry IV. Despite all her efforts, however, Agnes never succeeded in finding steadfast support either among the secular princes or in the imperial state church. In the spring of 1062, Archbishop Anno of Cologne (1056–75), an appointee still of Henry III, abducted the young heir to the throne from a vessel on the Rhine near Kaiserswerth. Henry's courageous attempt to escape by jumping into the river failed. Anno did not act alone but as the leader of a conspiracy that included several princes. Besides Anno, the sources clearly identify only two of the active conspirators: Count Ekbert of Brunswick and the Bavarian Duke Otto of Northeim. The reasons given for the rebellion, generally known as the coup of Kaiserswerth, are vague and sound rather lame: unhappiness with the regency government. Our most important source for the events of 1062, the chronicler Lampert of Hersfeld, relates in particular that the princes felt excluded from the government, because the empress would admit only the advice of Bishop Henry of Augsburg, and regarded the exclusion as an insult to their dignity and standing. Archbishop Anno himself is frequently accused of having arranged the abduction out of his own ambition and greed. More generous motives are implied occasionally: discontent with the education of the young king and with the style of government of the Empress Agnes, or more specifically, a concern for the welfare of the Empire.

Following the events of Kaiserswerth, Anno of Cologne headed the regency government. In 1065 Henry was declared of age through the ceremony of *Schwertleite*, and Anno's influence gave way to that of Archbishop Adalbert of Bremen (1043–72), who now became the foremost advisor to the king. The young king's episcopal advisors exploited their position to the advantage of the German dioceses, especially their own, accumulating on their behalf monasteries and monastic possessions. Abbeys lost the independence they had hitherto maintained under royal protection and lordship. In 1065, for instance, Anno was given Malmédy, Cornelimünster, and Vilich, while Adalbert obtained Lorsch and Corvey. Henry relied very heavily on the cathedrals and therefore the bishoprics for economic support. Thus it would be difficult to argue that imperial property was squandered in the grants to the bishops. Limitation of the independence of the monasteries, however, was a serious grievance in the respective monastic circles. Other complaints had their roots in unabashed episcopal nepotism, especially flagrant in Anno of Cologne, who pursued family politics without any scruple whatsoever. His nephew Burchard was appointed bishop of Halberstadt (1059–88) by Empress Agnes in 1059. Burchard may have owed his exalted position primarily to his personal qualifications, in strong contrast to Anno's brother Werner (1063–78), who was appointed to Magdeburg in 1063 at Anno's urging. In the elections to the archbishopric of Trier Anno likewise tried to replace the local candidate with a kinsman, a nephew named Cuno or Conrad. But Trier showed more determination than did Magdeburg. The citizens of Trier entered into a sworn association and murdered Conrad before the unfortunate candidate had even arrived in their city. Subsequently they elected Udo of Nellenburg (1066–78) as their new archbishop. The murderers were never apprehended, and for Archbishop Anno the disaster meant a severe loss of prestige and influence, which was immediately noted at the court. Despite his dynastic ambitions, however, Anno supported church reform, introducing, for example, the usages of Fruttuaria at Siegburg.

On the occasion of the diet of Tribur, held early in 1066, the princes forced Henry IV, whom they had taken by surprise, to banish Archbishop Adalbert of Bremen from his entourage. Adalbert's ever-increasing influence on the king was a thorn in the side of the Saxons particularly, but also of the ambitious prelate of Cologne. Adalbert was no less ambitious. In the beginning of his pontificate he had dreamed of turning his diocese, Bremen, into the seat of a patriarchate for northern Europe, a plan he was later forced to abandon. Hoping to forestall a further accumulation of power in the hands of the mighty Saxon nobility, Emperor Henry III had endowed Adalbert with comital rights over Saxon counties. Once he had gained influence under the young king, Adalbert continued his role as opponent of the Saxon nobility, and his fall at Tribur had profound repercussions. One immediate effect was a rebellion in the Slavic mission territory. The Obodrites penetrated to Hamburg and plundered the city. Magnus Billung, son of Duke Ordulf of Saxony, threatened Bremen with his army, forcing Adalbert to flee temporarily. The Billungs, however, did not have the strength to keep the rebellious Wends under control, and chaos ensued in the north and northeast of Germany. As we have seen, the episcopal nominations arranged by Anno of Cologne for his kinsmen encountered diocesan resistance. Those arranged by Adalbert also caused trouble. At first glance each unsuccessful nomination seems related to a particular set of circumstances. In the final analysis, however, the various reasons for diocesan rejection of a candidate proposed by the imperial government boiled down to the simple fact that the king, or rather his advisors, and the respective diocese were unable to reach a compromise on a candidate acceptable to both parties. Little does it matter whether the candidate, like Adalbero of Worms, a brother of Rudolf of Rheinfelden and monk at Saint Gall, was rejected because his huge girth rendered him incapable of fulfilling his episcopal obligations, or because, like Conrad at Trier, he had been appointed against the wishes of the prospective diocese. The picture hardly changed when Henry IV began to govern on his own, notwithstanding his efforts to follow the policies of his father. The period after 1065 was rather more frequently punctuated by disputes over nominations, specifically between cathedral chapters and bishops as well as between abbots and their monastic communities. These prelates had usually been appointed by the king and were often distinguished by their abilities as well as by their loyalty to the ruler. Some of the bishops, such as Hermann of Bamberg and Pibo of Toul, had administered their diocese successfully for several years without encountering opposition from the majority of their respective chapters. This situation changed in 1069. At that point the spread of church reform along with the coherent, stable, and uniformly applied policies of Henry IV, who was trying to strengthen royal authority by claiming inherited customary rights in the imperial church, led to lawsuits against bishops who were now accused of simony. Taking such accusations at face value, historians therefore assume that Henry IV lacked the empathy for church reform that had provided such secure foundations for his father's theocratic government.

Henry's attempts to use episcopal nominations to turn dioceses into reliable pillars of the imperial government found their parallel in his efforts to establish a strong center of royal power in the Harz mountains, a region of Saxony with a concentration of Salian property unusual for this duchy. As far as we know, royal rights in Saxony had received scant attention during the almost ten-year minority of the young king, when magnates did their best to strengthen their independence and augment their landed holdings. Henry's claims in the early 1070s, therefore, provoked bitter resistance and were pilloried as unheard-of novelties. "Saxon lay nobles demanded that lands which kings [Henry's direct ancestors as well as the Ottonians] had once given to them or to their ancestors in propriety or which they acquired during Henry IV's minority should permanently, unequivocally, and unconditionally be theirs and their heirs' for good. The Salians . . . clung to notions of reciprocity and reversibility, the conditional character of their and their Ottonian forebears' gifts in propriety, with an astonishing tenacity as a vital nerve of their kingship" (Leyser). Some of the local tensions had originally erupted in connection with efforts to expand episcopal authority. Such efforts might well, and frequently did, infringe on established local interests, depending for success on strong royal backing. "In the great Saxon rising of the later eleventh century the fronts had changed altogether. The bishops of the East Saxon dioceses were now aligned with the king's enemies" (idem). Theoretically, there was no objection yet to the royal investiture of bishops, but ever since the early seventies it had become increasingly popular to appeal unwelcome episcopal nominations to the pope should the king refuse to give in to the complaint of a chapter. In the case of Charles of Constance, for example, Pope Alexander had left the decision to a German synod that met in 1071 under the appropriate metropolitan, Archbishop Siegfried of Mainz, in the presence of two papal legates. But already earlier, several bishops had been bidden to Rome to defend themselves against accusations of simony. Without question, papal claims to primacy would encompass German dioceses and abbeys and especially the imperial Italian dioceses. In Italy as well as in Saxony royal claims to the loyalties of the episcopate were coming under increasing stress. At the last synod of Alexander II, held at Easter in Rome shortly before the pope's death (21 April 1073), five advisors of Henry IV were excommunicated due to events in Milan. Since 1072 two archbishops and their factions had confronted each other in that city: Archbishop Atto, supported by the Pataria and by the pope, and a royal candidate, Godfrey, who had been nominated earlier by the king. The excommunications were pronounced by the papal synod due to Henry's continued support for Godfrey.

2.   The Saxon Revolts

Imperial politics had provoked Saxon anger even in the lifetimes of Conrad II and Henry III, although it is probably untrue that nobles debated whether to elect another king instead of accepting Henry's minor son and heir, whose murder is said to have been contemplated. After Otto III died without leaving a direct male heir, crown estates and public rights in Saxony were largely appropriated by the secular magnates. From the very beginning, therefore, the Salian successors of the Liudolfings found themselves in a weakened position. Henry III tried to mend matters by creating strong bonds between the monarchy and the ecclesiastical princes, preferentially endowing them with choice imperial properties and rights. The comital rights with which the emperor had endowed Archbishop Adalbert of Hamburg/Bremen at the expense of the Billungs, constitute one example. He had also favored the bishops of Halberstadt and Hildesheim by enlarging their rights and properties through several important donations. The Harz region was largely Salian property, including numerous castles (*palatii*) and the silver mines at the Rammelsberg. Henry III's foundation of the collegiate chapter of Saints Simon and Juda at Goslar illustrates Salian dynastic ties to this part of Saxony and their corresponding concern for the area. Saints Simon and Juda was richly endowed and soon outshone many older foundations. The conclusion was inescapable that Henry would be unwilling to abandon royal rights to the Saxon nobility. During the minority of Henry IV royal influence in Saxony declined. Proof is hard to come by, but crown estates probably continued to be withdrawn from royal control. From the later 1060s on, however, Henry IV endeavored to vindicate royal rights in Saxony, probably employing juries of recognition, familiar from England, rather than the customary oath helpers or judicial duels. He reclaimed as inheritance from Henry III estates and rights that had been illegally alienated. Under certain circumstances Henry proved willing to confirm these possessions to their new tenants, provided these were willing to recompense the king either by payment of rents or fees, or through their services. Another essential item in Henry's plan to put Salian power on a secure footing in Saxony and neighboring areas, especially Thuringia, was the construction or rebuilding of strategic castles and forts. The fortresses were garrisoned by *ministeriales* or *milites* who were probably largely of Swabian origin; thus they were strangers in Saxony, where they acted in effect as standing representatives of the royal government, always ready to enforce judicial decisions on behalf of the king. The *liberi* and the peasants living in the vicinity of the castles who were called on to help with the construction as well as the upkeep of the garrisons became members of newly reorganized royal castle wards.

Kings had long enjoyed the rights now claimed by Henry IV, but the population most affected by these measures, identified in the sources as *milites, liberi homines,* or simply as the Saxon people, regarded Henry's claims as an arbitrary attempt to force them into unworthy dependence. The Saxon nobility under the leadership of Otto of Northeim took advantage of this mood. In late July 1073 at Hoetensleben (south of Helmstedt) "all of Saxony" entered into a conspiracy. Among the East Saxon and Thuringian nobles at the assembly were Archbishop Werner of Magdeburg, Bishop Burchard of Halberstadt, Otto of Northeim, Margrave Dedi, the Billung Count Hermann (an uncle of Magnus, still imprisoned by Henry IV), and Count Palatine Frederick. Among the ecclesiastical princes only Archbishop Liemar of Bremen (1072–101), Bishop Benno of Osnabrück (1068–88), and Bishop Eberhard of Naumburg (1045–78) were loyal supporters of the king. Among the lay magnates, the royal *Vogt* or *defensor* of Goslar, Bodo, as well as Count Burchard of Meissen stood by the king. During the night on 9 August 1073, Henry IV secretly fled from the Harzburg, his favorite stronghold and residence, to escape from a large Saxon army that was threateningly encamped before the fortress. A meeting between Henry and the Saxon magnates at Goslar in late June had apparently only further inflamed the disputes, and by August the Saxons were ready to use armed force against the king. "Already contemporaries felt that the Saxon rising was something quite novel in its scale and dimensions, something that surpassed all their experience of conflict and rift between a ruler and his *fideles*" (Leyser). Henry eventually made his way to the city of Worms whose citizens rallied to his side and overthrew their episcopal lord.

Up until 1073 the king had generally been able to have his way in disputes with individual discontented Saxon nobles. Margrave Dedi, for example, lost out to Henry in 1069 when he attempted to appropriate the imperial fiefs of Margrave Otto of Meissen (d. 1067), whose widow he had married against Henry's will. Otto of Northeim had lost his campaign to regain Bavaria, undertaken with the help of his ally, Magnus Billung, son and heir of Duke Ordulf of Saxony. In 1070, for reasons that are unclear, Otto had been accused of planning to murder Henry IV. In response, Otto had been declared an outlaw and was deprived of his possessions, including the duchy of Bavaria, which was granted to Welf IV in the same year. The united Saxon attack of 1073, however, was another matter. Henry was extremely vulnerable, especially because his relations with the southern German princes Rudolf of Swabia, Welf of Bavaria, and Berthold of Carinthia had also cooled.

With Henry's flight from the Harzburg in August 1073 the rebels quickly gained the upper hand throughout Saxony. Deprived of an alternative by his disadvantaged position, the king was forced to negotiate and accede to virtually all of the conspirators' demands. His accommodation laid the groundwork for the preliminary Peace of Gerstungen of 2 February 1074. When Henry seemed reluctant to carry out one of its conditions—the razing of all royal fortresses—on the Harzburg, the Saxons mounted a night assault on the castle in March 1074 and reduced it, its monastery, and its cemetery to a heap of rubble. The rebels did not shrink from tearing open the graves of both a son and a brother of Henry IV and scattering their bones. This desecration led to a shift in public opinion in Henry's favor. Henry made good use of this unexpected advantage and rejected the court of princes that had been suggested by the bishops of Magdeburg and Halberstadt, who were anxious to prove their innocence in the Harzburg attack. Skillfully, the king brought many of the conspirators over to his side, using amnesty, promises, and gifts as bait. Among the conspirators who changed allegiances were the German bishops, with the exception only of Magdeburg, Halberstadt, Merseburg, and Paderborn. When arms were joined in 1075 near Homburg, Henry's army under Rudolf of Rheinfelden emerged victorious. This victory was a first step in the defeat of the Saxons on 25 October, when much of the power and influence lost since the death of Henry III in 1056 was restored to the kingship. Henry IV was able to designate as successor his son Con-

rad, barely two years old. At Christmas 1075 he was reconciled with
Otto of Northeim and returned to him his fiefs, with the exception of Bavaria, and named him regent in Saxony. The other Saxon leaders remained in prison until the early summer of 1076.

3. The Struggle Between Henry IV and Pope Gregory VII

Tensions between Rome and the German court overshadowed the end of
the reign of Pope Alexander II. Unfortunately, the issues involved are not
precisely known, but whatever they were, they were responsible for the
excommunication of several of Henry's advisors at the Lenten synod of
1073 and a renewed break in diplomatic relations between pope and
king. The funeral of Alexander had not yet ended when a tumultuous
crowd of Romans proclaimed the archdeacon Hildebrand pope. A few
days later the election was solemnly repeated by the cardinals and the
clergy of Rome in conformance with the election decree of 1059. The
only omission was royal participation, as specified in the official text
promulgated by the Roman synod of that year. The new pope assumed
the name Gregory VII, probably out of reverence for Gregory the Great.
The excommunication of the royal advisors is the most likely explanation
for his failure to seek any kind of contact with the German king. One of
the best known and frequently cited canons from the Pseudo-Isidorian
Decretals stipulated automatic excommunication for anyone who maintained contact with excommunicated persons. Not even a brief greeting
could be exchanged between them. Rudolf Schieffer recently noted that in
the autumn of 1073 Gregory also prohibited the newly elected Bishop
Anselm of Lucca from requesting royal investiture with his bishopric, an
action considered necessary because Lucca was counted among the imperial dioceses. Bishop Anselm (1073–86), who was particularly close to
Gregory VII and wrote the most important canonical collection of the
Gregorian reform period, went on, however, to receive the investiture
with ring and crosier from the king in 1074. Gregory is said to have delayed the consecration of the new bishop of Lucca until harmonious relations between king and pope had resumed.

The first papal reference to the German king occurs in Gregory's response to Duke Rudolf of Swabia, who seems to have written to the pope
in the role of mediator. In the letter, which was entered into the register
of Gregory VII (a slender volume preserved to this day in the Archivio
Vaticano with the signature Reg. Vat. 2), the pope declared that he had
no quarrel with Henry IV. On the contrary, he wrote, he was beholden to
Henry for three reasons in particular: first, Gregory was present when

Henry was elected king (the exact date of this event is disputed); second, he, Gregory, had been honored by Emperor Henry and his court above other Italians: third, the dying emperor had entrusted his son to Pope Victor II. Gregory obviously regarded himself as Victor's legal successor in this respect. Finally, the pope proposed to Rudolf preliminary negotiations among himself, the Empress Agnes, Countess Matilda, Bishop Rainerius of Como, and other God-fearing men. They were to decide how best to heal the break between the monarchy (*regnum*) and the church (*sacerdotium*). This letter, as well as another of the same date (1 September 1073) to Bishop Rainerius, in which the pope speaks of Henry IV as the first among the laity and the future emperor, indicate that Gregory did not hold Henry IV responsible for the strains between the Roman church and the German court at the time of his election. The following spring, without major difficulties, Henry's advisors were absolved, Henry himself was completely reconciled with the church, and Gregory VII once again recognized Henry's hereditary customary right to invest bishops with their dioceses through the symbols of ring and staff. Although it seems probable that Pope Gregory VII discussed a prohibition of investiture—most likely in connection with Milan—at the synod of Rome held in February 1075, he nonetheless asked the king later that same year to have a successor to Bishop Hermann (1065–75) installed at Bamberg. Moreover, as far as we know, the pope did not object to Henry's investiture of Huzmann of Speyer (1075–90) in April or May 1075, to that of Henry of Liège (1075–91) in June or July 1075.

The beginning of the pontificate of Gregory VII (1073–85) thus shows him to have been not only successor to but also spiritual heir of the eleventh-century reforming popes. His basic approach to reform was much like theirs, but he promoted change much more impatiently and with far greater intensity. All of the known, relatively reliable biographical data for Hildebrand-Gregory have been brought together in a recent well-balanced study by Werner Goez. The pope probably came from the small town of Soana in beautiful, serene southern Tuscany. His family was not of noble origin, but still not without influence, for an uncle of his was abbot of Santa Maria del Priorato on the Aventine, reformed in the tenth century by Abbot Odo of Cluny at the urging of Duke Alberic. His parents gave Hildebrand, who was born between 1020 and 1025, as an oblate to an ecclesiastical institution in Rome, probably Santa Maria, where he grew up. There is no doubt that Hildebrand was a monk, although definitely not a Cluniac, and there is also no doubt that at Santa Maria, a monastery oriented to reform, Hildebrand was taught for a period by Lawrence of Amalfi. Lawrence died there in the spring of 1049.

The learned archbishop, who had a saintly reputation, knew both Latin and Greek. He was also a member of the circle of Roman reformers around John Gratian of the Church of San Giovanni a Porta Latina, who later became Pope Gregory VI and was deposed by Henry III in 1046. There is no telling, however, whether or to what extent Lawrence influenced Hildebrand. The first definite date we have for Hildebrand's life is January 1047, when he accompanied Gregory VI into exile as his chaplain. Hildebrand said later that he had been very unwilling to leave Rome at the time. And again according to his own testimony, he was just as unwilling to return to the Eternal City as a subdeacon in 1049 in the entourage of Pope Leo IX. Hildebrand was equally displeased when he was proclaimed pope more than twenty years later, in 1073. We must accept this statement at face value, so often did he call in his letters upon the Apostle Peter as a witness that he had never sought the heavy burden of the highest office in Christendom. His papal motto, which he used also to describe his initial, tumultuous election, is equally revealing: "For thou hadst cast me into the deep, in the midst of the seas; and the floods compassed me about" (Ps. 68:3).

During the long years that passed between his return to Rome and his own election to the papacy in 1073, Hildebrand was a faithful collaborator of the popes who appointed him first rector of San Paolo fuori le mura and, eventually, in 1059/60, archdeacon of the Roman church. He frequently served them as legate. In Rome, the financial affairs of the curia were his particular concern, although it remained for Pope Urban II, a former prior of Cluny, to introduce institutional changes. Hildebrand's ever-increasing prestige and extraordinary influence on Rome is attested to in a number of sources, among these the famous epigrams full of sarcasm of Peter Damian, prior of Fonte Avellana, whom Pope Stephen IX had elevated to cardinal-bishop of Ostia before Christmas 1057 at Hildebrand's urging. Although few details are known, the temptation must be resisted to consider as mere puppets the popes whom Hildebrand served. Even in those early days, however, Hildebrand seems to have been arrogant and domineering, vehemently defending his personal opinions even when these put him at odds with everybody else. His behavior at the Lenten synod of 1067 under Pope Alexander II is one example. The council debated the accusation of simony brought against Peter Mezzabarba, bishop of Florence, by the monks of Vallombrosa. Their opposition to Mezzabarba had occasioned fierce street battles in Florence. The delegation representing Vallombrosa in Rome in 1067 encountered a hostile assembly, and the zealous Vallombrosa monks were even accused of heresy. The bishops supported the Florentine, for the hierarchy seemed well aware of the danger to it and the church that might arise from the unre-strained fanatical activities of the monks of Vallombrosa. Peter Damian tried but failed to mediate between the monks and Peter Mezzabarba be-fore the official opening of the synod. During the negotiations Damian purportedly exclaimed before the assembled fathers: "My lord pope, these are the true locusts who utterly obliterate the green pastures of the holy church; would that a storm were to drive them all into the Red Sea!" (Goez). In the midst of this tumult only the archdeacon Hildebrand rose to the defense of the Vallombrosans, pointing out that they "had not looked to their own advantage but had acted in loving service to the church to further her purity" (idem). The monks were finally permitted to depart peacefully, although the bishop remained in office.

Even in those days religious passion was more comprehensible to the archdeacon Hildebrand than were the controlled, balanced, and serenely self-confident reforming efforts of one such as Hugh of Cluny, whom Hildebrand, as pope, once reproached for lack of a yet fiercer love for the Roman church burning in his heart. It should also be remembered that Gregory supported the Pataria movement in Milan to the very last, as he did the monks of Hirsau in Germany, who wandered through the country-side preaching upheaval and rebellion. For Gregory this burning love of the church was best, if not exclusively, reflected in incessant, feverish ac-tivity devoted to Christian charity for one's fellow man. Gregory inter-preted active service under the banner of the prince of the apostles, that is the pope, as such ministry. Hildebrand-Gregory knew no gray areas; all issues were black or white, one or the other. Indeed, there are many par-allels between his passionate zeal and that of certain Old Testament prophets. These parallels are pointed out in recent historiography, which rejects older, one-sided interpretations of Gregory's character. Gregory's determined manner won him few friends. The great pope was at one with Peter Damian in his emphasis on the primacy of the Roman church and, while still archdeacon, had enlisted Damian's active collaboration in the promotion of reform. Yet this same Damian referred to Hildebrand as "his holy Satan." It is appropriate that this epithet is frequently quoted, for Gregory's effect upon contemporaries—and upon historians as well—was equally self-contradictory. Elsewhere, Damian describes Gregory as an intrinsically worthless piece of iron but with the irresistible effect of the magnet, drawing everything into its field. He also compared him to a ti-ger tensed for the leap, to a wolf, and to the bone-chilling, icy north wind. One conclusion at least does seem obvious: Hildebrand was definitely not a mediocre personality.

As Gregory VII, Hildebrand ranks as one of the great popes in the history of the Roman church. His hotly debated actions certainly had their wellspring in his religious ideals and not in a craving for political dominance. However, one must add immediately that these ideals encompassed also the absolute, unquestioned obedience to the will of God as he, Gregory, had personally experienced it. Werner Goez points out appropriately that the terms *obedience* and *disobedience* are by far the most frequently encountered twin concepts in the more than four hundred extant letters of Gregory. "He felt as if being pressed into service constantly—and he expected the same willingness to serve from others. Personal desires and the personal will had to subject themselves to the overriding call of God to duty." By contrast, other familiar concepts evoked by the term *Gregorian reform* are surprisingly rare in the epistles, including references to the much-debated ecclesiastical Roman liberty (*libertas romana*). His third successor, Pope Paschal II (1099–118), again strongly emphasized obedience. The Roman council of 1102 declared disobedience an outright heresy, a meaning that had been implicit from the pontificate of Gregory VII on.

Gregory applied the required absolute obedience to God to himself as pope and as representative of the Apostle Peter. Gregory's self-identification with the prince of the apostles included his conviction that his papal actions were direct actions of Saint Peter himself. He argued that the recipients of his letters would hear in them the voice of Peter. In his famous letter to King Henry IV of 8 December 1075, Gregory wrote that whatever the king should write or should have delivered to the pope Peter himself would receive. "While the papal eye would scan the letters of Henry's messages or while he, Gregory, would listen to the voices of the messengers, the Apostle Peter with penetrating glance would discern the innermost spirit of the messages." Gregory's mystical identification with Saint Peter illuminated his whole being. Thus it seemed self-evident to him that his papal activities should be free of all error on the basis of Christ's prayer for Peter and the church. Gregory himself compiled the famous clauses on prerogatives and privileges of the pope and of the Roman church which were entered as the *dictatus papae* into the papal register in the spring of 1075 after the Lenten synod. One of its declarations expresses the conviction that by the merit of Peter the pope "would be raised to a better, saintlier level of being" (Kempf). As August Nitschke puts it, Gregory saw himself in a world where every being, not excluding monks and priests, "lived with the ever-present danger of being seized by the devil." The pope alone, by means of his identification with Peter, "would always be a 'true Christian,'" and thus able to recognize who was of God and who was of the devil. From this perspective it is easy to see why Gregory, firmly convinced of his divine mission, claimed the right to depose not only bishops but also secular rulers. Gregory's acting on this latter conviction by deposing Henry IV, when the king had provoked him with the renunciation of obedience in January 1076 at Worms, was wholly unprecedented. The result of Gregory's action was transformation of the Gelasian doctrine of royal and priestly power, pronouncing the superiority of the priestly power in the spiritual realm, into one of subjection of the secular to the ecclesiastical power; by the same token, church reform now became a fundamental struggle to determine the relationship between royal and priestly authority. In 1076/77 theocratic kingship became an anachronism. Gregory VII compared the relationship between the two powers to that between sun and moon, gold and lead. A disobedient prince was a member of the satanic realm. He stood far below the least among obedient Christians, and a vast chasm separated him from the members of the ecclesiastical hierarchy, including its doorkeeper.

To this day, Pope Gregory VII elicits conflicting judgments from historians. To some, he is the revolutionary genius, fighting for a new, just world order while advocating the overthrow of the old. To others, he is a saint, misunderstood by most of his contemporaries, dying a martyr's death in exile at Salerno because he had devoted his life to the zealous pursuit of justice to free the church from shameful slavery. Like all reformers, Gregory insisted that his undertakings were firmly rooted in the pronouncements of the fathers. It is indeed true that he expressly reserved for himself the papal right to promulgate new laws, or to alter old laws in accordance with the needs of the present. This prerogative, however, had been part of canon law as far back as the early centuries of the church. In fact, Gregory's pontificate carried forward the program of the eleventh-century reform unaltered. The struggle against simony and married clergy continued. The difference lay in Gregory's claiming the right to depose secular rulers and his general prohibition of investiture. This claim vastly expanded reforming activities and all but buried the old characteristics, which became barely recognizable in novel measures against crowned rulers. Another issue, intra-ecclesiastical papal primacy, now came to the fore, and has similarly given rise to differing evaluations of the pontiff. If Gregory himself did not introduce the issue altogether as something new, then—it has been suggested—he did at least provide a novel content for an old concept, enforcing it for the first time in history. This interpretation would surely have been greeted with whole-hearted approval by the French as well as the German clergy. The German bishops were in such an uproar over Gregory's direct intervention in their dioceses that they renounced their obedience to the pope in January 1076, and, furthermore, induced King Henry to do the same. Indeed, the history of the Roman primacy really cannot be imagined without Gregory VII. F. L. J. Meulenberg argues convincingly that it is primarily Gregory's charisma and energy and not the conscious departures from older models that has made him an indelible part of this history. Whenever possible the pope tried to preserve the juridical prerogatives of all the churches, provided these did not detract from the prerogatives of papal jurisdiction, a concept emphasized by the reformers in a new context. In the church at large Gregory partially transferred his papal rights to legates, including standing legates in particular countries. Thus he was in a position to enforce papal claims without, like Leo IX, traveling constantly. In a sense, then, Gregory was more conservative than is often thought. At the same time, however, he never shrank from the unconventional and radical. Famous is his appeal to the citizens of Constance to expel their bishop, Otto, and to appropriate his possessions. Otto had been excommunicated by the pontiff. However, the primatial and quasi-monarchical position of the papacy, intuitively grasped by Gregory VII, developed fully only under his twelfth-century successors, especially under Pope Innocent III (1198–216), when a vastly expanded bureaucracy with administrative and legal sophistication realized many of the ideas of Gregory VII (Tierney).

Royal investiture of several northern Italian bishops was the spark that ignited the bitter struggle between Henry IV and Gregory VII, as well as their respective successors, over the proper relationship between secular and priestly power. As far as historians can make out, Henry's renewed refusal to abandon his customary rights to the appointment of the archbishop of Milan was at fault. After a resounding victory over the Pataria by the majority citizen faction in Milan, Henry invested the cleric Tedald. Like Alexander II under seemingly similar circumstances, Gregory VII thereupon excommunicated five of Henry's advisors at the Lenten synod of 1075. In the last letter addressed to Henry before the renunciation of obedience at Worms, dated 8 December 1075, Gregory violently reproaches the king for maintaining contact with the men excommunicated in the spring. The pontiff complains that Henry's behavior in Milan stood in complete contrast to royal expressions of devotion and obedience expressed both in letters and in the negotiations with his mother, the Empress Agnes. Furthermore, Gregory continues, Henry now had appointed prelates to the churches of Fermo and Spoleto in contravention of the decrees of the Holy See. And what was worse, the appointees were entirely unknown to the pope, notwithstanding the scriptural prohibition of the

consecration of such persons—probably a reference to I Tim. 5 : 22. Ad-
monitions of a more general character follow. The letter concludes with a
report—unfortunately not at all clear—on the spring synod, which explains to the king that no new decisions had been passed. In this context
Gregory also mentions a decree that had been promulgated by the assembly, but he neither repeats nor describes this canon. A scriptural citation
that accompanies the reference implies that the decree concerned episcopal nominations in some way. Gregory adds the request to send legates to
Rome for negotiations and, finally, mentions oral messages entrusted to
the messengers carrying the papal missive. The nature of the messages is
unknown, but it is generally assumed that they threatened Henry with
excommunication or that they dealt with the question of investiture—
Gregory's letter does give us pause. Still, it is difficult to believe that this
missive should have caused the renunciation of obedience to the pope
declared at Worms in January 1076. The hortatory and abrupt tone of
the letter was nothing unusual. Gregory was far too busy—as he once
wrote—to worry much about courtesy and the usual niceties. We certainly have to assume that the king, just savoring the fruits of his great
victory over the Saxons, was not pleased by the papal messages. But
when all is said and done, the anti-papal letters dispatched from Worms
are more likely to have expressed the general mood of dissatisfaction with
the papal regime among the German bishops, whose customary independence was much reduced by direct papal intervention. In the words of one
of them, Archbishop Liemar of Bremen, they felt treated like servants, not
to say slaves.

   In general, historians tend to assume that the prohibition of lay investiture was the effective cause of the dispute between pope and king. The
chronicler Arnulf of Milan reports such a prohibition from the Lenten
synod of 1075, and one could assume that Gregory's letter of 8 December
1075 refers to it. That matters were more complicated than that was recently argued by Rudolf Schieffer. Schieffer points out that such a prohibition could at most have been pronounced for Milan, for in the
correspondence exchanged between Gregory and Henry during the summer of 1075, no reference to investiture problems can be found. Moreover, bishops later accused of having accepted investiture from Henry,
were able to swear that they knew nothing of an investiture prohibition
dating to the spring of 1075. The king had dispatched the bishops Adalbero of Würzburg and Hermann of Metz as his representatives to the
council, and they presumably would have informed their fellow bishops
of such a decision had it been promulgated. To solve the dilemma,
Schieffer hypothetically proposes to treat 1073, when Anselm of Lucca

had been temporarily prohibited from obtaining the royal investiture, as a precedent. Accordingly, at the Lenten synod of 1075, Henry might temporarily have been forbidden to invest bishops, should he continue his contacts with his excommunicated advisors. It is noteworthy that investiture is not mentioned once in connection with the events of Worms and Canossa, or with the election of Rudolf of Rheinfelden as anti-king. Schieffer's hypothesis seems to fit these facts better than do others, and it also tends to harmonize with Gregory's letter of 8 December. At any rate, we may conclude that no definite, unambiguous prohibition of investiture could have caused the great clash of 1076, for such a prohibition was first promulgated by Gregory VII at the autumn council of 1078 and repeated in 1080. The investiture prohibition thus emerges as a result of the dispute between pope and king and not as its underlying cause, for "*die Investiturfrage . . . befand sich damals noch in der Schwebe*" (Kempf, review of R. Schieffer).

Contemporaries date all the misfortunes that befell Germany after 1076 to the ill-fated diet of Worms of January of that year. On 24 January two archbishops and a majority of the German episcopate addressed a declaration to Gregory VII withdrawing their obedience from the pontiff, whom they reproached with an irregular election and ethics ill-becoming the head of Christendom. Simultaneously, the king sent messages both to the pope, whom he called Hildebrand, and to the Romans, calling upon Gregory to resign from the papal office. A little later, probably around Pentecost, Henry and his advisors publicized a somewhat expanded version of the January decree, now addressed to the "false monk Hildebrand," which concluded dramatically with a ringing "descend, descend!" It was the first salvo in a war of propaganda on both sides not to be silenced for many years.

Gregory received the letters from Worms during the Lenten synod of 1076, perhaps as early as 14 February, even though in the meantime a synod had met at Piacenza. At Piacenza the northern Italian bishops declared their solidarity with the German episcopate, and in their turn withdrew obedience from the pope. The pontiff reacted immediately and there at the synod of 1076 he excommunicated both bishops and king, the latter in a prayer addressed to the Apostle Peter. Through the mediation of Peter, Gregory declares, God had given him the power to loosen and to bind in heaven and on earth. Therefore he now prohibits Henry from governing either in Germany or in Italy, absolves all his subjects from their past or future oaths of fidelity, and prohibits them from serving Henry as king. Finally he pronounces anathema upon the king. When the excommunication became public knowledge it shook the earth to its foundations, in the words of a loyal Gregorian. Gregory's anger is comprehensible. Up until Worms, no emperor or king had ever pronounced a judgment against a pope from a distance. Moreover, Henry's reckless January decree was at the very least politically unwise. And yet, there is the precedent of earlier synods presided over by emperors that had judged or deposed popes. Henry and his advisors could cling to the belief that tradition was on their side when they opposed Gregory. Never, however, had a pope deposed a king. Later, in a letter to Hermann of Metz, Gregory claimed Saint Ambrose as a precedent, maintaining, furthermore, that Pope Zachary had deposed the last Merovingian, Childeric III. But contemporaries realized full well that these arguments did not correspond to the historical facts as described in the sources. The reasons given in Gregory's prayer of deposition—Henry's unheard-of pride and arrogance in his confrontation with the church, his disobedience, and his contact with the excommunicated—must have been more than sufficient cause in Gregory's eyes to justify a violent papal reaction, whether or not there were precedents.

Nobody in Germany at first questioned the papal deposition of Henry. As soon as it had become public knowledge, Henry was once again confronted by a hostile opposition. The Saxon princes, just recently released from captivity, together with Otto of Northeim, who had changed sides again, the southern German aristocracy, and the majority of the German bishops were the leaders of the revolt. Although it was the bishops who had persuaded the king to denounce Gregory and who had themselves been prominently engaged in the denunciation, they left the side of the excommunicated king and made every effort to become quickly reconciled with the pope. As early as the summer of 1076, the king's was the weakest faction by far. Henry IV had no choice but to negotiate from Oppenheim on the Rhine with the magnates and bishops who had been joined by the two papal legates in their camp at Tribur across from Oppenheim on the other side of the river. Negotiations were very difficult, for Henry's most implacable foes intended to proceed immediately with new elections. Henry was obliged to promise in writing that he would give satisfaction to the pope, that he would be obedient, and that he would do penance. Henry did, however, ask the pope to respond to the January accusations. The bishops and magnates at Tribur further agreed among themselves to hold elections if the king should be unable to obtain absolution from his excommunication within a year from the date of promulgation of the ban. Simultaneously, they invited the pope immediately to an assembly planned for February 1077 at Augsburg, where Gregory was to judge the dispute between Henry and the princes.

But the assembly of Augsburg under the presidency of the pope was never to meet. At this point Henry appraised the situation realistically. In the middle of winter, with the queen, his two-year old son Conrad, and a few companions, the king secretly crossed the Alps into the territory of his mother-in-law, Adelheid of Turin. Secrecy was necessary, for the southern German princes who were in a position to block the Alpine passes—Rudolf of Rheinfelden, Welf of Bavaria, and Berthold of Carinthia—were the leaders of the opposition. The news of Henry's arrival spread quickly, and his Italian supporters, assuming that he had come to lead a campaign, gathered around him. But Henry had come as a penitent to make submission to Gregory. The pontiff was on his way to Germany at the time, January 1077, but when he learned of the king's presence in Italy, he cautiously interrupted his journey and retired to Matilda's fortress at Canossa. There were preliminary negotiations, but still, when Henry appeared in penitential garb in the castle yard, the pope hesitated at first and refused to reconcile the penitent with the church. He yielded three days later to the entreaties of the papal entourage, especially those of Henry's godfather, Abbot Hugh of Cluny, and of the countesses Adelheid of Turin and Matilda of Canossa. The king promised in a written oath that he would abide by the papal judgment to be rendered in the near future, and that he would not attempt to hinder the papal journey across the Alps. Gregory then raised up the king who had prostrated himself in the form of a cross in front of the pope and celebrated the Eucharist with Henry and his followers, thus reconciling them to the church. It is a moot question whether this act reinstated Henry as sovereign. After the penance of Canossa, Gregory treated Henry as king although he was to declare in 1080 that he had not restored him to his royal office. More than anything else, Canossa was a pastoral event, notwithstanding the fact that as a consequence Gregory abandoned his visit to Germany. It is not that the pope now regarded the journey as superfluous, but that the German princes had failed to send him the promised escort to assure his safe passage—and Gregory could hardly arrive in Germany in the company of the king if he wished to maintain his role of impartial judge.

When Henry humbled himself before the pope at Canossa he had won part of his battle: the pontiff abandoned his plans for an immediate intervention in Germany. This provided Henry with breathing space. The king, now absolved together with his most loyal supporters, could fight for his crown and do his best to gather adherents. But this political success came at a high price. By his public and spectacularly solemn penance, Henry in effect recognized the sentence from the February synod and acknowledged the papal right to judge secular princes as well as secular affairs. Gregory assumed that this right belonged to him as a matter of principle and that it constituted a natural component of the papal office. As a matter of fact, however, it turned the ancient concept of the duality of church and monarchy upside down, introduced profound changes, and destroyed forever the medieval ideal of the one Christian *res publica,* although Gregory VII himself was still entirely wedded to this concept. The immediate accountability of the ruler to God ceased to exist. The monarchy was thus deprived of its sacrality, with which it had entered a seemingly indissoluble bond in the Carolingian period in the west of the former Roman Empire, and earlier still in the east. The venerable formula of the king as the servant of the church became under Gregory VII a much more precise and realistic formula of the princes as vassals of Saint Peter, that is, the pope; true enough, this political conception could only be realized to a very limited extent, but it should not be underestimated for this reason.

Henry's most bitter enemies felt deserted by the pope. As soon as the events of Canossa became known, they elected Rudolf of Rheinfelden as their new king, perhaps after an official deposition of Henry IV. The election took place in March 1077 in the Franconian city of Forchheim in the presence of a small but influential group of princes. Present were the dukes Berthold of Carinthia and Welf of Bavaria, apart from Rudolf himself, who had had a crown made for himself in advance since the royal insignia were not at his disposal. Otto of Northeim was there as well, still fighting for the return of his former duchy of Bavaria, as were the archbishops Siegfried of Mainz, Gebhard of Salzburg, and Werner of Magdeburg, together with four bishops. Perhaps also at the assembly was Duke Magnus of Saxony. Gregory VII was represented by two legates who eventually agreed to the new election and mediated among the assembled magnates. Their suggestion, that personal claims on Rudolf be postponed, won approval. Rudolf had to swear an oath to permit free canonical episcopal elections and to refrain from any attempt to make the royal dignity hereditary in his family. Kings, like bishops, were to be freely elected, that is, freely designated.

The absolution of Canossa now proved very valuable to Henry. The pope would not immediately recognize Rudolf, and Rudolf had to fight for recognition in Germany as well. The battles at Mellrichstedt in August 1078, at Flarchheim (Thuringia) in January 1080, and at the river Elster in October 1080, depleted the ranks of Henry's enemies. As a result of Mellrichstedt, Rudolf's influence was largely restricted to Saxony, and even before the battle at Flarchheim, several Saxon magnates, including the Billungs, transferred their allegience to Henry IV. At the battle of the

Elster, finally, Rudolf lost his right hand in battle, the oath hand, and eventually died from the injury. Contemporaries looked upon the event as a divine judgment, for had it not been this very hand which once had sworn fidelity to Henry IV, a fidelity later broken? At least one chronicler expanded upon Rudolf's death with the most gruesome details. It took almost a year after the death of Rudolf before the Swabians and the Saxons agreed on Count Hermann of Salm as the new anti-king. Hermann was crowned at Goslar in 1081 but never attained much influence at all, and at no time did he seriously threaten Henry's kingship. Hermann was not replaced when he died fighting for his patrimony in Lotharingia in 1088.

Henry had won the battle for the crown. Apart from the absolution of Canossa, Gregory's long hesitation in recognizing Rudolf of Rheinfelden as the only legitimate king probably contributed most to the favorable outcome. For a long time the pope had persisted in his plan to arbitrate between the opposition and King Henry IV. When he at last excommunicated and deposed Henry for a second and final time at the Lenten synod of 1080, the decision came too late, and neither aided Rudolf nor seriously harmed Henry. Gregory was absolutely convinced that his judgment represented the decision of God and of the prince of the apostles. He afterward went so far as to prophecy the destruction of Henry before the feast of Saint Peter in Chains (1 August). The second excommunication of the king received far less attention than the first, perhaps an indication of a loss of papal authority in Germany, where many regions had for years suffered repeated devastation by armies of both sides. A general war-weariness had set in. In June 1080 Henry could already strike his first counter blow. At a synod held at Brixen, Gregory was formally deposed. Among the participants was Cardinal-Priest Hugh Candidus, who had by then finally deserted Gregory's cause. Hugh claimed to represent the Roman cardinalate and signed the sentence of deposition together with twenty-seven bishops and King Henry IV. Because of a few scurrilous accusations, for example, that Gregory was responsible for the poisoning of several popes, it is customary to reject the entire document as a fabrication for purposes of propaganda. There is no denying, however, that one or the other of the accusations it makes against Gregory was entirely justified from the vantage point of the king and his supporters. Examples are the accusation that the pope subverted the ecclesiastical order (perhaps a reference to the double nominations to bishoprics such as Constance, Augsburg, and Paderborn, sees that were simultaneously claimed by an imperial and a papal nominee each), that he nourished strife, supported a perjurer as king, and tried to deprive the legitimate

king of body and soul—surely a reference to Gregory's prediction of
Henry's defeat or death before the first of August. After Gregory's deposition the synod of Brixen nominated Archbishop Wibert of Ravenna as
pope. Almost four years later thirteen cardinals as well as other prelates
and members of the papal administration deserted Pope Gregory VII, unable to fathom and to support further the pope's obdurate refusal to
make any kind of concession to Henry, even in the face of modest royal
requests. The Romans opened the city gates to the king and his army, and
Gregory withdrew to the impenetrable fortress of Sant'Angelo. Only
then, in 1084, and probably after a formal Roman election, was Wibert
consecrated in Saint Peter's basilica as Clement III. On Easter day Henry
and his queen, Adelheid, received the imperial coronation. When the
Normans, vassals of the papacy since 1059, freed the pope from the
Castello Sant'Angelo, they plundered and devastated Rome to such an
extent that Gregory was obliged to leave the city together with his allies.
Under their protection, he died on 25 May 1085 in the city of Salerno.
His last words, "I have loved justice, hated iniquity, that is why I die in
exile," found many commentators. P. E. Hübinger more recently connected the pontiff's words not only with Psalm 44 but also with one of the
clauses of the Sermon on the Mount: "Blessed are they which are per-
secuted for righteousness' sake: for theirs is the kingdom of heaven"
(Matt. 5:10).

After the death of the great pope, Henry met no difficulty in being recognized everywhere, including Saxony, as legitimate king. In July 1085,
when he approached Saxony at the head of an army, his most inflexible
opponents among Saxony's bishops fled to the Danes, together with anti-
king Hermann. By the autumn of the same year Archbishop Hartwig of
Magdeburg and Bishop Burchard of Halberstadt had already returned to
their dioceses, but the peace concluded in 1088 after the murder of Burchard nonetheless favored Henry, who had been able to have his eldest
son, Conrad, crowned king a year earlier. Otto of Northeim had died in
1083, and in 1090 Margrave Ekbert of Meissen was killed. He had been
outlawed by a court of princes. In Rome, too, everyone was weary of war.
Not until a year after the death of Gregory VII did the reformers agree on
a new pope, Abbot Desiderius of Montecassino. But the abbot hesitated
until March 1087 before accepting the high office. Gregory's successor
was then enthroned in Saint Peter's as Pope Victor III (1086–87). Nothing could be more deceptive, however, than the superficial impression
that Gregory had failed completely. True, the decrees of this pontiff
echoed but little in the canonical collections of his contemporaries; nor
could Gregory transmit to his successors his unique sense of prophetic

mission. But by his determined efforts Gregory had channeled church reform into a new direction. That direction did not change with his death. The deposition of the king, and even more the investiture prohibition at the synods of 1078 and 1080, overshadowed the pontificates of his successors until the Worms agreements, and forced the issues of simony and nicolaitism into the background. The struggle over investiture had begun.

Bibliography for Chapter 4

General

The best introduction to the literature is provided by the series Studi Gregoriani (Rome, 1947–). Twelve volumes have appeared so far, no. 8 is an index volume. Furthermore, see Christopher Brooke, *The Investiture Disputes*, Historical Association Pamphlet (London, 1958). The titles below provide a very small selection.

Benson, Robert L. *The Bishop-Elect: A Study in Medieval Ecclesiastical Office.* Princeton, 1968.

———. "Plenitudo potestatis: Evolution of a formula from Gregory IV to Gratian." *Studia Gratiana* 14 (1967): 196–217.

———. "The Gelasian Doctrine: Uses and Transformations." In *La notion d'autorité au Moyen Age; Islam, Byzance, Occident.* Colloque de la Napoule 1978, 13–44. Paris, 1982.

Berges, Wilhelm. "Gregor VII. und das deutsche Designationsrecht." *Studi Gregoriani* 2 (1947): 189–209.

Borino, Giovanni B. "Il decreto di Gregorio VII contro le investiture fu 'promulgato' nel 1075." *Studi Gregoriani* 6 (1959): 329–48.

Bosl, Karl. "'Noble unfreedom': The Rise of the Ministeriales in Germany." In *The Medieval Nobility: Studies on the Ruling Classes of France and Germany from the Sixth to the Twelfth Centuries.* Edited by Timothy Reuter, 291–311. Amsterdam, 1978.

Brackmann, Albert. "Die Ursachen der geistigen und politischen Wandlung Europas im 11. und 12. Jahrhundert." *HZ* 149 (1934): 229–39.

Brooke, Christopher. "Hildebrand." In *Medieval Church and Society: Collected Essays,* 57–68. London, 1971.

Brooke, Zachary N. "Lay Investiture and Its Relation to the Conflict of Empire and Papacy." Annual Raleigh Lecture 1939. *Proceedings of the British Academy.* London, 1939.

Classen, Peter. "Heinrichs IV. Briefe im Codex Udalrici." *DA* 20 (1964): 115–29.

Cowdrey, H. E. J. "The Papacy, the Patarenes and the Church of Milan." *Transactions of the Royal Historical Society,* 5th ser., 18 (1968): 25–48.

Erdmann, Carl. *Die Entstehung des Kreuzzugsgedankens.* Stuttgart, 1935. Chapters 4–8 in particular pertain to Pope Gregory VII.

Erdmann, Carl, and D. von Gladiss. "Gottschalk von Aachen im Dienste Heinrichs IV." *DA* 3 (1939): 115–74.

Fliche, Augustin. "Premiers résultats d'une enquête sur la réforme grégorienne dans le diocèse français de Narbonne." *Académie des inscriptions et de belles-lettres. Comptes rendus* 1944, 162ff.

Fornasari, Giuseppe. "Coscienza ecclesiale e storia della spiritualità: Per una ridefinizione della riforma di Gregorio VII." *Benedictina* 33 (1986): 25–50.

Fuhrmann, Horst. "Das Reformpapsttum und die Rechtswissenschaft." In *Investiturstreit und Reichsverfassung*, 175–203.

———. "Pseudoisidor, Otto von Ostia (Urban II.) und der Zitatenkampf von Gerstungen (1085)." *ZRG Kan. Abt.* 68 (1982): 52–69.

———. "Rex canonicus—Rex clericus?" In *Institutionen, Kultur und Gesellschaft im Mittelalter. Festschrift für Josef Fleckenstein zu seinem 65. Geburtstag.* Edited by Lutz Fenske, Werner Rösener, and Thomas Zotz, 321–26. Sigmaringen, 1984.

Hageneder, Othmar. "Das päpstliche Recht der Fürstenabsetzung: seine kanonistische Grundlegung." *Archivum Historiae Pontificiae* 1 (1963): 53–95.

Heidrich, Ingrid. *Ravenna unter Erzbischof Wibert (1073–1100): Untersuchungen zur Stellung des Erzbischofs und Gegenpapstes Clemens III in seiner Metropole.* Vorträge und Forschungen herausgegeben vom Konstanzer Arbeitskreis für mittalalterliche Geschichte. Sonderband 32. Sigmaringen, 1984.

Hirsch, Ferdinand. "Die rechtliche Stellung der römischen Kirche und des Papstes nach Kardinal Deusdedit." *Archiv für katholisches Kirchenrecht* 8 (1908): 34–49.

Hirsch, Hans. "Reichskanzlei und Reichspolitik im Zeitalter der salischen Kaiser." *MIÖG* 42 (1927): 14ff.

———. "The Constitutional History of the Reformed Monasteries During the Investiture Contest." In *Medieval Germany*, 131–73.

Hoffmann, Hartmut. "Die beiden Schwerter im hohen Mittelalter." *DA* 20 (1964): 78–114.

———. "Die Unveräusserlichkeit der Kronrechte im Mittelalter." *DA* 20 (1964): 389–474.

Jordan, Karl. *Das Eindringen des Lehnswesens in das Rechtsleben der römischen Kurie.* Darmstadt, 1971. With a very helpful bibliographical postscript.

———. "Der Kaisergedanke in Ravenna zur Zeit Heinrichs IV., ein Beitrag zur Vorgeschichte der staufischen Reichsidee." *DA* 2 (1938): 85–128. The most recent paper on the Ravenna forgeries with an updated bibliography is Ovidio Capitani, "Hadrianum e Privilegium minus: Una rilettura," in *Aus Kirche und Reich: Festschrift für Friedrich Kempf,* edited by Hubert Mordek, 187–200 (Sigmaringen, 1983).

Keller, Hagen. "Schwäbische Herzöge als Thronbewerber: Hermann II (1002), Rudolf von Rheinfelden (1077), Friedrich von Staufen (1125). Zur Entwicklung von Reichsidee und Fürstenverantwortung, Wahlverständnis und Wahlverfahren im 11. und 12. Jahrhundert." *Zeitschrift für die Geschichte des Oberrheins* 131 (1983): 123–62.

Knabe, Lotte. *Die gelasianische Zweigewaltentheorie bis zum Ende des Investiturstreits.* Berlin, 1936.

Koch, Gottfried. *Auf dem Wege zum Sacrum imperium: Studien zur ideologischen Herrschaftsbegründung der deutschen Zentralgewalt im 11. und 12. Jahrhundert.* Vienna, 1972.

Ladner, Gerhart Buridan. *The Concepts of Ecclesia and Christianitas and Their*

Relation to the Idea of Papal Plenitudo potestatis from Gregory VII to Boniface VIII. Miscellanea historiae pontificiae, vol. 18. Rome, 1954.

Liebermann, Felix. "Lanfranc and the Antipope." *EHR* 16 (1901):328–32.

Lynch, Joseph. "Hugh I of Cluny's Sponsorship of Henry IV: Its Context and Consequences." *Speculum* 60 (1985):800–826.

Moore, R. I. "Family, Community and Cult on the Eve of the Gregorian Reform." *Transactions of the Royal Historical Society,* 5th ser., 30 (1980): 49–69.

Mordek, Hubert. "Kanonistik und gregorianische Reform; Marginalien zu einem nichtmarginalen Thema." In *Reich und Kirche vor dem Investiturstreit.* Edited by Karl Schmid, 65–82. Sigmaringen, 1985.

Morrison, Karl F. *Tradition and Authority in the Western Church, 300–1140.* Princeton, 1969.

Pasztor, Edith. "Sacerdocio e regno nella 'Vita Anselmi episcopi Lucensis.'" *Archivum Historiae Pontificiae* 2 (1964):91ff.

Salmon, Pierre. *Mitra und Stab, die Pontfikalinsignien im römischen Ritus.* Rome, 1960.

Schieffer, Rudolf. "Von Mailand nach Canossa: Ein Beitrag zur Geschichte der christlichen Herrscherbusse von Theodosius d. Gr. bis zu Heinrich IV." *DA* 28 (1972):333–70.

———. *Die Entstehung des päpstlichen Investiturverbots für den deutschen König.* MGH 28. Stuttgart, 1981. Arguments against Schieffer's thesis of the earliest official prohibition of investiture for the German king in 1078 have been marshalled magisterially by Friedrich Kempf, S.J., *Archivum Historiae Ponficiae* 20 (1982):409–14.

———. "Rechtstexte des Reformpapsttums und ihre zeitgenössische Resonanz." In *Überlieferung und Geltung normativer Texte des frühen und hohen Mittelalters.* Edited by Hubert Mordek, 51–69. Quellen und Forschungen zum Recht im Mittelalter, vol. 4. Sigmaringen, 1986.

Schieffer, Theodor. *Die päpstlichen Legaten in Frankreich vom Vertrage von Meersen (870) bis zum Schisma von 1130.* Berlin, 1935.

Schlesinger, Walter. "Die Wahl Rudolfs von Schwaben zum Gegenkönig 1077 in Forchheim." In *Investiturstreit und Reichsverfassung,* 61–85.

Schmale, Franz-Josef. "Papsttum und Kurie zwischen Gregor VII. und Innocenz II." *HZ* 193 (1961):265–85.

Schneider, Christian. *Prophetisches Sacerdotium und heilsgeschichtliches Regnum im Dialog 1073–1077; zur Geschichte Gregors VII. und Heinrichs IV.* Munich, 1972.

Schumann, Otto. *Die päpstlichen Legaten in Deutschland zur Zeit Heinrichs IV. und Heinrichs V. (1056–1125).* Marburg, 1912.

Von den Steinen, Wolfram. *Canossa, Heinrich IV. und die Kirche.* Munich, 1957.

Struve, Tilmann. "Lampert von Hersfeld, Persönlichkeit und Weltbild eines Geschichtsschreibers am Beginn des Investiturstreits." *Hessisches Jahrbuch für Landesgeschichte* 19 (1960):1ff.; 20 (1970):32ff.

Szabó-Bechstein, Brigitte. *Libertas ecclesiae: Ein Schlüsselbegriff des Investiturstreits und seine Vorgeschichte; 4. bis 11. Jahrhundert.* Studi Gregoriani, no. 12. Rome, 1985.

Tellenbach, Gerd. "'Gregorianische Reform' Kritische Besinnungen." In *Reich und Kirche vor dem Investiturstreit.* Edited by Karl Schmid, 99–113. Sigmaringen, 1985.

Whitney, James P. *Hildebrandine Essays.* Cambridge, Mass., 1932.

Zema, D. B. "The Houses of Tuscany and of Pierleoni in the Crisis of Rome in the Eleventh Century." *Traditio* 2 (1944) : 155–75.

———. *"Economic Reorganization of the Roman See During the Gregorian Reform."* *Studi Gregoriani* 1 (1947) : 137–68.

Zerbi, Pietro. "Monasteri e riforma a Milano." *Aevum* 24 (1950) : 44ff.

Ziese, Jürgen. *Wibert von Ravenna: Der Gegenpapst Clemens III. (1084–1100).* Päpste und Papsttum, no. 20. Stuttgart, 1982.

The Episcopacy

Bogumil, Karlotto. *Das Bistum Halberstadt im 12. Jahrhundert.* Cologne, 1972.

Claude, Dietrich. *Geschichte des Erzbistums Magdeburg bis in das 12. Jahrhundert.* 2 vols. Cologne 1972, 1975.

Fleckenstein, Josef. "Hofkapelle und Reichsepiskopat unter Heinrich IV." In *Investiturstreit und Reichsverfassung,* 117–40.

Glaeske, Günter. *Die Erzbischöfe von Hamburg-Bremen als Reichsfürsten, 937–1258.* Hildesheim, 1962.

Jenal, Georg. *Erzbischof Anno II. von Köln (1056–75) und sein politisches Wirken.* 2 vols. Stuttgart, 1974, 1975.

Johnson, Edward. "Bishop Benno II of Osnabrück." *Speculum* 16 (1941) : 389–403.

Lück, Dieter. "Die Kölner Erzbischöfe Hermann II. und Anno II. als Erzkanzler der Römischen Kirche." *Archiv für Diplomatik* 16 (1969) : 1ff.

———. "Erzbischof Anno II. von Köln: Standesverhältnisse, verwandtschaftliche Beziehungen und Werdegang bis zur Bischofsweihe." *Annalen des Historischen Vereins für den Niederrhein* 172 (1970) : 69ff.

———. "Die Vita Annonis und die Annalen des Lampert von Hersfeld." *Rheinische Vierteljahrblätter* 37 (1973) : 117ff.

Robinson, Ian Stuart. "Periculosus homo: Pope Gregory VII and Episcopal Authority." *Viator* 9 (1978) : 103–31.

Schieffer, Rudolf. "Die Romreise deutscher Bischöfe im Frühjahr 1070: Anno von Köln, Siegfried von Mainz und Hermann von Bamberg bei Alexander II." *Rheinische Vierteljahrblätter* 35 (1971) : 152ff.

———. "Spirituales Latrones: Zu den Hintergründen der Simonieprozesse in Deutschland zwischen 1069 und 1075." *Historisches Jahrbuch* 92 (1972) : 19–60.

Tangl, Michael. *Das Leben des Bischofs Benno II. von Osnabrück.* Leipzig, 1911.

Thomas, Heinz. "Erzbischof Siegfried I. von Mainz und die Tradition seiner Kirche." *DA* 26 (1970) : 368–99.

Weinfurter, Stefan. "Reformkanoniker und Reichsepiskopat im Hochmittelalter." *Historisches Jahrbuch* 97/98 (1978) : 158–93.

Ziese, Jürgen. "Bischofsamt und Königtum." *Historisches Jahrbuch* 97/98 (1978) : 108–30.

Pope Gregory VII

Arquillière, Henri Xavier. *Saint Grégoire VII: Essai sur sa conception du pouvoir pontifical.* Paris, 1934.

Borino, Giovanni B. "Quando e dove si fece monaco Ildebrando." *Studi e testi* 125 (1946):218ff.

———. "L'Arcidiaconato di Ildebrando." *Studi Gregoriani* 3 (1948):463–516.

Caspar, Erich. "Gregor VII. in seinen Briefen." *HZ* 130 (1924):1–30.

Cowdrey, H. E. J., ed. *The Epistolae vagantes of Pope Gregory VII.* Oxford, 1972.

Dereine, Charles. "La prétendue règle de Grégoire VII pour chanoines réguliers." *Revue bénédictine* 71 (1961):108–18.

Fuhrmann, Horst. "Zur Benutzung des Registers Gregors VII. durch Paul von Bernried." *Studi Gregoriani* 5 (1956):299–312.

Gilchrist, John T. "Gregory VII and the Juristic Sources of his Ideology." *Studia Gratiana* 12 (1967):3–37.

———. "Gregory VII and the Primacy of the Roman Church." *Tijdschrift voor Rechtsgeschiedenis* 36 (1968):123–35. A review of the book by Meulenberg (see below) and of the date of the *Collection in 74-Titles.*

Goez, Werner. "Zur Erhebung und ersten Absetzung Papst Gregors VII." *Römische Quartalschrift* 63 (1968):117–44.

———. "Zur Persönlichkeit Gregors VII." *Römische Quartalschrift* 73 (1978): 193–216.

Hilpert, Hans-Eberhard. "Zu den Rubriken im Register Gregors VII." *DA* 40 (1984):606–11.

Hoffmann, Hartmut. "Zum Register und zu den Briefen Papst Gregors VII." *DA* 32 (1976):86–130.

Hübinger, Paul Egon. *Die letzten Worte Papst Gregors VII.* Opladen, 1973.

Ladner, Gerhart Buridan. "Two Gregorian Letters: On the Sources and Nature of Gregory VII's Reform Ideology." *Studi Gregoriani* 5 (1956):221–42.

———. "Gregory the Great and Gregory VII: A Comparison of Their Concepts of Renewal." With "A Note on the Computer Methods Used," by David W. Packard. *Viator* 4 (1973):1–31.

Meulenberg, L. F. J. *Der Primat der römischen Kirche im Denken und Handeln Gregors VII.* Rome, 1956.

Miccoli, Giovanni. "Le ordinazioni simoniache nel pensiero di Gregorio VII." *Studi medievali* 3d ser., 4 (1963):104–35. Reprinted in idem, *Chiesa gregoriana,* 169–201. Florence, 1966.

Morghen, Raffaello. *Gregorio VII.* Turin, 1942.

Murray, Alexander. "Pope Gregory VII and his Letters." *Traditio* 22 (1966): 149–202.

Nitschke, August. "Die Wirksamkeit Gottes in der Welt Gregors II." *Studi Gregoriani* 5 (1956):115–219. A remarkable essay, albeit somewhat one-sided, that has found general acceptance.

Robinson, Ian Stuart. "Gregory VII and the Soldiers of Christ." *History* 58 (1973):184–91.

———. "Pope Gregory VII, the Princes and the Pactum 1077–1080." *EHR* 94 (1979):721–56.

Santifaller, Leo. *Quellen und Forschungen zum Urkunden- und Kanzleiwesen Papst Gregors VII.* Studi e testi 190. Vatican City, 1957.

Schieffer, Rudolf. "Tomus Gregorii papae." *Archiv für Diplomatik* 17 (1971): 169–84.

———. "Gregor VII.-Ein Versuch über die historische Grösse." *Historisches Jahrbuch* 97–98 (1978): 87–107.

Wühr, Wilhelm. *Studien zu Gregor VII. Kirchenreform und Weltpolitik.* München and Freising, 1930.

Zafarana, Z. "Sul 'conventus' del clero romano nel maggio 1082." *Studi medievali.* 3d ser., 7 (1966): 399–403.

Dictatus Papae

Fuhrmann, Horst. "'Quod catholicus non habeatur, qui non concordat Romanae ecclesiae,' Randnotizen zum Dictatus Papae." In *Festschrift Helmut Beumann,* edited by K. U. Jäschke and R. Wenskus, 263–87. Sigmaringen, 1977.

Hofmann, Karl. *Der "Dictatus Papae" Gregors VII.* Paderborn, 1933.

Kempf, Friedrich. "Ein zweiter Dictatus Papae Gregors VII.? Ein Beitrag zum Depositionsanspruch Gregors VII." *Archivum Historiae Pontificum* 13 (1975): 119–39. Reviews the article by H. Mordek (see below).

Kuttner, Stephan. "Liber canonicus." *Studi Gregoriani* 2 (1947): 387–401.

Meulenberg, Leo. "Une question toujours ouverte: Grégoire VII et l'infaillibilité du pape." In *Aus Kirche und Reich. Festschrift für Friedrich Kempf,* edited by Hubert Mordek, 159–71. Sigmaringen, 1983.

Mordek, Hubert. "Proprie auctoritates apostolice sedis: Ein zweiter dictatus papae Gregors VII.?" *DA* 28 (1972): 105–32.

Ullmann, Walter. "Romanus Pontifex indubitanter efficitur sanctus: Dictatus Papae 23 in retrospect and prospect." *Studi Gregoriani* 6 (1959–61): 229–64.

Wojtowytsch, Myron. "Proprie auctoritates apostolice sedis: Bemerkungen zu einer bisher unbeachteten überlieferung." *DA* 40 (1984): 612–21.

Canossa

A good introduction to the events is provided by the collected essays in the volume *Canossa als Wende,* edited by Hellmut Kämpf. Wege der Forschung, no. 12. Darmstadt, 1969.

Beumann, Helmut. "Tribur, Rom und Canossa." In *Investiturstreit und Reichsverfassung,* 33–60.

Consiglia de Matteis, Maria. "La riconciliazione di Canossa." *Studi Medievali* 19 (1978): 681ff.

Elze, Reinhard. "Über die Leistungsfähigkeit von Gesandschaften und Boten im 11. Jahrhundert: Aus der Vorgeschichte von Canossa (1075–1077)." *Beihefte der Francia* 9 (1980): 3–10.

Morrison, Karl F. "Canossa, a Revision." *Traditio* 18 (1962): 121–48.

Vogel, Jörgen. *Gregor VII. und Heinrich IV. nach Canossa.* Schriftenreihe des Instituts für Frühmittelalterforschung der Universität Münster, no. 9. Berlin and New York, 1983.

Zimmermann, Harald. *Der Canossagang von 1077: Wirkungen und Wirklich-*

keit. Akademie der Wissenschaften und der Literatur in Mainz. Abhandlungen, vol. 5. Mainz, 1975.

Monastic Reform and the Nobility

Bulst, Neithard. *Untersuchungen zu den Klosterreformen Wilhelms von Dijon (962–1031).* Bonn, 1973.
Hils, Kurt. *Die Grafen von Nellenburg im elften Jahrhundert.* Freiburg/Br., 1967.
Jakobs, Hermann. *Der Adel in der Klosterreform von St. Blasien.* Cologne, 1968.
———. *Die Hirsauer, ihre Ausbreitung und Rechtsstellung im Zeitalter des Investiturstreites.* Cologne, 1961.
———. "Rudolf von Rheinfelden und die Kirchenreform." In *Investiturstreit und Reichsverfassung,* 87–115. Includes a detailed bibliography for the general topic.
Semmler, Josef. *Die Klosterreform von Siegburg.* Rheinisches Archiv, no. 53. Bonn, 1959.

Saxony

Baaken, Gerhard. *Königtum, Burgen und Königsfreie.* Constance, 1961.
Fenske, Lutz. *Adelsopposition und kirchliche Reformbewegung im östlichen Sachsen; Entstehung und Wirkung des sächsischen Widerstandes gegen das salische Königtum während des Investiturstreits.* Göttingen, 1977.
Freed, John. "The Origins of the European Nobility: The Problem of the Ministerials." *Viator* 7 (1976): 211–42.
Kost, Otto-Hubert. *Das östliche Niedersachsen im Investiturstreit: Studien zu Brunos Buch vom Sachsenkrieg.* Göttingen, 1962.
Lange, Karl-Heinz. "Die Stellung der Grafen von Northeim in der Reichsgeschichte des 11. und frühen 12. Jahrhunderts." *Niedersächsisches Jahrbuch für Landesgeschichte* 33 (1961): 1ff.
———. *Der Herrschaftsbereich der Grafen von Northeim 950 bis 1144.* Studien und Vorarbeiten, vol. 24. Göttingen, 1969.
Leyser, Karl J. *Rule and Conflict in an Early Medieval Society: Ottonian Saxony.* Bloomington, Ind., and London, 1979.
———. "The Crisis of Medieval Germany." Raleigh Lecture on History." *Proceedings: British Academy* 69 (1983): 409–43.

Polemics

Affeldt, Werner. "Königserhebung Pippins und Unlösbarkeit des Eides im Liber de unitate ecclesiae conservanda." *DA* 25 (1969): 313–46.
Berschin, Walter. *Bonizo von Sutri.* Berlin, 1972.
Beumann, Jutta. *Sigebert von Gembloux und der Traktat de investitura episcoporum.* Vorträge und Forschungen herausgegeben vom Konstanzer Arbeitskreis für mittelalterliche Geschichte, no. 20. Sigmaringen, 1976.
Cantarella, Glauco Maria. "Placibo di Nonantola. Un progetto di ideologia." *Rivista di storia della Chiesa in Italia* 37 (1983): 117–42, 406–36.

Jordan, Karl. "Die Stellung Wiberts von Ravenna in der Publizistik des Investiturstreites." *MIÖG* 62 (1954):155ff.

Leyser, Karl J. "The Polemics of the Papal Revolution." In *Medieval Germany and Its Neighbours, 900–1200*, 138–60. London, 1982.

Mirbt, Carl. *Die Publizistik im Zeitalter Gregors VII*. Leipzig, 1894. The volume is still an essential introduction.

Robinson, Ian Stuart. "Colores rhetorici im Investiturstreit." *Traditio* 32 (1976): 209–38.

―――. "Eine unbekannte Streitschrift über die Sakramente von Exkommunizierten im Münchener Kodex lat. 618." *Studi Gregoriani* 11 (1978):303–95.

―――. *Authority and Resistance in the Investiture Contest: The Polemical Literature of the Late Eleventh Century*. Manchester, 1978.

Schnitzer, Joseph. *Die Gesta Romanae ecclesiae des Kardinals Beno und andere Streitschriften der schismatischen Kardinäle wider Gregor VII*. Bamberg, 1892.

Zafarana, Z. "Ricerche sul'Libre de unitate ecclesiae conservanda." *Studi medievali*, 3d ser., 7 (1966):617–700.

Ziese, Jürgen. *Historische Beweisführung in Streitschriften des Investiturstreites*. Munich, 1972.

CHAPTER 5

The Controversy Over Investitures in England, France, and Germany Under Gregory's Successors

1. Pope Urban II, Investiture, and *Hominium*

The death of Gregory VII in May 1085 at Salerno sowed confusion and seemed to spell disaster for the church. The division of the cardinals and the lower Roman clergy into two factions, one of which supported Henry's anti-pope Clement III, was the most obvious but not the only sign. But Pope Urban II (1088–99), Gregory's second successor after the brief reign of Victor III (1086–87), spectacularly reversed the trend of the mid-eighties and led the papacy to new heights.

Urban, an aristocratic Frenchman with important family connections, had been archdeacon of the archdiocese of Reims since the late fifties. He entered Cluny, probably between 1067 and 1070, and soon became prior under Abbot Hugh. Prior Odo—Urban's name before his election to the papacy—was among the monks Hugh sent to Rome to assist Gregory VII. Gregory appointed Odo cardinal-bishop of Ostia. Both Gregory and Victor III recommended Odo to the papal electors. Victor's recommendation was taken up, and in 1088, at Terracina, Odo was elected pope. He adopted the name Urban II. The difficult beginnings of Urban's pontificate tested the skills of the Cluniac monk. Clement III was an able opponent with a secure power base in his archdiocese of Ravenna, who from 1084 to 1089 was supported by a clear majority of the Roman clergy. Wibert of Ravenna/Clement III was a personality in his own right, certainly not a creature of Henry IV. Nevertheless, approaching with an army from southern Italy, Urban eventually succeeded in the summer of 1089 in driving the anti-pope from the city. Almost five years later, in 1094, Urban was finally able to enter the Lateran palace and in 1098 the

Castello Sant'Angelo, both times without bloodshed. Urban had paid
compensation to the Roman adherents of Clement III and had satisfied
their claims. The pillars of the papal party in those days were Countess
Matilda of Tuscany and the Normans of southern Italy who provided the
pope with ready sanctuary should he need it. In 1089 Urban persuaded
Matilda to enter into a political marriage with the seventeen-year-old
Welf V, son of the deposed Bavarian Duke Welf IV and her junior by
twenty-six years. The marriage cemented an alliance that effectively
blocked the emperor's passage to Rome.

Rome nevertheless once again became a campaign goal after Henry IV
had stabilized and strengthened his position in Germany. He set out in
1090. At first his recent strain of good luck promised to hold in Italy as
well. In 1092, however, at the fortress of Canossa, the emperor suffered a
disastrous defeat with far-reaching implications. The northern Italian
cities of Milan, Cremona, Lodi, and Piacenza formed an anti-imperial alliance in their drive for independence. Moreover, in 1093, Henry's son
Conrad rebelled against him. Conrad had been crowned as successor and
heir at Aachen in 1087. Joining forces with Matilda and young Welf V,
Conrad was now crowned king of Italy in Milan. As cardinal and legate
to Germany, Pope Urban II had never paid any attention to the anti-king
Hermann of Salm, but in 1095 the pope recognized Conrad, presumably
in the belief that the young Salian could count on German as well as Italian support. At a meeting in Cremona, Conrad acted as honorary squire
to the pope. He held the pope's stirrup, led his horse by the bridle, and
swore the customary oath of security that was adapted to the occasion.
Urban on his part promised to assist Conrad in every way to achieve his
aims—provided these would not infringe on Roman ecclesiastical rights,
a significant limitation of papal aid since investiture was specifically mentioned and stressed. In the end, however, Urban merely helped arrange
the marriage of Conrad and a daughter of his old ally, Count Roger of
Sicily. The emperor was powerless to stem this veritable tide of misfor-
tune. His enemies had effectively isolated him in the region of Padua and
Verona. As a final insult, Henry's second wife, Praxedis, or Adelheid,
daughter of a Russian and widow of the margrave of the Nordmark, publicly humiliated Henry before Pope Urban II at the council of Piacenza in
1095 by accusing him of sexual depravity. Urban permitted her continued
separation from Henry without imposing a penance. Henry's fortunes did
not take a turn for the better until young Welf deserted his wife, Matilda,
who, as Welf complained everywhere, was unwilling to grant him con-
jugal rights. With the breakup of this unnatural marriage also came the
end of the alliance between the houses of Canossa and of the Welfs. In

1097 Henry could finally return to Germany where he had reinstated Welf IV as duke of Bavaria the preceding year. In the meantime, however, Urban II had won general recognition as legitimate pope, outdistancing by far the corresponding efforts of Clement III whose significance was now much reduced.

The years 1095–96 represent the apex of the pontificate of Urban II. In the letter announcing his election Urban had declared unhesitatingly that he stood fully behind the policies of Gregory VII, a claim borne out by his pontificate as a whole. In carrying out these policies, however, Urban was more flexible and lenient than his great predecessor. The councils of Piacenza (March 1095) and Clermont (November 1095) are a striking illustration. Conscious of the dignity of his papal office Urban tried to remedy schism and strife. He made generous use of the papal prerogative to grant dispensations when necessary for the well-being of the church. At the same time Urban emphasized that his dispensations were not to prejudice traditional ecclesiastical regulations. Concessions would be abrogated once the situation had improved. Urban was particularly concerned about the schism within the church. In Germany as well as in Italy numerous ecclesiastical dignities had two claimants each, one nominated by the imperial party and the other by the reformers. Under such conditions intraecclesiastical problems accumulated rapidly. Three proved particularly thorny: reconciliations with the church, encounters with excommunicated persons, and the validity of sacraments conferred by schismatics. Historians today are agreed that both the papal and the imperial factions were deeply committed to ecclesiastical reform. Nicolaitism and simony were evils detested by all. Moreover, allegiances shifted constantly. Nevertheless, adherents on both sides mutually anathemized each other as heretics and schismatics—the latter a term that was interpreted differently—with complete disregard for the effect of such anathemas on their pastoral or administrative activities. Was there no standard for their validity? What was to be done, for example, about the activities of bishops like Hermann of Metz or Hartwig of Magdeburg, loyal Gregorians and supporters of reform, who had come to an agreement with the emperor, largely to maintain themselves in their dioceses? Did not any contact with the excommunicated entrain automatic excommunication for the offender? Urban II had hardly any contact with the German clergy. Bishop Gebhard of Constance, whom he had consecrated and named papal vicar for all of Germany side by side with Altmann of Passau (d. 1091), was one exception; several southern German princes, and the monasteries of Hirsau and All Saints at Schaffhausen, were others. In an effort to reduce the confusion, Urban provided some specific instructions to

Gebhard in a letter of April 1089. Wibert of Ravenna as well as Henry IV, the originators of the schism, were to be considered excluded from the church on principle. The same basic decision, the pope declared, applied to simonists who had obtained their offices from either Wibert or Henry. Persons, however, who had only come into contact with the excommunicated could be reconciled with the church through an act of penance to be determined by the legate. In the same letter the pontiff agreed to a preliminary recognition of at least some of the nonsimoniacal clergy who had been ordained by schismatic bishops who were not guilty of simony themselves. Evidently, the problems were complex and it should not cause surprise that the pope reserved a final decision for all such cases for a general council.

As far as we know, the first synod to deal with such intraecclesiastical problems was the council of Piacenza of March 1095. The assembly became a triumphal success for the papacy. The transmission of the conciliar canons promulgated at Piacenza is still unclear, because several versions circulated. Certainly, however, the decrees contained the usual condemnations of simonists, but they elaborated numerous distinctions. Nonsimoniacal clergy, ordained or consecrated by simonists, were allowed to remain in their rank provided they were unaware at the time that their consecrator had committed simony. A further condition applied: their manner of life had to be blameless. A similar limitation pertained to the recognition of clergy who had been consecrated by bishops who only later came to be schismatics. Consecrations were also accepted as licit when a cleric was unaware at the time of ordination or consecration that the ordaining bishop had been excommunicated by name. Such clergy could continue in their offices, were to be reconciled with the church, and might eventually even attain a higher rank. Another canon stipulated that in case of future consecrations by schismatics or simonists no exceptions were to be made. Piacenza evidently was to alleviate an intolerable situation and to draw the line. The conditional amnesty proclaimed at the assembly naturally made it much easier for clergy to join the ranks of the adherents of the legitimate pope than did the final years of the pontificate of Pope Gregory VII. The degree of success of Urban's policies renders the failure of a reconciliation between pope and emperor all the more regrettable. Clement III, who continued to hold his office of archbishop of Ravenna, remained a stranger to the German bishops, and they managed to combine loyalty to Henry IV with recognition of Urban II, or at least with neutrality toward the claimants to the papal throne. Nothing, however, is known about any kind of rapprochement between the two chief adversaries.

About Urban's pontificate, many questions still await answers. Among these are his policies concerning investitures. Did investiture constitute a stumbling block and how much of a stumbling block? Urban's reticence in this respect is noteworthy. At the autumn synod of 1078 Gregory VII had prohibited clergy under threat of excommunication from receiving investiture with a bishopric (*episcopatus*), with an abbey, or with a church from the hands of an emperor, of a king, or of any other member of the laity of whichever sex. In March 1080, when Henry IV was excommunicated and deposed for a second time, the pope and the assembled synod strengthened a similar decree by a second canon stipulating excommunication also for secular powers and persons who dared to perform such an investiture. At his first synod at Melfi, in September 1089, Urban II seems only to have repeated part of Gregory's original condemnation dealing with the clergy. In contrast to Gregory at the synod of 1078, Urban made no mention at Melfi of excommunication. Clerics and monks who had been invested by the laity were to be deposed: their investiture was invalid. A mild punishment indeed! And even this canon was omitted when Urban II informed Bishop Pibo of Toul of the 1089 conciliar decisions. Even the great council of Piacenza may have been only marginally interested in the investiture problem. Only a single codex in one of the several known and edited manuscript groups transmits a fragmentary canon against lay investiture of clerics or monks with bishoprics, abbeys, or other offices. Alfons Becker has hypothesized that Gregory's prohibition of investiture was not repeated at Piacenza; he may be closest to the truth.

There are, however, two occasions when Urban II is known to have addressed investiture: at Cremona, where he concluded an agreement with Henry's rebellious son Conrad, and at the council of Clermont held in late November 1095. The council is famous for its association with the First Crusade, for it was on that occasion that Urban publicly called for a crusade against the Seljuk Turks and evoked an enthusiastic response among all ranks of the populace. The studies of Robert Somerville emphasize, however, that the conciliar fathers dealt with a far greater range of issues: pope and assembly proclaimed a peace of God, certainly a very familiar institution for the French pope, including the usual regulations for the protection of the unarmed population and of the churches. In other canons, besides prohibiting simony, Urban dealt with clerical morals, emphasized rules stipulating celibacy and prohibiting the clergy from carrying arms, and confirmed that the canonical sequence of ecclesiastical grades had to be observed in promotions. He also spelled out in detail fasting practices in the Roman church and prohibited the laity from possessing tithes or churches. Three of the Clermont canons prohibit investiture and, for the first time, the homage of clergy to the king and other laity. Soon after the council of Clermont, in February 1096, the provincial synod of Rouen repeated the decrees against investiture and homage. Urban II himself apparently prohibited both investiture and homage once again at his last synod in Rome, which he celebrated in the spring of 1099 shortly before his death.

If one examines Urban's pontificate as a whole, it is difficult to agree with Augustin Fliche and other historians who argue that the pontiff turned from the "opportunistic policies" of his early years to rigoristic "Gregorian policies" once he had attained general recognition as the legitimate pope. They suggest that he subsequently pursued the designs of his great predecessor unflinchingly and even exceeded Gregory's severity by prohibiting homage. Considering especially the consequences of Urban's decrees in England, which are discussed in the following section, this seems like a reasonable interpretation. Nevertheless, the prohibition of homage should be interpreted with great caution. Sources from around the time of the council of Clermont reveal the first traces of the use of the word *hominium* or *homagium* (homage). The word occurs in the decrees of a synod held at Poitiers in 1100 by two legates of Pope Paschal II with the intention of confirming Urban's Clermont canons. The synod of Rouen of 1096, as well as the council of Clermont itself, still used circumlocutions to describe the ceremony of rendering homage. Pope Paschal II himself used *hominium* when he prohibited feudal homage at his 1102 council held in the Lateran. The circumlocutions used, however, permit no doubt about the meaning of the word *hominium*. According to François Ganshof's classic analysis, *hominium* corresponds to commendation with a double hand gesture: the future lord grasps the hands of his future vassal, folded together in a gesture of prayer. What is not known, however, is how frequently investiture was accompanied by commendation, Monika Minninger's helpful summaries notwithstanding. *Investitura,* too, was an expression for the deliverance of ring and crosier into the hands of the prelate which shows up for the first time in late eleventh-century sources. The sources are unfortunately too often either silent or extremely vague. As Ganshof is at pains to point out, commendation was merely the framework of a contractual relationship that might encompass a great variety of forms and degrees of dependence. Thus it is almost impossible to calculate the effect of Urban's prohibition. The single most important element of the ceremony of investiture with a bishopric or an abbey was the oath of fealty or loyalty sworn by the invested cleric or monk. It was this oath that had already occasioned several disputes in the reign of Emperor Henry III, because both the Bible and the Rule of Saint

Benedict forbade oathtaking for clergy and monks. Neither Gregory VII nor his successors, however, forbade fealty oaths directly. Gregory's dispensation from all such oaths when he deposed Henry IV is a different matter.

In summary, despite continuing uncertainty among historians, it is apparent that in the relationship between the royal and the ecclesiastical power during the pontificate of Urban II, the prohibition of investiture carried greater weight than did the prohibition of homage. As Becker noted for France, it is not certain "that the monarch in fact and always required the prohibited homage, or that the French bishops did more than swear fealty. After 1095 references to homage disappeared in ecclesiastical legal and administrative sources." In England matters were different. Since the Norman Conquest the ecclesiastical hierarchy as landholders was firmly integrated into the feudal system. Commendation during investiture was important. Thus it is ironic that the Clermont prohibition was never promulgated beyond the Channel. The provincial synod of Rouen was but a weak substitute, especially because England and Normandy were at the time ruled independently by William Rufus and Duke Robert Curthose, respectively.

Urban II died on 29 July 1099, probably without having heard that Jerusalem had been taken fourteen days earlier by the predominantly French Crusaders. The Holy City had been turned into a bloodbath, to the utter horror of the far more civilized and sophisticated Arabs. Murder and looting tarnished the fame of most of the "Frankish" knights, with the exception of the Lotharingian Godfrey of Bouillon. Still, at least in Latin eyes, the bloodshed was negligible compared with the glorious success of the Christian army. Urban's public address at Clermont calling for the Crusade had not only elicited boundless enthusiasm but also evoked ideals in Western Christendom that lasted well into the early modern period, although religious ideals were soon partly superseded by more concrete economic interests. The desperate military straits of the Byzantine Emperor Alexios were readily forgotten in the West. Alexios had had a troop of knights in mind when his emissaries first approached Urban with a request for help, probably at Piacenza. It was instead the idea of an armed pilgrimage that spread like wildfire among many groups of the population. As early as the winter of 1095 huge crowds (by medieval standards) set out for Jerusalem, having fallen under the spell of charismatic and fanatical popular preachers like Peter of Amiens, who claimed that his role had been thrust upon him by a heavenly letter and whose very donkey was thought by the adoring multitude to be holy. The pilgrims began by unleashing pogroms against Jews in the Rhenish cities.

Probably none of them managed to reach Jerusalem; the sad remnants of the disorganized bands who had so far survived the incredible difficulties and strains of the arduous march on foot through Europe were annihilated by the Turks in Asia Minor. Only the knights, departing in 1096 after complex and extremely expensive preparations, eventually reached Jerusalem and founded the Latin Kingdom of Jerusalem. In our context this remarkable feat is noteworthy because it suggests a scene far removed from historical reality: united Christendom under the leadership of the papacy victoriously propagating the Christian faith and overcoming the infidels. The kings of Europe were reduced to marginal players: the French king, Philip I (1060–108) was excommunicated because of his second marriage, to Bertrada of Montfort; Henry IV, the German emperor, was under anathema and cut off in a corner of northern Italy, surrounded by his enemies; the English king, William Rufus (1087–100), was barely willing to recognize Urban as legitimate. Such a scene of united Christendom must earlier have animated Gregory VII, but it was not to be his destiny to lead a united Christian army to the East. Paschal II celebrated "the triumph of the Christian armies in Asia" in one of his earliest letters, a triumph that owed everything to Pope Urban II.

2.   The Investiture Conflict in England

Earlier chapters focused largely on events in the Empire, but the papally led church reform complicated the relationship between *regnum* and *sacerdotium* elsewhere as well and caused ominous confrontations. Urban's successor, Pope Paschal II (1099–118), was able however, to come to understandings—stopping just short of formal agreements—with both England and France, and to put an end to simmering conflicts in both countries. In Germany, on the other hand, difficulties centering on the prohibition of investiture increased rather than lessened under this pontiff, who is usually described as a dour old monk or, at best, a naive weakling, his permanent successes in England and France that were advantageous for both church and monarchy notwithstanding.

The relations between Anglo-Saxon England and Rome had been close ever since Pope Gregory the Great (590–604) had sent Augustine, who before his departure had been prior of Gregory's own monastery of Saint Andrew in Rome, as missionary to King Aethelbert of Kent. When Augustine had been halfway there, his companions had sent him back to Rome to beg release from the enterprise. Rumors about the fierce barbarians, whose language the monks did not speak, had thoroughly unsettled them. Augustine and his group of about forty companions were obliged, however, to continue their journey, fortified by additional letters of recommendation to the Frankish court and to Aethelbert's queen, Bertha, daughter of the Frankish King Charibert. In Kent Augustine was well received. The king took the missionaries under royal protection and provided all necessities, including a dwelling at Canterbury, where they led a simple and communal life. They used an ancient British church, dedicated to Saint Martin, for their liturgies. Most important, the king gave them permission to preach. Their success was impressive. According to a letter of Gregory the Great, Aethelbert was baptized on Christmas Day 597 with "more than ten thousand of the English." The basic ecclesiastical organization of the English church into the two archdioceses of Canterbury and York dates from these years, for from Kent, Christianity spread slowly to the east and north of England, a long process, accompanied by many setbacks, even in Kent. One such setback occurred in the time of Augustine himself. On papal authority he tried to obtain the collaboration of the bishops of Wales and other British territories. The Britons, heirs to the proud tradition of Patrick and Ninian, were in a quandary and hesitant to abandon their own customs, which had served them well. The Celtic church was organized along nondiocesan, monastic lines. It used an antiquated method of dating Easter and differed from the Roman church also in penitential practices and in customs such as the shape of the tonsure. Bede relates that negotiations between Augustine and the British church failed in the end because at a meeting Augustine had arrogantly remained seated instead of rising to welcome the arriving Britons with the humility that Celtic tradition customarily regarded as the sign of a true Christian.

That Celtic ideals nonetheless came to exert their profoundly enriching influence on English Christianity is due to the Irish church. This offshoot of the British church, equally marked by simplicity, austerity, love of learning, and self-abnegation, was distinguished by its missionary zeal. The Irish Christians regarded exile for the love of God as a particularly severe form of asceticism. Beneficiaries of the Celtic ideals were the Frankish as well as the English kingdoms of the seventh and the eighth centuries. As Columbanus founded Luxeuil and Bobbio, so Columba established the great monastic center of Iona, and it was primarily from there that at first Northumbria, and subsequently also the Midlands and Essex, were converted. Until the synod of Whitby in 663, East Anglia and Kent under the archbishop of Canterbury as well as Wessex followed Roman practices, whereas the rest of the country, with the exception of some heathen pockets, looked to Iona. At Whitby King Oswy was swayed by the classical statement of the Petrine primacy to decide that Roman practices should be uniformly observed: "since they all hoped for one kingdom in heaven, they should not differ in celebrating the sacraments of heaven" (Bede). Still, the Roman victory did not cause the wholescale exodus of British monks from England. By the time of Bede (c. 673–735), Roman ecclesiastical institutions and learning had become firmly integrated throughout England with the strands of British Christianity. In about 716 even the monks of Iona finally accepted the Roman date for Easter. Abbots Adamnàn and Aidan were arguably as beloved by Bede as was his own Benedict Biscop. British traditions impressed themselves not only on English religion but also on the arts and learning, witness the magnificent Lindisfarne Gospels and the missionary work of Boniface on the continent.

The description of the Anglo-Saxon church as corrupt and decadent before the Conquest by William of Malmesbury can no longer be accepted without some challenge. The achievements of the tenth-century monastic revival, linked particularly with the names of Dunstan (d. 988), Aethelwold (d. 984), and Oswald (d. 992), continued to affect the English church—at least in the south—until well after the Norman Conquest. The religious houses they had restored or that had been restored under their inspiration remained influential (Glastonbury, Ramsey, Abingdon, Ely, Peterborough, Thorney, Winchcombe, Crowland, and others), and the men they had trained continued to provide leadership. Many rose to bishoprics and served as foremost advisors to kings and nobles. Dunstan, exiled in 956 from Glastonbury, where he had brought together the first community of monks in two generations, had found refuge at the abbey of Saint Peter (Blandigny) at Ghent. His contemporary, Archbishop Oda of Canterbury (d. 958), had professed at Saint Benoît-sur-Loire, Fleury, where his nephew Oswald was also trained. We know, too, of Continental clerks and monks who at least visited England. Among these are the chanters from Corbie who were invited by Abbot Aethelwold to Abingdon. Abbo of Fleury came to Ramsey at the invitation of Oswald and taught in the monastic school for two years (986–88). His influence on learning there lasted into the twelfth century. The *Regularis Concordia* drawn up by Bishop Aethelwold and approved by the council of Winchester (between 963 and 975) mentions as advisors monks from Fleury and Ghent. The fact that there was interaction between England and the Continent is well documented.

In England, however, foreign impulses from as far away as Einsiedeln essentially only furthered a movement already under way that was an expression of native piety. By the year 1000 there were over forty Benedictine monasteries in England, only two of which, Saint Augustine at

Canterbury and the nunnery at Shaftesbury, had unbroken histories going back to the period before the tenth-century revival (Barlow). The influence of this revival at the parish level was direct and strong. Sir Frank M. Stenton estimates that "between 975 and 1066 every English diocese came for a time, if only for a short time, under the rule of a bishop who was a professed monk." The Domesday survey shows that Anglo-Saxon churches, typically small, in towns and in the countryside were numerous: in Norwich alone there were almost fifty (Clanchy). The monastic bishops instructed as well as ruled their clergy. They firmly upheld priestly ideals and tried hard, albeit with little success (possibly because of the influence of Danish customs), to move the lower clergy toward a celibate life as well. A vernacular religious literature was developed, not so much for monastic readers as for parish priests and the laity. This included Aelfric's *Lives of the Saints* and his translations from the Bible. Aelfric had been trained by Aethelwold at Winchester. His *Catholic Homilies* illuminate the characteristic emphasis on pastoral care, also expressed in collections of vernacular prayers and manuals on penance. The literature of this period is preserved in a good number of manuscripts, some of them from the twelfth century. The fact that there are still so many indicates that the literature had wide appeal and was not displaced entirely by the Latin and more legalistic culture dominant after the Conquest. The work of Wulfstan, another reformer of the second generation, emphasizes that if Anglo-Saxon was used to achieve a wider circulation for local literature, then it cannot be said that the use of the vernacular indicates a parochial outlook or a limitation to learning. Wulfstan I, bishop of London in 996, archbishop of York in 1002–23, bishop of Worcester in 1002–16, and a friend of Aelfric, is best known for his admonition to all of the English people in the year 1014. His diocese of York, remote and forbidding as it was at the time, required a practical man who was able to establish and keep order. He turned therefore to legal writings, homilies, and a formulary of penitential letters, using manuscripts at the library of Worcester cathedral and conceivably some remnants of Alcuin's library at York. The Northumbrian priests' law as well as the *Rectitudines singularum personarum* (duties of all ranks and orders) have been attributed to him, and he is responsible for the royal law codes from Aethelred to Cnut, either because he actually drafted them or because he inspired them. As advisor and friend of kings he was able to carry over to secular life the reform begun by Dunstan at the monastic level. His homilies, later incorporated into the homiliary of his sainted namesake, Wulfstan II of Worcester (1062–95), were still copied in the twelfth century and still read in the thirteenth century. It can be shown that Aelfric and Wulfstan

relied on traditional theological and legal literature, in particular Carolingian ninth-century writings, material that was still very suitable two
centuries later for England, where the cooperation between kings and
bishops in the interest of church reform was and remained a hallmark of
politics. The Conquest did nothing to change this outlook, the much live-
lier and more varied scene of learning on the Continent notwithstanding.

Duke William of Normandy set out to conquer England not so that he
might reform the church but so that he might claim the kingdom as his
inheritance. Among William's preparations was an embassy to Rome to
request papal support for the enterprise. He received help from Gregory
VII, who was then an archdeacon. When Gregory became pope he pointedly reminded William that he was responsible for Pope Alexander II's
giving his blessing to the enterprise despite opposition at the curia because of the expected bloodshed. As ruler of Normandy William was in
firm control of the church. Although he had not categorically excluded
papal interventions (two Norman bishops, for example, were repri-
manded by the council of Reims of 1049 by Pope Leo IX), he did not
encourage it. Under his guidance, at regular synods where William presided, the Norman church was reformed and centrally reorganized around
the see of Rouen. It is not easy to explain, then, why William had dispatched Bishop Gisilbert of Lisieux to Rome in 1066—ten years before
Henry IV was excommunicated and deposed. This question suggests a
second one: Why did Gregory VII treat William with much more defer-
ence than he did other kings of Europe, at least until about 1080? Gregory's first letter to William, written in April 1074, seems to provide an
answer. The pontiff declares that William is the only one among kings to
place the precepts of his mother, the church, before all other considerations. Five years later Gregory was to threaten in a letter to Archbishop
Lanfranc that should William, "whom he has always loved best among
kings," turn against the church, he would deal all the more harshly with
him. But nevertheless, as late as 1081 Gregory VII withdrew sentences of
excommunication imposed by his legates on Norman clergy because of
William's support of reform, "although he did not behave as religiously in
some things as we would like him to." Even Gregory's last letter to William was warm and amicable. It shows "how lasting was his undertone of
official confidence in William, despite their many differences" (Cowdrey).
Papal support and praise added luster to the reign of a man who had been
despised as a bastard at the outset. Gregory seems to have admired William's prowess and his success. He was most of all persuaded that William
loved "justice," a term made famous by Gregory's dying words.

William had manifested love of justice by judicious support of reform in Normandy. He appointed his relatives Odo and Hugh, probably neither yet of canonical age, to the sees of Bayeux and Lisieux, respectively, but balancing nepotism with reform, he gave the highest ecclesiastical office in the duchy, the see of Rouen, to Maurilius (1054–67), a monk of Fécamp. Maurilius, who came from Reims, had studied at Liège and for a time had been abbot of an Italian monastery. Pope Leo IX at Reims in 1049 had criticized the planned marriage of William and Matilda of Flanders because of consanguinity, although how they were related was never explained. The marriage was solemnized in 1050 or 1051, and because of embroidered accounts of the incident in twelfth-century chronicles, it has been argued that the marriage was not papally sanctioned until 1059. There was probably an early and amicable settlement, however, for Lanfranc, prior of Bec, was in Leo's company for almost a year beginning in late 1049, and Bishop Geoffrey of Coutances attended Leo's Roman synod of April 1050. Moreover, at about the same time, Abbot John of Fécamp was in Rome as William's emissary (Bates). As penance William and Matilda founded two abbeys at Caen, one for women and one for men, where Lanfranc became abbot in 1063. Throughout his reign William seems to have valued good relations with the head of Christendom. His consultation with Rome before the invasion of England is in keeping with this policy.

After the death of the childless Edward the Confessor (1042–66) the English had acclaimed and anointed as their king Harold Godwinson, brother-in-law to Edward, and for years the most powerful of the English earls. William had good reasons, therefore, to rally as much support as possible for his invasion, although the deaths of Count Geoffrey Martel of Anjou and of King Henry I of France, both in 1060, had freed him from threats to his duchy. From the papacy he can have expected only spiritual and moral support. Neither Norman nor Anglo-Saxon contemporary chronicles are always reliable, but it is generally agreed that Edward at some point had promised the English crown to William of Normandy (1051?), that Harold, the later king, had sworn an oath of loyalty or friendship to William in late 1065, and that Edward on his deathbed designated Harold as king—or, in a less likely interpretation, as a regent for the kingdom. The crucial issue in the present context is Harold's oath to William of Normandy. The sources are either ambiguous or partisan. William of Poitiers, writing in about 1073–74, states that Harold did homage accepting William as his future king. By becoming king himself, Harold, again according to William of Poitiers, committed perjury. The perjury charge was the reason, or pretext—depending on one's perspective—for William's invasion and perhaps lay at the heart of William's legation to Rome.

The undated fragment of a letter of Pope Alexander II (1061–73) and a request for fealty from William, which was probably verbally transmitted by Pope Gregory VII's legate, Hugh, in 1080, suggest that if the perjury charge did indeed come up in Rome, it was not the only topic debated in 1065. The Alexander fragment, preserved in the canonical collection of Deusdedit, is not very helpful, for in it the pope merely declares that England since the conversion has existed "in the care and wardship of the prince of the apostles" (*sub apostolorum principis manu et tutela*). The vagueness of this phrase leaves it open/to a range of interpretations. The exact terms of the request for fealty will never be known. It is nonetheless clear that for Gregory VII more was at issue than subjection in spiritual matters. There was precedent for his request. In 1059 an oath of vassalage to the papacy had legitimized Norman conquests in southern Italy. Both Richard of Capua (14 September 1073) and Robert Guiscard (6 June 1080) repeated the oath for Gregory VII. Robert did so just a month after the legate, Hugh, departed for England. William curtly rejected fealty "because I did not promise it and my predecessors never did fealty to earlier popes," but he engaged himself to continue the payment of Peter's Pence, a custom since Alfred's reign. William's famous response to Hugh's request is a reliable fact. The precise nature of the 1065 negotiations as well as of Gregory's demands in 1080 remain uncertain.

William's victory at the Battle of Hastings in 1066 secured him the English crown. He certainly enjoyed Roman protection—whether he had obtained a papal banner or not—and Gregory had every reason to expect that the new king of England would later show his gratitude. By 1070 William had brought the country under control by building castles and using Norman knights and could turn his attention to the church. The problem of the church had become urgent since the death of Ealdred, archbishop of York, on 11 September 1069, during a general rising of the English. Ealdred rather than the archbishop of Canterbury, Stigand, had crowned William at Westminster on Christmas Day 1066. Stigand's position was ambiguous: he had been transferred from Winchester to Canterbury in 1052 without papal sanction to replace the Norman, Robert of Jumièges, who had very recently obtained his pallium in Rome (spring 1051) and had appealed to the papacy. Stigand held Winchester and Canterbury in plurality, not unusual at the time, and more important, had become archbishop during the lifetime of his predecessor. Stigand thus was unable to obtain his pallium until 1058 from the intruder Benedict X

(April 1058–January 1059) and was probably excommunicated by Leo IX. It seems certain that the majority of English bishops, for example, Wulfstan II of Worcester, avoided consecration by Stigand throughout his pontificate. The exception was Remigius of Dorchester, who was sent by William to Stigand for consecration in 1067 or 1068. With the death of Ealdred, however, the disorganization of the English hierarchy under an excommunicated metropolitan could no longer be tolerated. In April 1070 at Winchester and in May at Windsor two papal legates and Bishop Ermenfrid of Sion (Canton Valais, Switzerland) held councils attended by most of the bishops and abbots of English sees. Stigand appeared at the council of Winchester, but it was a foregone conclusion that he and his brother, Bishop Aethelmaer of Elmham, would both be deposed, as was Bishop Aethelric of Selsey at Windsor. Leofwine of Lichfield, a married man with sons, and Aethelwine of Durham resigned or left their respective sees. From the native English clergy only Siward of Rochester, the smallest English see, and Wulfstan of Worcester remained in office. Returning to France, Bishop Ermenfrid held a council in Normandy that imposed a remarkable set of penances on all ranks of William's army and included separate provisions for those who had wanted to but had failed to injure anyone and those who had fought at the Conqueror's side as mercenaries. The way was open for a thorough reorganization of the English church.

William's choice for archbishop of Canterbury was Lanfranc, formerly prior of Bec and since 1063 abbot of Saint Stephen's at Caen. Born in about 1010 at Pavia, Lanfranc was a scholar, educated probably during the years 1020–30 at Pavia and perhaps also at Vercelli or Ravenna. There is some evidence that he had gained legal expertise, but according to Gibson, his basic training was in the conventional fields of rhetoric, grammar, and logic. For unknown reasons he eventually left Italy. He may have studied at Tours in about 1035 with Bérengar, a pupil of Fulbert of Chartres, before studying by himself at Avranches, in keeping with a tradition that Gibson convincingly connects with Mont-Saint-Michel, an island in the Channel just north of Avranches and accessible from there at low tide. But instead of continuing his scholarly career along these lines, Lanfranc decided in 1042 to enter the monastery of Bec. The community had only been founded a few years earlier and was still an austere and extremely poor little place, not at all comparable with such great Norman ducal foundations as Mont-Saint-Michel, Fécamp, Jumièges, Saint Wandrille, or Saint Ouen. Lanfranc, however, thought that life at the community was not strict enough and planned to take up the life of a hermit. He never did. In the end he settled down at Bec, where he became prior by 1045. One of Lanfranc's duties was teaching. Tradition has it that he persuaded Abbot Herluin, founder of Bec, to open the school to outside pupils in order to cover the expenses for rebuilding the church and monastery. Under Lanfranc's teaching the school quickly gained an international reputation: Pope Nicholas II sent clerics to Lanfranc, Germans are known to have attended Bec, and, of course, Anselm, Lanfranc's successor at Bec and Canterbury, first came to Bec to study with Lanfranc. Not among the young men flocking to the school, however, was Anselm da Baggio, later Pope Alexander II: and the canonist Ivo of Chartres at most may have crossed Lanfranc's path before the latter went to Bec.

It is not known how Lanfranc came to the attention of Duke William, but Lanfranc became one of his close advisors in the 1050s. William's respect for Lanfranc is strikingly expressed by his appointment of him as the first abbot of the duke's foundation, the abbey of Saint Stephen at Caen in 1063. Saint Stephen's replaced Fécamp as the ducal family monastery, and William was buried there. Together with Saint Stephen's, its twin foundation, the abbey of Holy Trinity for women, and the stone castle built in 1060 became symbols of ducal authority and largesse. Lanfranc hesitated to accept the archbishopric of Canterbury, and it took a papal command to persuade him to leave his abbey in 1070. Earlier Lanfranc had refused invitations by Nicholas II and Alexander II to remain in Rome at the papal court, and he declined also his 1067 election to the archbishopric of Rouen. Even after his consecration as archbishop of Canterbury in August 1070, he asked Rome for release. The permission never came, and because of the insistence of the archdeacon Hildebrand that he come in person, he traveled with his colleague Thomas of York in 1071 to Rome to obtain the pallium, customary emblem of the metropolitan dignity. Nevertheless, his successor as archbishop of Canterbury, Anselm, referred to the collaboration of king and archbishop in the government of the Anglo-Norman church with the well-known simile of two well-matched oxen, a picture that can only have been suggested to him by the harmonious collaboration of king and archbishop. There can be no doubt that William's confidence in Lanfranc was well founded. Both men were of the same mind about order and reform in the English church; both seemed agreed that the church would be served best if control rested in the hands of a strong ruler.

Lanfranc set to work centralizing the English church. His chief instrument was to be ecclesiastical councils like those that had served William so well in Normandy. First, however, the assumed primacy of Canterbury over England's second archdiocese, York, had to be firmly established. Although Thomas of York had been elected before Lanfranc's arrival in England, at William's request his consecration was delayed so that it could be conferred by Lanfranc. Lanfranc used the occasion to demand a written profession of obedience from Thomas, who at first indignantly refused. He eventually gave in under royal pressure but limited his promise of obedience to Lanfranc and then reopened the issue when he was in Rome with Lanfranc in 1071. This time he claimed not only that he had parity in rank with Canterbury but also that the dioceses of Lichfield, Worcester, and Dorchester were part of the archdiocese of York. Alexander referred both questions to a council that was to be held in England in the presence of a papal legate. The council of Winchester of April 1072 brought Lanfranc victory on both issues, not only thanks to William's support, confirmed in a royal privilege, but also thanks to a series of papal privileges from the seventh to the ninth centuries, perhaps among the Canterbury forgeries. The forgeries may already have been compiled at Christchurch, Canterbury, before Lanfranc used them (Gibson), or possibly vague allusions to the primacy were only later inserted into authentic papal letters (Southern). Whatever the origin of the forgeries, historians generally agree that Lanfranc himself cannot have been responsible for them, although the debate has now been reopened by Sally Vaughn, who concludes that it was Lanfranc who "launched the conflict between Canterbury and York that echoed across future generations and embittered Anselm's last days."

Once Lanfranc was recognized as primate of all Britain, the conciliar decisions from his councils obtained validity throughout England as well as in British regions then in contact with Canterbury. Most of the synods met in conjunction with meetings of the royal court, but clerical deliberations were held separately; conciliar decisions had to have the approval of the king. It is also clear that councils could only be held if permitted by the king, provided, we may assume, that William II followed his father's customs in this respect. One of Anselm's chief reasons for his profound unhappiness with his position under William II was his inability to hold a kingdomwide reform synod. The Conqueror's often cited ordinance on church courts has perhaps some connection to Lanfranc's council of 1076. A decree promulgated by that synod assumes that a bishop has jurisdiction over the offenses of laymen who are accused before him. In the past, the ordinance, in the form of a Latin writ, has been seen as establishing separate ecclesiastical and secular courts. But as Barlow argued recently, "the writ cannot be used to prove that there was little true ecclesiastical jurisdiction in the Anglo-Saxon period." The text refers only to the hundred courts—omitting any reference to the important shire courts—and does not name the court where the bishops were to decide ecclesiastical cases in accordance with the canons and with episcopal laws. The ordinance instructs royal officials not to take ecclesiastical cases under their own jurisdiction except at the request of the bishop, but if necessary they are to insure appearance before the bishops.

An important witness to Lanfranc's attitude toward church government is still extant. Z. N. Brooke identified a manuscript at Trinity College, Cambridge, as the original exemplar of a canonical collection that was used almost exclusively in Lanfranc's letters and at his councils. It was widely and systematically distributed. The *Collectio Lanfranci,* as it is appropriately named whether it was compiled by him at Bec or compiled at his instruction, was almost the first lawbook to introduce the Pseudo-Isidorian Decretals to England, although it abbreviated them by about one third by omitting mostly pastoral material. "We seem to see the hand that cut down those unmanageable Carolingian commentaries on the Pauline Epistles" (Gibson). The codex also includes the conciliar texts associated with the forged Decretals, but in different recensions. It is further individualized by additions such as documents from the papal council of 1059 and three letters addressed to Lanfranc by Clement III, the anti-pope. Brooke has already shown that the abbreviation of the decretals did not alter the basic character of Pseudo-Isidore with its emphasis on papal and primatial authority in favor of the bishops and at the expense of the metropolitans. Lanfranc obviously felt entirely at ease in applying ancient canon law selectively; it is likely that the ingenious concept of the dual loyalties in the persons of clerics and monks, to the king as well as to the pope, enabled him to overlook the contradictions between his own very reserved and distant relationship with the papacy under Gregory VII (England probably for a time seriously considered the official recognition of Clement III) and the Pseudo-Isidorian attitude to the successor of Saint Peter.

The twin positions of clerics as servants of both *regnum* and *sacerdotium* was a commonplace in early medieval Europe. In the Conqueror's England, however, the concept was for the first time given a juridical definition and application. William the Conqueror stressed that England was his both by right of conquest and legally by right of inheritance. There is much continuity, therefore, in English institutional and administrative arrangements. But even though Anglo-Saxon England was moving rapidly toward feudalism, thoroughgoing feudalization along the lines of the Norman pattern of landholding and military service was at best a rarity before 1066. It was only introduced by the Conquest. The military summons of about 1072 to Abbot Aethelwig of Evesham as well as the estate records of Peterborough and Abingdon link Henry II's *cartae baronum* of 1166 not only to the end of the reign of Henry I (1100–1135) but even to the reign of the Conqueror. Legislation of William I is poorly preserved, but it is nonetheless clear that the lands of churches and abbeys were treated like secular fiefs. Bishops and abbots were subject to the *servitium debitum* calculated in quotas of knights' fees. That does not mean that bishops and abbots were expected to serve on campaigns in person, but they were responsible for equipping and providing prompt service with their quota of knights, regardless of how many knights they had actually enfeoffed with church lands. Some of the incidents of feudal tenure illustrated by the coronation charter of Henry I did not, strictly speaking, apply to the church, characterized in later legal terms as an undying corporation, but others, such as aid and counsel, clearly did. Still others, such as wardship, were adapted for use in connection with churches and abbeys (spoils system). William Rufus, like Henry I in the later years of his reign, persistently kept bishoprics and abbeys vacant for prolonged periods and used their income for the maintenance of court and followers. During such vacancies canons and monks had to subsist on a small fraction of the income ordinarily available. After the death of Lanfranc in 1089, for example, some of the monks of Christchurch were dispersed to avoid their being a burden on Canterbury income at the disposal of Rufus. Finally, like the secular magnates, ecclesiastics were invited by the king and did homage. As a consequence clergy as tenants could be accused before the royal court regardless of their clerical status. In 1082, for unknown reasons (perhaps plans for a campaign with English knights in Italy), William ordered the arrest, forfeiture, and imprisonment of his half-brother, Bishop Odo of Bayeux. At his trial, apparently on Lanfranc's advice, Odo was treated as an earl and tenant-in-chief. References to his ecclesiastical position were studiously avoided. Lanfranc used the proceedings of 1082 as a precedent at the trial of William of Saint Carilef, bishop of Durham, in 1088. The archbishop was present in court as a royal counselor assisting in the conviction of the bishop on suspicion of complicity in a baronial revolt against William Rufus. Again, the accused was not allowed to plead as a member of the clergy, for, argued Lanfranc, the king had deprived him not of the *episcopatus* but only of his fief.

William the Conqueror, his sons, and perhaps his grandson, Henry II, dominated until 1170 what could be called a national church. The "new usages" attributed with hindsight to William I by Eadmer, the companion and biographer of Anselm, were far-reaching. The king could determine whether a pope, or which pope if there were a disputed election, should be recognized; nobody was allowed to receive letters from the

pope without first submitting them to the king; councils held by the archbishop of Canterbury could not promulgate decrees without prior royal
approval; neither barons nor royal officials could be excommunicated
without express royal permission. Eadmer should have added that papal
legates could only be welcomed if invited by the king, although it was
"the archbishop who appears as the principal advocate of the barriers so
often said to have been raised by the king" (Brett). Furthermore, appeals
to the papacy came to be seen as treasonable activity. Eadmer should
have mentioned as well that all ecclesiastics of the realm holding of the
king in chief "have their possessions of the king as baronies and are an-
swerable for them to the king's justices and ministers" (Constitution of
Clarendon, c. 11). Owing to the mutual understanding between Lanfranc
and William, however, "the Conqueror's power over the English church
strengthened rather than weakened Lanfranc's archiepiscopal authority"
(Vaughn). When Lanfranc died in 1089 he had established an unprecedented degree of primatial control over the English church and, just as
important, had vastly increased the landed wealth of Canterbury, not
only by a determined process of recuperation with the lawsuit of Penen-
den Heath against Odo of Bayeux as a beginning, but also by new ac-
quisitions that were carefully protected.

   On both English primacy and Canterbury property, Archbishop Anselm
of Canterbury (1093–109) felt compelled at least to equal Lanfranc's
record, just as he saw the harmonious relationship between Lanfranc and
the Conqueror as an ideal to be imitated in his own collaboration with
King William Rufus (1087–100) and King Henry I. A brilliant and original theologian, Anselm had been a monk at Bec for thirty years before his
election to the archbishopric, and since 1078 he had been abbot of Bec.
He deeply distrusted the world with its blandishments and generally
lacked any interest in secular affairs or advancement. At times, however,
Anselm's "practical policies could have the same sharp edge as his theological insights" (Southern). On the Canterbury primacy, Anselm certainly perceived his duties clearly and reacted with characteristic passion
and zeal, never ceding an inch for the sake of peace and harmony—compromise was for lesser men. Skillfully using every opportunity, and often
thanks to his friends among the Norman magnates, Anselm could expand
Canterbury's authority in Wales and in Ireland. To the chagrin of the
monks of Christchurch, however, he was unable to overcome the shortcomings of Lanfranc's 1072 agreement with York, which had secured
Canterbury's primatial rank in all of Britain. It was once again the king,
now Henry I, who settled the issue in favor of Canterbury on the basis of
the records of 1072—but not until after the death of Anselm in 1109,

because according to Hugh the Chanter of York, the king never forgave Anselm for forcing his hand over investiture in 1105. However, the delay was not due to lack of trying on Anselm's part. At least on paper the high-point of recognition for Canterbury's claims was a privilege Anselm obtained from Pope Paschal II during a Rome visit in 1103—only it was too vague to be enforced when the need arose. On a smaller scale Anselm could also show considerable persistence and practical skill. Once he had decided to accept the archbishopric of Canterbury—Sally Vaughn argues this occurred at the latest during his election on 6 March 1093 at what was assumed to be the deathbed of William Rufus—"Anselm was taking active measures to assure his advancement." Anselm secured his release from Robert, duke of Normandy, from the archbishop of Rouen, from William *Bona Anima,* and from the Bec community. He attained his release from Bec only with difficulty. Bec opposition also confronted Anselm when he proposed William of Beaumont as new abbot instead of permitting free elections at Bec. William was a cousin of Robert of Meulan, master of the castle of Brionne that dominated Bec. William would be able to provide Bec with peace, economic prosperity, and security, which would be conducive to a strict observance of the Rule of Saint Benedict.

According to Eadmer, Anselm, before his election, warned the magnates and ecclesiastics at Gloucester of likely difficulties between himself and Rufus, since they were as different from each other as a wild bull and a feeble old sheep. Different they certainly were. Ironically, however, it was the sheep who showed the greatest determination in disputes with the king. For more than thirty years obedience had characterized Anselm's life as a monk, and his service as archbishop left obedience to his monastic profession as a guiding principle firmly in place. The impact of his actions, however, was now much enlarged. Anselm never doubted that after God he owed obedience first of all to the pope as successor of Saint Peter, however poorly the pontiff might be informed on English issues. This conviction alone sufficed to separate Anselm from most of his episcopal colleagues. It is also the root of Anselm's conflicts with both Rufus and Henry. Furthermore, Anselm was generally more familiar with the requirements of church reform than were his episcopal colleagues. He may not always have been informed on the most recent legislation from papal and legatine councils, but he certainly shared the condemnation of nicolaitism and simony. How could he, then, square the demands of Rufus, his feudal lord, with the demands of his conscience?

As soon as Anselm had been consecrated, disagreements with the king began to accumulate rapidly. The first major issue was the pallium, by then considered necessary before a metropolitan could officially take up his duties. As abbot of Bec, Anselm had followed the French example and recognized Pope Urban II. Since at least 1083, however, English contacts with the papacy had ceased, and England may have toyed with the possibility of recognizing the anti-pope Clement III. At the Rockingham Court of February 1095 the quarrels between king and archbishop burst into the open. The assembly was to decide on Anselm's request for permission to travel to Rome, where he wanted to obtain the pallium from Pope Urban II. This would have equaled England's official recognition of Urban, and William Rufus therefore had refused to grant permission for the journey. At Rockingham the king together with his secular and ecclesiastical magnates insisted that Anselm's overriding loyalty was to the king; submission to the pope had to take second place. At the request of William the majority of the assembled ecclesiastics withdrew their obedience from Anselm, but the secular nobles in particular had no wish to depose Anselm and to send him into exile. Accordingly, the proceedings were prorogued. In the meantime William had sent two emissaries to Rome. They returned in the company of a papal legate, Cardinal Walter of Albano, who was bringing Anselm's metropolitan pall. Walter obliged the king in every conceivable way, even offending Anselm, to obtain England's official recognition of Urban II. He confirmed to William far-reaching powers over the English church and agreed on behalf of the pope that no legates would be sent to the kingdom without express royal permission and that no English cleric should receive papal letters without royal permission. In addition, Walter consented to the stipulation that no English cleric should have to obey the pope without royal orders. Even Walter, however, was not willing to depose Anselm. After lengthy negotiations, Anselm agreed to take the pallium from the altar of Canterbury Cathedral after it had been deposited by the legate, but he categorically refused to accept it from the hands of the king.

Willy-nilly king and primate had been reconciled, but a new confrontation did not take long to develop. William criticized the equipment of the knights Anselm had sent to the king in early 1097 for the royal campaign against Wales. By then Anselm had realized that the fundamental incompatibility between himself and the king precluded a beneficial relationship and harmonious cooperation. He decided, therefore, to ask Urban personally for advice and support. In 1097, at Pentecost he asked the surprised king and the *curia regis* for leave to go to Rome. At first, despite his repeated requests, the leave was refused. Finally, exasperated by Anselm's persistence, the king gave him the choice of either accepting the decision of the king and never again appealing to the pope or of resigning the archbishopric. He decided to resign. In November he left Dover and did not return until after the death of William II in a hunting accident in August 1100. He returned at the urging of Henry I, youngest son of the Conqueror. The legitimate heir of William II would have been Robert Curthose, duke of Normandy. Henry, therefore, was vitally dependent on Anselm's support.

Henry's coronation charter, solemnly promising old liberties to the church and to the barons of England and abrogating the abuses introduced by William Rufus, might be seen as a most promising beginning for the productive cooperation between king and archbishop. But a new obstacle, not of their making, arose. Anselm's years of exile had been spent on the Continent in Rome and at Lyons as guest of the zealous Gregorian archbishop, Hugh. In Rome Anselm had participated in Urban's spring synod of 1099, and thus had witnessed the reconfirmation of the Clermont decrees against investiture and homage. Because they had been promulgated in his presence Anselm felt bound to observe them to the letter. As a consequence he refused both homage and investiture from Henry. Anselm appreciated the royal position to a degree and offered to intercede with Pope Paschal II, who, as Urban's successor, had been in office since August 1099. Anselm interceded by asking the pope to relax the prohibitions for England. Henry badly needed Anselm's support, and both sides showed goodwill. Still, there was no easy solution to the startling prohibitions Anselm introduced into England. Continuous negotiations ended in failure just before Easter in 1103 when Anselm went into exile for the second time. At the Lateran council of 1102 Paschal had once again prohibited both investiture and homage. Even at this point, however, Henry and Anselm as well as the pope shied away from a full-blown confrontation over investiture: "Anselm naturally inclined to peace, the king shrewdly calculating political risk, and the curia unwilling to lose Peter's Pence and England's recognition" (Böhmer). In 1105, finally, Anselm made some headway in Rome. The pope himself reported to Anselm the results of his recent Lateran synod: Henry's advisors who had persuaded the king to invest clerics (Robert of Meulan was mentioned by name) and clerics who had received investiture were excommunicated; the king was under threat of anathema. The pontiff separately instructed Archbishop Gerard of York to publicize the excommunications in the absence of the primate. It is generally assumed that at this point Anselm also threatened the king with excommunication on his archdiocesan authority because Henry had confiscated Canterbury estates. Eadmer declares that Anselm told Adela of Blois "that he had come to excommunicate her brother Henry, king of England, for the wrong which now for two years and more he had been doing to God and to the archbishop himself." In the spring of 1105 Henry was in Normandy, on the verge of conquering Normandy, his brother Robert's duchy. He certainly could not afford an excommunication. On the contrary, he required every ounce of support he could find, and in particular that of Robert of Meulan. Robert had been excommunicated by name, and according to canon law, Henry himself, by his continued association with his powerful advisor, would automatically fall under excommunication. Anselm was very much aware of this particular difficulty, which was a major reason for his lengthy exile. Under these ominous circumstances, in July 1105 Henry's sister, Countess Adela of Blois, arranged a meeting at Laigle between Anselm and the king. A truce was agreed upon. The archbishop obtained Robert's promise to change his ways and therefore absolved him in accordance with the terms of the excommunication, as Anselm explained later in a letter to Paschal. The king restored the Canterbury estates. Both sides agreed in addition to send an embassy to the pontiff in an attempt to resolve the remaining issues.

The evidence pertaining to the negotiations at Laigle as well as subsequent discussions is obscure. With a great deal of ingenuity historians have tried to determine who could have introduced the terms of the compromise soon to be reached. There is, of course, Eadmer's *Historia Novorum,* but he is almost silent on the details of the discussions between the archbishop, the king, and perhaps the countess of Blois at Laigle. Eadmer never mentions the absolution of Roger of Meulan in the context of the talks at Laigle. There is not even a hint in his narrative that a compromise had been discussed, let alone reached: "They [the archbishop and the countess] found that he [Henry] was overjoyed at Anselm's coming and had to a considerable extent given up his former brusqueness. Then, when they had had their talk together, the king restored to Anselm the revenues of his archbishopric and their former friendship for one another was re-established." Eadmer goes on to explain that the embassy to Rome was agreed on because Anselm would not return to England as long as Henry I insisted that he "should not in any respect withhold his fellowship from any of those who had accepted from the king investitures of churches or from those who had consecrated them." This is an unmistakable reference to Paschal's 1105 legislation and to the canonical prohibition of contact in any form with the excommunicated if excommunication was to be avoided. Norman Cantor's study allows us to lay to rest at least one hypothesis. Cantor illustrates convincingly that the views of Bishop Ivo of Chartres differed profoundly from those of the English settlement reached after Laigle. Ivo, therefore, did not contribute to the compromise.

The only reliable witnesses to the stages of negotiations after Laigle are the letters of Anselm and of Paschal II. In December 1105 Anselm informed his friend and advisor Hugh of Lyons that now the chief disagreement between the king and himself was homage. Henry, so Anselm wrote, would let himself be persuaded of the illegitimacy of royal investiture of prelates, but he absolutely refused to abandon his claims to their homage. A letter of Paschal, dated 23 March 1106, already includes precise instructions for Archbishop Anselm. The pontiff wrote in response to proposals submitted to him by royal emissaries and absolved Anselm of the obligation to observe Urban's prohibition of investiture and homage. At the same time, Paschal absolved from excommunication bishops who had been invested by the king in the intervening period and instructed the archbishop to consecrate prelates who had done homage to the king provided they had not received investiture as well. This dispensation was to be valid only temporarily: "until such time when God through the words of Anselm should have softened the heart of the king." Finally, in August 1107, this compromise was publicized at a meeting of the royal court; the king would no longer insist on the investiture of prelates who had been duly elected in his presence. In return for the temporalities of their sees or abbeys they would render homage. Henry abandoned investiture only grudgingly; his court paid the utmost attention to events in the Empire, and the rumor of 1108 that the pope was willing to permit investiture to Henry V caused lively English protests. As it turned out, however, the temporary compromise of 1105/7 in no way lessened royal authority within the English church. Roman influence did not increase markedly until the anarchy of Stephen's reign (1135–54). In fact, only the murder of Archbishop Thomas Becket by overzealous courtiers of King Henry II prevented the renewed isolation of the English church in the twelfth century.

3. France and the Investiture Question

The eventful pontificate of Paschal II included the solemn meeting of 1107 at Saint Denis with the French kings Philip I (1060–108) and Louis VI (1108–37). The result was a compromise on investitures but its terms are nowhere described. Contemporary France differed from both Germany and England because the Capetians, the undisputed heirs of the royal Carolingian tradition since 987, effectively dominated only a few of the French bishoprics—twenty-five out of a total of seventy-seven, in Becker's estimate. Royal sovereignty was still limited to a small area of France. Most French bishoprics, therefore, were in the hands of numerous nobles. Moreover, the French kings could not always impose their authority, even within their own domain. Their power often depended on whether or not they could influence episcopal elections in favor of candidates of their choice. Nonetheless, the power of the kings of France depended as much on the bishoprics as did that of the German rulers. The Capetians relied on the economic and military aid of the bishops in their efforts to expand their sovereignty over their nominal vassals. Tenaciously they clung to their claims but were compelled at the same time to proceed cautiously and pragmatically. Grand proclamations of theocratic doctrine had no room on their agendas. The final result, the support of yet another bishop, mattered much more than the particular circumstances that led to his appointment. The church approved of the royal efforts. Faced by the choice of either supporting kingship or falling under the domination of numerous feudal powers, the church usually selected the first alternative as the lesser evil.

The great council of Pope Leo IX in 1049, rightly described as the beginning of the Gregorian reform, gathered at Reims in the border region of France and the Empire, an area to which the movement was indebted for many impulses. One reason Leo chose Reims was that he had concern about conditions prevailing in the French church. For good reasons one of the canons promulgated at Reims demanded canonical election of prelates. Many of the French bishops were accused of simony. In Germany and Italy reformers could rely on the active intervention of Emperor Henry III. King Henry I of France (1031–60) had little inclination to heed canonical prescriptions. The wealth and political reliability of a candidate rather than ecclesiastical suitability were his primary considerations. In France, therefore, the popes themselves had to take up the fight for canonical elections and against simony and married clergy. Leo's successors preferably used legates to promulgate and enforce Roman decrees at local French councils. Occasionally papal emissaries were dispatched for a specific purpose, usually to arbitrate intra-ecclesiastical disputes. The intervention of Peter Damian, legate of Alexander II, on behalf of Cluny in the abbey's legal wrangles with the bishop of Mâcon is well known. Damian also used his influence to secure the submission of the abbey of Saint Martial at Limoges, a monastery recently transferred to Cluny. Evidently, even in the early period the reform relations between Rome and France were lively. Episcopal appointments were frequently disputed and often provided opportunities for the popes to intervene. Occasionally there were royal objections and some resistance to the activity of the legates or the papacy, but again and again both sides were prepared to retreat from their maximum demands.

The pontificate of Gregory VII brought changes, but not with regard to the ruler, now Philip I. In letters dating from 1073 and 1074 Gregory had threatened Philip repeatedly with excommunication and deposition— without any effect. The pope also encountered the passive resistance of the French nobles and of Abbot Hugh of Cluny. In November 1074 and again in early 1075, Gregory had urged them to pressure the king and force him to mend his ways. In another letter he castigated the French bishops for their lukewarm attitude and compared them to dumb dogs unable even to bark. The bishops had rallied to the support of the king and opposed reform. In part as response to these failures, Gregory, hoping to bring the French episcopate into closer dependence on Rome, proceeded at the Lenten synod of Rome of 1075 to nominate Hugh of Die and Amat of Oleron as permanent legates in France.

On papal authority Hugh intervened in a series of episcopal nominations including the appointment for Le Puy, a diocese under royal patronage, and without great difficulty succeeded in excluding simonists. Throughout both interventions, the king and Gregory VII remained very much in the background. Hugh's promulgation of the first prohibition of investiture in September 1077 at the council of Autun, held to settle the disputed election to the bishopric of Cambrai, caused hardly a ripple. The episcopal city as well as a section of the diocese of Cambrai were politically part of the Empire and an important point d'appui in the Flemish region for the German king. Ecclesiastically, however, Cambrai belonged to the archdiocese of Reims. In the episcopal election held in the fall of 1076 the clergy and people of Cambrai named their former archdeacon Gerard as bishop and, according to custom, sent him to Henry IV with a request for investiture. Gerard was duly invested, but Archbishop Manasses of Reims refused consecration, having heard of Henry's excommunication at Gregory's Lenten synod of 1076. In the spring of 1077 Gerard arrived in Rome and asked for consecration by the pope. Gerard claimed not to have known either of Henry's excommunication or of the prohibition of lay investiture. The bishop-elect offered to resign, but after some hesitation Gregory accepted Gerard's apology yet left the final decision to Hugh of Die. Hugh was to hold a general council, if possible in agreement with King Philip and at a location on French royal territory, with the participation of Abbot Hugh of Cluny and Archbishop Manasses of Reims. The synod was also to proclaim the prohibition of lay investiture, a decision the participants were to confirm. The synod eventually gathered at Autun in the duchy of Burgundy. Its decree against lay investiture has not been preserved, but Gregory's instructions to the legate together with a letter of the archbishop of Reims to Gregory referring to the synod, provide at least partial information. The synod prohibited metropolitans and bishops under threat of deposition from consecrating clerics who had been invested by a layman. Another canon must have stipulated that no secular power was allowed to interfere in episcopal elections. Still further, we know that Hugh suspended the archbishops of Reims, Sens, and Bourges for failure to attend the legatine synod. Manasses had duly sent his excuses but they were rejected by Hugh. Disregarding Manasses's metropolitan rights, he himself consecrated Gerard of Cambrai during the synod.

Hugh's determined measures to introduce reform into the French church continued after the synod. He arranged for another synod on 15 January 1078 at Poitiers, the capital of the duke of Aquitaine, a strong supporter of the Roman reforms. Although King Philip I of France had instructed his bishops as well as the duke not to attend such councils, the assembly convened as appointed. Archbishop Rudolf of Tours vainly tried to interrupt the proceedings by force when the assembly examined the background of his episcopal nomination. The legate promulgated a new prohibition of investiture whose text has been preserved, and he suspended a whole series of bishops for uncanonical promotion. Rudolf had interrupted the synod for purely selfish reasons, but his action also expressed a more general mood of anger directed against Hugh and Roman reform policies. Complaints against the legate came to the attention of the pope when most of the suspended bishops arrived in Rome in the spring. They were reinstated by the pope at the Lenten synod; bishops who had not traveled to Rome—those of Thérouanne, Beauvais, Noyon, Laon, and Senlis—simply continued in their offices, with the exception of the bishop of Amiens. French protests were caused primarily by Hugh's behavior. It was difficult for men like the archbishop of Reims, who claimed the primacy over the French church at least since the time of Hincmar, or the archbishop of Sens, who was since the ninth century "primate of Gaul" and "papal vicar for France," to submit to a legate from the little town of Die.

In April 1079 Gregory VII established a new primacy at Lyons, a city beyond the French borders. He entrusted the new office to Archbishop Gebuin of Lyons and, after Gebuin's death in late 1082 or early 1083, to Hugh of Die, because he believed that the new arrangement in the French church reflected its ancient organization. The change was drastic. It subordinated the archbishops of Rouen, Tours, and Sens to the new primate. Manasses, not apparently a very likable person, tried and failed to unite the French episcopal opposition since the bishops, usually loyal adherents of the king, preferred neutrality. After the archbishop had lost the support of the king, Gregory deposed him in December 1080. The resistance of the archbishop of Sens, by contrast, continued unabated for many years. The conflict exerted a powerful influence on the French church, particularly because Ivo, bishop of Chartres and thus suffragan of the archbishop of Sens, took on the task of defending the primacy of Sens after the archbishop had been excommunicated.

Hugh of Lyons led the opposition to Abbot Desiderius of Montecassino, whom the cardinals had elected Pope Victor III as Gregory's successor. Owing to his relentless hostility Hugh was eventually excommunicated. Victor's successor, the French Cluniac monk Urban II, conscious of the extent of Hugh's opposition to the curia, divided the primacy. He endowed the archbishops of Reims and Narbonne, in addition to the archbishop of Lyons, with primatial powers, which were now much diluted. In other ways Urban's policy toward France differed little from that of Gregory. The great issues continued to be avoided. It is conceivable that Urban did not necessarily always object to investiture, provided it was possible to withdraw a diocese from the king's influence. At least this is the conclusion to be drawn from the election of Ivo, abbot of Saint Quentin at Beauvais. The clergy and people of Chartres elected Ivo as their bishop with the approval of the pope. The king had allowed the election as well, without protesting the deposition of Ivo's predecessor by the papal legate, and he seems to have invested Ivo in accordance with the wishes of the cathedral chapter. One reason that investiture continued to receive little attention was Philip's marital situation. In 1092 Philip had abandoned the queen to marry Bertrada of Montfort, wife of Count Fulk of Anjou. The only French bishop who seriously opposed the royal wish for a legitimization of this marriage was Ivo of Chartres, who was imprisoned by the king for his opposition. Largely because of Ivo's absence, a council held at Reims in the fall of 1094 by Archbishop Richer of Sens decided the proceedings in the king's favor. Hugh of Lyons quickly excommunicated the king in a decision that was only confirmed by Urban at the council of Clermont in November 1095. Urban's reasoning was based exclusively on Philip's desertion of the queen and his illegitimate marriage. It is not necessary to discuss Philip's difficulties in detail. Suffice it to say that Urban had absolved Philip even before he left France in 1095. When the king did not keep his promise to separate from Bertrada, the excommunication was quickly renewed. Philip found himself still excommunicated at the accession of Pope Paschal II.

The Frenchman Ivo of Chartres was one of the few "Gregorians" who analyzed in the context of church reform the complexities of royal participation in episcopal elections. He suggested a solution that would go far to accommodate both ecclesiastical demands for noninterference (*liber-*

tas) and royal demands for recognition of justified claims. Ivo's attitude, however, underwent changes (Hoffmann). Moreover, Ivo was not the first who tried to delimit purely ecclesiastical components of elections from those of a mixed ecclesiastical-secular nature, nor did he fully succeed. Still, such observations do not lessen the significance of his famous letter to Archbishop Hugh of Lyons about the investiture of Archbishop Daimbert of Sens. The substance of the letter is less significant than the fact that an eminent bishop addressed the investiture problem publicly in the late 1090s. Ivo was a man of rare learning and distinction who enjoyed "an unusual status as friend of the popes and defender of the monarchy, holding a position between the two opponents" (Hoffmann). It is wrong, however, to assume that he created the theoretical foundation for the compromise that reconciled Rome with the kings of Europe. By the time of Ivo the differentiation of temporalities (rights and properties) and spiritualities (ecclesiastical office and sacramental powers) attached to a bishopric or an abbey was already very old. Since the mid-eleventh century the argument had been most often brought forward by simonists. According to Guido of Arezzo, the simonists excused their payments with the argument that the payments did not purchase the spiritual office. They only bought the "unholy" secular property. An admonition not to be tricked by such declarations is frequently found in canonical collections of this period, including the *Panormia* of Ivo of Chartres. The investiture decrees of Pope Gregory VII certainly did not differentiate between temporalities and spiritualities of an episcopal see, nor did the writings of Humbert of Silva Candida. Hugh of Lyons, in fact, referred specifically to the material property of a bishopric when he prohibited lay investiture at the council of Poitiers (1078).

The conceptual distinction between temporalities and spiritualities was applied in practice by the adherents of the anti-king Rudolf of Rheinfelden. His supporters claimed that on the occasion of the investiture of Bishop Wigold of Augsburg they had observed the 1078 decree of Gregory VII precisely: after the archbishop of Mainz had handed Wigold ring and crosier, Rudolf went on to invest him with the ecclesiastical properties in fulfillment of his royal duties. Nothing was heard from Rome in response to this assertion. However, the *scholasticus* Wenric of Trier, one of the most important royal publicists, pointed out immediately that it would be unjust to prohibit from Henry IV what was permitted to Rudolf. Apparently Henry's supporters did not yet see any difference between the customary investiture with ring and crosier and Rudolf's investiture of Wigold with the temporal appurtenances of a see.

Manegold of Lautenbach took a further step toward conceptual differentiation. He did not merely distinguish temporalities and spiritualities; he further distinguished two types of temporalities: *regalia* and other church property, perhaps under the influence of Norman and Anglo-Norman conceptions (Hoffmann). It is certainly correct that the feudal system was nowhere more clearly thought out and organized than in Britain, as we have seen. The arguments used in the proceedings against Odo of Bayeux and William of Saint Carilef certainly represent a step toward the ultimate solution, already more accurately adumbrated in Manegold's arguments than in the English distinction between spiritualities and temporalities. It was only at this point that a major obstacle emerged in full: Roman as well as canon law described church property as an inalienable, permanent endowment. Once spiritualities and temporalities could be distinguished it became necessary to define anew ecclesiastical property rights if any royal prerogatives were to be recognized. This intellectual position proved as yet unattainable. As a way out of the dilemma rulers were allowed to participate in the transfer of the temporalities by way of dispensation, thus circumventing the issue of the legal status of ecclesiastical property for the time being.

In 1097 when Pope Urban II rejected remarks that Ivo of Chartres had evolved in his dispute with Hugh of Lyons, it was not yet accepted that there was some justification in allowing secular rulers certain rights with respect to ecclesiastical property. In contrast, Urban's successor, Pope Paschal II, seems to have appropriated the notion when he temporarily permitted Anselm of Canterbury to consecrate prelates even if they should have done feudal homage to the king. The compromise was skillfully selected. Without permanently abandoning any of the ecclesiastical reform demands, Paschal recognized the legal aspects of the Anglo-Norman political settlement and gained at the same time an important objective with Henry's renunciation of his customary right of investiture with ring and crosier. Contemporaries saw ring and crosier as purely ecclesiastical symbols, and it is for this reason that they were so important. The ring symbolized the marriage of Christ with the church, his bride—thus bishops could not leave their original diocese without dispensation—and the crosier symbolized the care of souls. The presentation of these symbols, investiture, was regarded as the conferral of a sacrament, and therefore laymen could not confer sacraments, not even kings, once their office had been denuded of its theocratic foundation. To the great credit of Henry I he was able to grasp this essential fact. The relations between England and the Empire were close. Henry V married Henry's daughter Matilda, but more than a decade passed before the German king could no longer ignore the importunities of his magnates.

German rulers insisted on customary prerogatives in part because Germany was less feudalized than England. William's military conquest of England had permitted the introduction of a strictly centralized feudal regime. In theory the king was the only proprietor of landed property, which he distributed as fiefs to his secular and ecclesiastical tenants-in-chief in return for specific services. Patronage at the time of Henry I was distributed according to the same principles. Henry IV of Germany had no similar opportunities and was therefore obliged to imitate the methods of government developed by his predecessors. There was no room for compromise. At the time of Henry IV the feudal oath was largely absent in Germany and was thus not available to replace investiture. Rudolf of Rheinfelden's procedure at the investiture of Bishop Wigold of Augsburg is proof. As will be seen, even Pope Calixtus II was eventually obliged to permit Henry V an investiture with the temporalities through the symbol of the sceptre.

Compared with both England and Germany, the situation in France might be called murky. Customs and traditions in the territories of the various noble families differed greatly. What might be acceptable depended on local circumstances. Only in this context could Ivo publicly declare that investiture could be tolerated if necessary because it did not pertain to eternal salvation. When Ivo was writing and Urban prohibited homage at the council of Clermont, "French sources for some time had no longer mentioned investiture with ring and crosier" (Becker, *Frankreich*). It is impossible, therefore, to know whether Philip still invested bishops despite Urban's at least theoretical prohibition. "The French king perhaps, always depending on a local set of circumstances, on some occasions conferred investiture using the crosier (for example when he invested Ivo at Chartres) and on others simply permitted a bishop to enter into possession of the appurtenances of his see either with or without a different kind of ceremony, or simply allowed him to take over" (ibid.).

In December 1104 a council held in Paris reconciled King Philip I with the church. He had at long last separated from Bertrada. Two years later, in 1106, in the tradition of his predecessors Leo IX and Urban II, Paschal II traveled north into France after his council of Guastalla. In the course of his journey he held a solemn meeting at Saint Denis with Philip and his son, Louis VI, joint rulers at the time. An account written with the hindsight of more than three decades is preserved in the writings of the famous Abbot Suger of Saint Denis. Suger tells us that ecclesiastical affairs (they are not described in any way) were amicably discussed and that the pontiff eventually asked the French kings for their support of his German policy. The kings agreed; as a consequence, Paschal was able to meet the emissaries of Henry V at Châlons-sur-Marne in the midst of an impressive entourage of ecclesiastical and secular French magnates before the opening of his council of Troyes (May 1107). Suger's scanty narrative is all we have as a description of the alliance concluded between Rome and France. Perhaps we may assume that the pontiff and the kings agreed to accept as satisfactory "contemporary ecclesiastical policies in France and basically to continue the current practice in filling the bishoprics" (Becker).

4. The Peace Between Church and Empire: The Concordat of Worms

The German emissaries at Châlons, led by Archbishop Bruno of Trier, no longer represented the old opponent of the popes, Emperor Henry IV, but his son, Henry V (1106–25). At the turn of the year 1104–5 Henry had defied his father and entered into an alliance with a group of nobles, mainly from Bavaria, Saxony, and Thuringia. The rebel had immediately contacted Pope Paschal II, and the pontiff had absolved him from the oath he had sworn to his father (at his coronation in 1099 at Aachen) never to intervene in the government during his father's lifetime, except at the emperor's request. A year earlier the diet of Mainz had elected Henry V to the kingship, simultaneously deposing his elder brother, Conrad, the anti-king who had never found much of a following in Germany and who died, perhaps in 1101, forgotten by all in Italy. Henry V placed himself in the vanguard of the ecclesiastical party. Paschal II, who had exchanged frequent embassies with the young king, had reason to hope that Rome might be able to reach an understanding with the Empire as well as with France and England. On 7 August 1106 Emperor Henry IV had died at Liège. Paschal's great synod of Guastalla (October 1106) in the territory of the Countess Matilda of Canossa paid particular attention to the Empire.

Paschal's famous letter to Anselm of Canterbury, granting the archbishop permission to consecrate clerics who had done homage to the king, had been sent in the spring. Paschal had not relaxed the prohibition against investiture, and the council of Guastalla maintained the same attitude in response to observers sent by Henry V. Homage was not mentioned. Like his predecessor Urban II, however, Paschal showed leniency. Citing decrees of the fathers of the early church, pope and synod recognized bishops who had been consecrated by schismatics provided that the prelates had not committed simony, had been canonically elected, and were not guilty of criminal behavior. Their morals had to be beyond reproach. But no concession was forthcoming from Henry V, who insisted on investiture with ring and crosier. Nonetheless, it is likely that some compromise was arranged behind the scenes with the leader of the German delegation at Guastalla, Archbishop Bruno of Trier, who seems to have had the support of Matilda. It is noteworthy that the council did not excommunicate Henry V and, moreover, only postponed the negotiations instead of breaking off contact with Henry. The negotiations resumed at Châlons, where Paschal arrived fresh from his conference with the French kings at Saint Denis. Not surprisingly the papal resolve had stiffened, presumably because Henry V, in contrast to the rulers of France and England, categorically rejected any kind of compromise. Suger's description of the negotiations of Châlons is clearly colored by the terminology of the Worms agreements of 1122, and it remains uncertain, therefore, what Henry actually demanded in 1107. Nevertheless, the negotiations of Châlons were a complete failure, at least at the moment. For it might well be argued that as a result of the apparently failed negotiations at Châlons, royal circles began to realize that the pope would never concede the hotly contested right of investiture to the German king, even though Paschal was ready to accept a reasonable compromise.

The *Tractatus de investituris,* which has been dated to 1109 and is most likely attributable to the imperialist author Sigebert of Gembloux, seems to have been given to emissaries of Henry V who were on their way to Rome to conduct discussions with the pope about the imperial coronation. The treatise still insists on investiture as a royal prerogative, but, reminiscent of the letter of Ivo of Chartres to Hugh, it at least hints that the particular symbols used for investiture are irrelevant, provided investiture takes place before consecration. Investiture, the *Tractatus* points out, protects church property, and the king or emperor may effect it "by word or command or staff or any other matter." The bishop should take ring and crosier from the altar on the day of his consecration. The treatise also mentions homage, and suggests that it should best take place before consecration. In this treatise the word *hominium* makes its first appearance in the Empire, betraying, as Peter Classen argues, the influence of the English precedent on Henry's policies. The *Tractatus de investituris,* in short, attempted to show the way out of the dilemma that had handicapped politics in Germany for so long. But the possibilities offered by "the feudal interpretation of the relationship between bishop and king resting materially on the regalia and personally on homage" (Classen) remained unused in 1110/11. The negotiations with the pope failed once again. The Lateran council of March 1110 promulgated widely publicized decrees prohibiting not only investiture with churches or ecclesiastical dignities (recipient, consecrator, and the layman giving investiture were all subject to excommunication) but also the conveyance of ecclesiastical property. The only aspect not covered by the investiture canons of 1110 is homage, very likely because Paschal had no intention of abrogating his agreement with King Henry I of England. It is also possible that Henry's envoys had refrained from referring to the respective passage in the *Tractatus,* which was often considered to be their instructions for negotiations.

In the summer of 1110, despite the failure of the negotiations Henry V set out for Rome at the head of a large army. His aim was the imperial coronation. The ill-fated agreements of February 1111 were the result of renewed discussions held between representatives of the two sides at Sutri, just north of Rome, and in a little church just outside Saint Peter's basilica in Rome. For once we know what was said, for the documents have been preserved. Paschal II obtained Henry's promise to declare in a solemn oath on the day of the imperial coronation that he would abandon investiture with ring and staff and that all non-regalian possessions of the church would become her outright property. In return, the pontiff would instruct the German bishops to return to the king *regalia* (rights and property) that pertained by inalienable right to the Empire but which had been transferred to the churches since the time of Charlemagne. The secret agreements, in particular Paschal's proposal to return the *regalia,* are usually described as utopian and unrealistic. The pontiff is thought of as an early precursor of the twelfth-century movement advocating apostolic poverty for the church, exemplified later by Saint Francis of Assisi. However, these and similar arguments overlook the fact that Henry V had to swear to the pope that he would restore the Papal States as described in the old imperial donations. Such views also fail to distinguish accurately enough between *regalia* and other church property. The concept of *regalia* was very ambiguous and was interpreted differently north and south of the Alps. Not all secular rights and properties in the hands of German or Italian bishops were regalian in character. Nevertheless, when the agreements became public knowledge on Henry's coronation day, 12 February 1111, they caused an uproar among the magnates in Saint Peter's. The details are sketchy, but Paschal's proposal was certainly rejected as unacceptable and perhaps heretical. In the end, when Paschal refused to crown Henry V without the exchange of documents, the pontiff and his entourage of cardinals, other clergy, and Roman nobles were captured and led away as prisoners of Henry and his army. Two months' captivity wore down Paschal's resistance and that of the cardinals. Henry succeeded in extorting the privilege of Ponte Mammolo—henceforth

known as *pravilegium*—granting Henry V the imperial coronation and
investiture with ring and crosier before consecration. In addition, Paschal
swore never to excommunicate Henry.

It soon became obvious that Henry, now emperor, had gained nothing
with the extorted privilege. Strong opposition within the church forced
Paschal to revoke the grant in 1112 and the relations between Rome and
the Empire returned to their nadir. After the death of Paschal II (21 January 1118), his loyal chancellor and supporter, John of Gaeta, succeeded
to the papacy as Gelasius II but died after a very brief reign (24 January
1118–28 January 1119), having fled to Cluny because of the hostility of
the powerful Roman family of Frangipani. Under Calixtus II (1119–24),
a noble from Burgundy who had been archbishop of Vienne before his
election, negotiations with the emperor resumed. In February 1119, Calixtus addressed a conciliatory letter to Henry V, who had been excommunicated by Gelasius. The imperial diet meeting in June of that year
near Mainz agreed to seek a reconciliation with the pontiff, and already
in the autumn of 1119 at Strasbourg discussions were held between
Henry V and papal envoys, William of Champeaux—the famous Paris
theologian and teacher of Abelard—and Abbot Pons of Cluny.

William of Champeaux referred to himself as an example to explain
that loss of investiture did not mean loss of services. William was bishop
of Châlons and, according to the narrative by Hesso, a papal supporter
and not unbiased, he pointed out that he faithfully fulfilled all the obligations owed to the state, using *res publica* instead of the ordinary *regnum,*
without having received "anything" (presumably the investiture) from
the French king either before or after his consecration (1113). The bishops of Henry V would do the same. The king, therefore, should abandon
investiture with ring and crosier for bishoprics and abbeys. Eventually
Henry reluctantly agreed. Pons of Cluny and William reported immediately to Calixtus, who was staying at Paris. The pope added two cardinals, Lambert of Ostia and Gregory of Sant'Angelo, to the negotiating
committee, and sent the delegation back to Henry to conclude a written
treaty. They were also to arrange a meeting between pope and emperor
that was to take place before the convening of a papal council that had
been convoked for Reims. The encounter was finally scheduled for 24
October at Mouzon, and Calixtus interrupted the conciliar proceedings
at Reims to set out with his entourage to meet Henry V on the way. Hesso
reports that sudden fear brought everything to a halt. The emperor, it was
said, might intend to interpret the new treaty in the sense of the proposal
of 1111, thus making himself master of church property or at least de-

manding a feudal oath for such property. Moreover, the papal party wished to exclude from the peace imperial rivals in the bishoprics. The intention was presumably to obtain from the emperor a specific declaration renouncing "secular investiture"—according to Theodor Schieffer, probably meaning homage as used for English ecclesiastics.

Henry, claiming that he had to consult the princes, rejected these newly formulated papal demands. Once again negotiations were postponed. The council fathers at Reims, after being told by Cardinal John of Crema that Henry V had intended to repeat the outrage of 1111, reacted promptly by excommunicating the emperor, the anti-pope Burdinus (set up by Henry V in 1118 but completely disregarded since negotiations were initiated with Calixtus II), and numerous imperial supporters, including the famous jurist Irnerius of Bologna. But the council also disappointed the new pontiff. The assembly refused to endorse a canon reflecting the position of Calixtus at the negotiations with Henry; the decree would have outlawed not only investiture with ecclesiastical office but also the investiture with ecclesiastical possessions.

Theodor Schieffer emphasizes that the negotiations of Mouzon, despite failure, meant "a step toward Worms where the parties were largely represented by the same envoys and the treaty of 1119 was used as a working paper." Since Mouzon both sides had accepted the continuity of episcopal obligations toward the Empire, known as *servitium* but irreducible to feudal dues. The tumultuous scenes at the council of Reims are an excellent indicator that the majority of the participants were ready to compromise. When the pontiff returned from Mouzon he was so close to a physical breakdown that John of Crema had to represent him at the council. And even under these trying circumstances the council fathers were unwilling to jeopardize a hoped-for peace and thus did not consent to the investiture decrees proposed by Calixtus and his advisors. One may assume that the mood at the council corresponded to the mood of many ecclesiastical partisans of reform. The council of Reims was ready to accept lay rights in ecclesiastical property at least tacitly even if such rights should be expressed in Germany in antiquated form by investiture with the temporalities.

The German nobility was equally anxious for peace with the church although the anti-imperial opposition under the leadership of Archbishop Adalbert of Mainz could be satisfied in general with its position. Actively involved in the events of 1110–11 as arch-chancellor of Henry V, Adalbert lost royal favor soon afterward because of his wholly unscrupulous dynastic ambitions. He participated in the council of Reims in the company of five hundred of his knights. Calixtus named him papal legate. After the failure of the negotiations at Mouzon, Adalbert thus led the opposition to Henry V in the double capacity of high-ranking member of the German nobility and of representative of the church. Until 1121, however, when military skirmishes on both sides created new hostilities, Adalbert's party, including the archbishop of Cologne as well as magnates from Saxony and the lower Rhine, suspended its activities. The new spate of hostilities, involving struggles over ecclesiastical rights and over dominance in the area of the middle Rhine, ended in late September–early October 1121 with the diet of Würzburg. The assembly concluded a formal treaty establishing peace between Henry V and the noble opposition (Büttner). Adalbert and his party apparently were able to dictate the conditions: the emperor was to submit to the pope. Calixtus seems to have been expected in Germany for a final settlement of the dispute between the papacy and the Empire. Until his arrival, canonically elected bishops were to remain in office even if they had not been appointed by Henry. This stipulation was specifically geared to protect two prominent adherents of Adalbert of Mainz, his brother Bruno of Speyer and Bishop Burchard of Worms. For the first time in history, the Würzburg agreement clearly differentiated between emperor and empire. The context identifies the Empire with the princes, "designating them equal partners with the king" (Büttner).

In July 1122 German envoys returned in the company of a papal delegation, including once again the two cardinals who had participated in the talks of Mouzon: Cardinal Lambert of Ostia (later Pope Honorius II) and Cardinal deacon Gregory (later Pope Innocent II). They immediately convoked a general synod for Mainz, Adalbert's see, scheduling it for early September. It was apparently expected that Henry V would simply bow to the demands of Adalbert and his party. If such should indeed have been the impression in Rome, politics in Germany quickly persuaded the legates otherwise. Throughout the month of August they were in close contact with the emperor. When the synod convened at Mainz as planned, emissaries of Henry V, Archbishop Bruno of Trier, Bishop Otto of Bamberg, and an imperial chaplain, Arnold, probably participated. During the synod and the negotiations, the emperor remained in the imperial city of Worms. On 23 September 1122 the conciliation between Henry V and the church took place outside the walls of the city. No formal act of penance was required and the papal legates had to content themselves with relatively small gains. Envoys and emperor exchanged brief documents, charters embodying concessions and assurances by each party to the other. "The simple brevity of the Concordat's two charters was deliberate" (Benson). The number of details that were not settled is extraordinary, and it is therefore not surprising that the concordat (a term only introduced in the seventeenth century) provided no fundamental remedies for the underlying conflict that had caused so much havoc for almost half a century. Like the agreement with Henry I of England, the charters of Worms were originally intended as a compromise. "They had both the virtues and the defects of an armistice" (idem). Nevertheless, they fulfilled their purpose. The emperor renounced investiture with ring and crosier, thus allowing free canonical election and consecration. The pope, in turn, conceded for German bishoprics and abbeys elections in the presence of the king or his representatives. The king had the right to intervene in disputed elections, and most important, the emperor could invest candidates for German sees before consecration with the *regalia* (not defined in the document) of the diocese, using the sceptre instead of ring and crosier. In Burgundy and imperial Italy *regalia* were to be transferred only after the new bishop or abbot had already been consecrated. On receipt of the *regalia* the prelates were to fulfill their legal obligations (these again were not defined) toward the ruler. Both sides promised each other peace.

Like contemporary observers, historians have long debated the precise legal implications of the Worms documents. The original charter of Henry V is still preserved in the Vatican archives. In the Middle Ages the document could also be read on one of the famous frescoes of the Lateran palace, depicting Henry V in the act of handing the document to the pontiff. Today, the fact that copies of only the papal charter exist raises a host of issues to intrigue specialists. Many questions will never be answered. We are certain, however, that Calixtus II presented his agreement with the emperor to the great Lateran council assembled in 1123. Despite the stormy opposition of the old adherents of Pope Paschal II who were disinclined to allow any compromise after the fiasco of 1111, Calixtus managed to obtain the council's official acceptance of the treaty. He persuaded the assembly that contemporary political conditions required a dispensation from the strict immediate application of ecclesiastical regulations. Despite an epilogue under Lothar III, who demanded the restoration of investiture with ring and crosier, and despite all of its shortcomings, the "temporary" settlement of Worms succeeded in restoring peace between *regnum* and *sacerdotium* in the Empire and thus freeing the two powers from antiquated concepts with their increasingly anachronistic restrictions.

Bibliography for Chapter 5

General

Arduini, Maria Lodovica. *Non fabula sed res: Politische Dichtung und dramatische Gestalt in den Carmina Ruperts von Deutz*. Rome, 1985.
Becker, Alfons. *Papst Urban II. (1088–1099). Part 1, Herkunft und kirchliche Laufbahn: Der Papst und die lateinische Christenheit*. MGH Schriften, vol. 19, part 1. Stuttgart, 1964.
———. "Urban II. und die deutsche Kirche." In *Investiturstreit und Reichsverfassung*, 241–75.
———, and Dietrich Lohrmann. "Ein erschlichenes Privileg Papst Urbans II. für Erzbischof Guido von Vienne (Calixt II.)." *DA* 38 (1982): 66–111.
Berschin, Walter. *Os meum aperui: Die Autobiographie Ruperts von Deutz*. Schriftenreihe des Zentrums patristischer Spiritualität Koinonia Oriens im Erzbistum Köln 18. Cologne, 1985.
Blumenthal, Uta-Renate. *The Early Councils of Pope Paschal II (1100–1110)*. Pontifical Institute of Mediaeval Studies. Studies and Texts, vol. 43. Toronto, 1978.
Brackmann, Albert. "The Beginnings of the National State in Mediaeval Germany and the Norman Monarchies." In *Medieval Germany*, 281–99.
Cantarella, Glauco Maria. *Ecclesiologia e politica nel papato di Pasquale II. Linee di una interpretazione*. Istituto storico italiano per il medio evo. Studi storici, vol. 131. Rome, 1982.
Cartellieri, Otto. *Abt Suger von Saint-Denis (1081–1151)*. Berlin, 1897.
Cauchie, Alfred. *La querelle des investitures dans les diocèses de Liège et de Cambrai*. Louvain, 1889–91.
Chodorow, Stanley A. "Ecclesiastical Politics and the Ending of the Investiture Contest." *Speculum* 46 (1971): 613–40.
———. *Christian Political Theory and Church Politics in the Mid-Twelfth Century*. Berkeley and Los Angeles, 1971.
———. "Ideology and Canon Law." *Proceedings, Fourth International Congress of Medieval Canon Law*. Monumenta iuris canonici. Ser. C, Subsidia 5, 55–80. Vatican City, 1976.
Classen, Peter. *Gerhoch von Reichersberg: Eine Biographie*. Wiesbaden, 1960.
Cowdrey, H. E. J. *The Age of Abbot Desiderius: Montecassino, the Papacy, and the Normans in the Eleventh and Early Twelfth Centuries*. Oxford, 1983.
Dereine, Charles. "L'Elaboration du statut canonique des chanoines réguliers spécialement sous Urban II." *Revue d'Histoire Ecclésiastique* 46 (1951): 534–65.
Dormeier, Heinrich. *Montecassino und die Laien im 11. und 12. Jahrhundert*. MGH Schriften 27. Stuttgart, 1979.
Erdmann, Carl. "Mauricius Burdinus." *Quellen und Forschungen aus italienischen Archiven und Bibliotheken* 19 (1927): 205ff.
Fliche, Augustin. "Y-a-t-il eu en France et en Angleterre une querelle des investitures?" *Revue bénédictine* 46 (1934): 283–95.
Fried, Johannes. *Die Entstehung des Juristenstandes im 12. Jahrhundert*. For-

schungen zur neueren Privatrechtsgeschichte, vol. 21. Cologne and Vienna, 1974.

————. "Der Regalienbegriff im 11. und 12. Jahrhundert." *DA* 29 (1973): 450–528. With a detailed bibliography for earlier literature.

Gossman, Francis J. *Pope Urban II and the Canon Law*. Washington, D.C., 1960.

Gottlob, Theodor. *Der kirchliche Amtseid der Bischöfe*. Bonn, 1936.

Hallinger, Kassius. "Die Anfänge von Cîteaux." In *Aus Kirche und Reich. Festschrift für Friedrich Kempf*. Edited by Hubert Mordek, 225–35. Sigmaringen, 1983.

Hausmann, Friedrich. *Reichskanzlei und Hofkapelle unter Heinrich V. und Konrad III*. MGH Schriften 14. Stuttgart, 1956.

Heinemann, Wolfgang. *Das Bistum Hildesheim im Kräftespiel der Reichs- und Territorialpolitik vornehmlich des 12. Jahrhunderts*. Hildesheim, 1958.

Henking, Carl. *Gebhard III., Bischof von Constanz: 1084–1110*. Constanz, 1880.

Hiestand, Rudolf. "Legat, Kaiser und Basileus: Bischof Kuno von Praeneste und die Krise des Papsttums von 1111/1112." In *Aus Reichsgeschichte und Nordischer Geschichte. Kieler Historische Studien* 16 (1972): 141ff.

Hoffmann, Hartmut. *Gottesfriede und Treuga Dei*. MGH Schriften 20. Stuttgart, 1964.

Holtzmann, Walther. "Zur Geschichte des Investiturstreits (= englische Analekten II)." *Neues Archiv* 50 (1933–35): 246–319. See especially pt. 3, "England, Unteritalien und der Vertrag von Ponte Mammolo"; pt. 4, "Eine Bannsentenz des Konzils von Reims 1119."

Joachimsen, Paul. "The Investiture Contest and the German Constitution. In *Medieval Germany*, 95–129.

Klewitz, Hans-Walter. "Das Ende des Reformpapsttums." *DA* 3 (1939): 372–412. Reprinted in Klewitz, *Reformpapsttum und Kardinalkolleg*. Darmstadt, 1957.

Kretzschmar, Robert. *Alger von Lüttichs Traktat "De misericordia et iustitia": Ein kanonistischer Konkordanzversuch aus der Zeit des Investiturstreits*. Quellen und Forschungen zum Recht im Mittelalter, vol. 2. Sigmaringen, 1985.

Ladner, Gerhart Buridan. "I mosaici e gli affreschi ecclesiasticopolitici nell'antico palazzo Lateranense. *Rivista di archeologia cristiana* 12 (1935): 265–92.

Leyser, Karl J. "England and the Empire in the Early Twelfth Century." *Transactions of the Royal Historical Society*, 5th ser., 10 (1960): 61–83.

Liebermann, Felix. "Anselm von Canterbury und Hugo von Lyon." In *Historische Aufsätze dem Andenken an Georg Waitz gewidmet*. Leipzig, 1886.

Lohrmann, Dietrich. "Die Jugendwerke des Johannes von Gaeta." *Quellen und Forschungen aus italienischen Archiven und Bibliotheken* 47 (1967): 355–445.

————. "Energieprobleme im Mittelalter: Zur Verknappung von Wasserkraft und Holz in Westeuropa bis zum Ende des 12. Jahrhunderts." *Vierteljahrschrift für Sozial- und Wirtschaftsgeschichte* 66 (1979): 297–316.

Loud, G. A. "Abbot Desiderius of Montecassino and the Gregorian Papacy". *Journal of Ecclesiastical History* 30 (1979): 305–26.

Lühe, Wilhelm. *Hugo von Die und Lyon, Legat von Gallien*. Breslau, 1898.

Minninger, Monika. *Von Clermont zum Wormser Konkordat: Die Auseinander-*

setzungen um den Lehnsnexus zwischen König und Episkopat. Cologne and Vienna, 1978.

Mordek, Hubert. "Urban II., St. Blasien und die Anfänge des Basler Klosters St. Alban." *Zeitschrift für die Geschichte des Oberrheins* 131 (1983):199–224.

Morin, G. "Lettre inédite de Pascal II, notifiant la déposition de Turold, éveque de Bayeux, puis moine du Bec (8 oct. 1104). *Revue d'Histoire Ecclésiastique 5* (1904):284–89.

Ott, Irene. "Der Regalienbegriff im 12. Jahrhundert." *ZRG Kan. Abt.* 35 (1948): 234–304.

Palumbo, P. F. "Nuovi studi (1942–1962) sullo scisma di Anacleto II." *Bullettino istorico italiano* 75 (1963):77ff.

Robert, Ulysse. *Histoire du Pape Calixte II.* Paris, 1891.

Schieffer, Theodor. "Nochmals die Verhandlungen von Mouzon 1119." In *Festschrift Edmund Stengel*, 324–41. Münster, 1952.

Schmale, Franz-Josef. *Studien zum Schisma des Jahres 1130.* Cologne, 1961.

Servatius, Carlo. *Paschalis II. (1099–1118): Studien zu seiner Person und seiner Politik.* Päpste und Papsttum, vol. 14. Stuttgart, 1979.

Somerville, Robert. *The Councils of Urban II. Part 1, Decreta Claromontensia.* Annuarium Historiae Conciliorum Supplementary vol. 1. Amsterdam, 1972.

———. "Cardinal Stephan of St. Grisogono: Some Remarks on Legates and Legatine Councils in the Eleventh Century." In *Law, Church, and Society: Essays in Honor of Stephan Kuttner.* Edited by Kenneth Pennington and Robert Somerville, 157–66. Philadelphia, 1977.

Stroll, Mary. "New Perspectives on the Struggle Between Guy of Vienne and Henry V." *Archivum Historiae Pontificiae* 18 (1980):97–116.

Van Engen, John H. *Rupert of Deutz.* Berkeley and Los Angeles, 1983.

Weinfurter, Stefan. *Salzburger Bistumsreform und Bischofspolitik im 12. Jahrhundert. Der Erzbischof Konrad I. von Salzburg (1106–1147) und die Regularkanoniker.* Cologne, 1975.

White, Hayden V. "The Gregorian Ideal and Saint Bernard of Clairvaux." *Journal of the History of Ideas* 21 (1960):321–48.

———. "Pontius of Cluny, the *curia romana* and the end of Gregorianism in Rome." *Church History* 27 (1958):195–219.

Wilks, Michael J. "Ecclesiastica and Regalia: Papal Investiture Policy from the Council of Guastalla to the First Latern Council, 1106–1123." In *Councils and Assemblies.* Studies in Church History, vol. 7. Edited by G. J. Cuming and Derek Baker, 69–85. Cambridge, 1971.

Wolter, Hans. *Ordericus Vitalis. Ein Beitrag zur kluniazensischen Geschichts-Schreibung.* Wiesbaden, 1955.

Zatschek, Heinz. "Beiträge zur Beurteilung Heinrichs V., 1: Die Verhandlungen des Jahres 1119." *DA* 7 (1944):48–78.

Zèrbi, Pietro. "Pasquale II e l'Ideale della povertà della Chiesa." *Annuario dell'Università Cattolica del Sacro Cuore*, 203ff. Milan, 1965.

England and Normandy

Barlow, Frank. *The Feudal Kingdom of England.* 3d rev. ed. London, 1972.

———. *The English Church, 1066–1154.* London and New York, 1963.

————. "A View of Archbishop Lanfranc." *Journal of Ecclesiastical History* 16 (1965):163–77.

————. *William I and the Norman Conquest.* London, 1965.

————. *The English Church 1000–1066: A History of the Later Anglo-Saxon Church.* 2d rev. ed. New York and London, 1979.

————. *The Norman Conquest and Beyond.* London, 1983. A collection of essays, 1936–81.

————. *William Rufus.* Berkeley and Los Angeles, 1983.

————. *Edward the Confessor.* Berkeley and Los Angeles, 1984.

Bates, David R. "The Character and Career of Odo, Bishop of Bayeux (1049/50–1097) *Speculum* 50 (1975):1–20.

————. *Normandy Before 1066.* London and New York, 1982.

Böhmer, Heinrich. *Kirche und Staat in England und der Normandie im XI. und XII. Jahrhundert.* Leipzig, 1899.

Brett, Martin. *The English Church Under Henry I.* Oxford, 1975.

Brooke, Christopher N. L. "The Canterbury Forgeries and Their Author." *Downside Review* 68 (1950):462–76; 69 (1951):210–31.

————. "Gregorian Reform in Action: Clerical Marriage in England, 1050–1200." *Cambridge Historical Journal* 13 (1956):1–21. Reprinted in Brooke, *Medieval Church and Society,* 69–99. London, 1971.

————. "Archbishop Lanfranc, the English Bishops and the Council of London of 1075." *Studia Gratiana* 12 (1967):39–60.

————. "The Archdeacon and the Norman Conquest." In *Tradition and Change: Essays in Honour of Marjorie Chibnall Presented by Her Friends on the Occasion of Her Seventieth Birthday.* Edited by Diana Greenway, Christopher Holdsworth, and Jane Sayers, 1–19. Cambridge, 1985.

Brooke, Zachary N. *The English Church and the Papacy from the Conquest to the Reign of John.* Cambridge, 1931.

————. "Pope Gregory VII's Demand for Fealty from William the Conqueror." *EHR* 26 (1911):225–38.

Brown, R. Allen. *The Normans and the Norman Conquest.* London, 1985.

Cantor, Norman F. *Church, Kingship and Lay-Investiture in England 1089–1135.* Princeton, 1958. See Theodor Schieffer, *HZ* 192 (1961):690ff. for a review.

Clanchy, Michael T. *England and its Rulers. 1066–1272.* Totowa, N.J., 1983.

Cowdrey, J. E. H. "Bishop Ermenfrid of Sion and the Penitential Ordinance Following the Battle of Hastings." *Journal of Ecclesiastical History* 20 (1969): 225–42.

————. "Pope Gregory VII and the Anglo-Norman Church and Kingdom." *Studi Gregoriani* 9 (1972):79–114.

————. "The Anglo-Norman Laudes Regiae." *Viator* 12 (1981):37–78.

Darlington, Richard R. "Ecclesiastical Reform in the Late Old English Period." *EHR* 51 (1936):385ff.

Davis, R. H. C. "William of Jumièges, Robert Curthose and the Norman Succession." *EHR* 95 (1980):597–606.

Duggan, Charles. *Twelfth-Century Decretal Collections and their Importance in English History.* London, 1963.

————. "From the Conquest to the Death of John." In *The English Church and the Papacy in the Middle Ages*. Edited by C. H. Lawrence and David Knowles, 63–115. London, 1965.

Evans, Gillian R. "Schools and Scholars: The Study of the Abacus in English Schools c. 980–c. 1150." *EHR* 94 (1979):71–89.

Finucane, Ronald C. *Miracles and Pilgrims: Popular Beliefs in Medieval England*. London, 1977.

Garnett, George. "Coronation and Propaganda: Some Implications of the Norman Claim to the Throne of England in 1066." *Transactions of the Royal Historical Society,* 5th ser., 36 (1986):91–116.

Gibson, Margaret. *Lanfranc of Bec*. Oxford, 1978.

Gransden, Antonia. "The Legends and Traditions Concerning the Origins of the Abbey of Bury St. Edmunds." *EHR* 100 (1985):1–24.

Green, Judith A. *The Government of England Under Henry I*. Cambridge Studies in Medieval Life and Thought. Fourth Series, vol. 3. Cambridge, 1986.

Hartmann, Wilfried. "Beziehungen des Normannischen Anonymus zu frühscholastischen Bildungszentren." *DA* 31 (1975):108–43. Significant additions and corrections to Pellens, below.

Hollister, C. Warren. "1066: The 'Feudal Revolution'." *American Historical Review* 73 (1968):708–23.

———. "Henry I and Robert Malet." *Viator* 4 (1973):115–22.

———. *Monarchy, Magnates and Institutions in the Anglo-Norman World*. London, 1986.

Holt, John C. "Feudal Society and the Family in Early Medieval England, I: The Revolution of 1066." *Transactions of the Royal Historical Society,* 5th ser., 32 (1982):193–212.

John, Eric. *Orbis Britanniae and Other Studies*. Leicester, 1966.

———. "Edward the Confessor and the Norman Succession." *EHR* 94 (1979): 241–67.

Kapelle, William E. *The Norman Conquest of the North: The Region and Its Transformation 1000–1135*. Chapel Hill, N.C., 1979.

Lapidge, Michael and Helmut Gneuss, eds. *Learning and Literature in Anglo-Saxon England: Studies Presented to Peter Clemoes on the Occasion of His Sixty-Fifth Birthday*. Cambridge, 1985.

Matthew, Donald. *The Norman Monasteries and Their English Possessions*. Westport, Conn., 1979.

Morris, Colin. "William I and the Church Courts." *EHR* 82 (1967):449–63.

Nicholl, David. *Thurstan, Archbishop of York*. York, 1964.

Pellens, Karl. *Das Kirchendenken des Normannischen Anonymus*. Wiesbaden, 1973.

———. *Die Texte des Normannischen Anonymus*. Wiesbaden, 1966. See the articles by W. Hartmann, and Reynolds in this list.

Petersohn, Jürgen. "Normannische Bildungsreform im hochmittelalterlichen England." *HZ* 213 (1971):265–95.

Reynolds, Roger E. "The Unidentified Sources of the Norman Anonymous C.C.C.C. MS 415." *Transactions of the Cambridge Bibliographical Society,* no. 5, 2 (1970):122ff.

Richter, Michael. *Canterbury Professions*. Torquay, Devon, 1973.

Somerville, Robert. "Lanfranc's Canonical Collection and Exeter." *Bulletin of the Institute of Historical Research,* 45 (1972): 303–6.

Southern, Sir Richard W. "The Canterbury Forgeries." *EHR* 73 (1958): 193–226.

———. "The Place of Henry I in English History." Raleigh Lecture in History. *Proceedings of the British Academy,* 127–69. London, 1962.

———. *St. Anselm and His Biographer.* Cambridge, 1963.

Stenton, Sir Frank M. *The First Century of English Feudalism,* (1066–1166). 2d ed. Oxford, 1961.

Tenth-Century Studies: Essays in Commemoration of the Millennium of the Council of Winchester and Regularis Concordia. Edited by David Parsons. London, 1975.

Tillmann, Helene. *Die päpstlichen Legaten in England bis zur Beendigung der Legation Gualas (1218).* Bonn, 1926.

Vaughn, Sally N. *Anselm of Bec and Robert of Meulan: The Innocence of the Dove and the Wisdom of the Serpent.* Berkeley and Los Angeles, 1987.

Ward, George. "Saxon Churches in the Domesday Monachorum and White Book of St. Augustine". *Archaeologia Cantiana* 45 (1933): 60–89.

Warren, W. L. "The Myth of Norman Administrative Efficiency." *Transactions of the Royal Historical Society,* 5th ser., 34 (1984): 113–32.

Williams, George H. *The Norman Anonymous of 1100 A.D.* Harvard Theological Studies, no. 18. Cambridge, Mass., 1951.

France

Becker, Alfons. *Studien zum Investiturproblem in Frankreich.* Saarbrücken, 1955.

Bournazel, E. *Le gouvernment Capétien au XIIe siècle, 1108–1180.* Paris, 1975.

Cauchie, Alfred. *La querelle des investitures dans les diocèses de Liège et de Cambrai.* Louvain, 1889–91.

Choux, Jacques. *L'episcopat de Pibon (1069–1107): Recherches sur le diocèse de Toul au temps de la réforme grégorienne.* Paris, 1952.

Fliche, Augustin. "Premiers resultats d'une enquête sur la réforme grégorienne dans les diocèses français." *Comptes rendus des séances de l'Académie des Inscriptions et Belles Lettres,* 162ff. Paris, 1944.

Imbart de la Tour, Pierre. *Les elections épiscopales dans l'église de France du IXe au Xe siècle.* Geneva, 1974.

Lemarignier, Jean-François. *La France médiévale: Institutions et sociétés.* Collection U. Paris, 1970. A basic introduction, but a bibliography is given.

———. *Le gouvernement royal aux premiers temps Capétiens (987–1108).* Paris, 1965. Includes a detailed bibliography.

Luchaire, Achille. *Louis VI, le Gros, Annales de sa vie et de son règne (1081–1137).* Paris, 1890.

Monod, Bernard. "L'election épiscopale de Beauvais de 1100 à 1104." *Mémoires de la Société Académique . . . du Département de l'Oise* 19 (1904–6).

———. *Essai sur les rapports de Pascal II avec Philippe Ier (1099–1108).* Paris, 1907.

Pacaut, Marcel. *Louis VII et les élections épiscopales dans le royaume de France.* Paris, 1957.

———. *Louis VII et son royaume.* Paris, 1964.

Schramm, Percy Ernst. *Der König von Frankreich: Das Wesen der Monarchie vom 9. bis zum 16. Jahrhundert.* Weimar, 1939.

The Crusades

Atiya, Aziz Suryal. *The Crusade, Historiography and Bibliography.* Bloomington, 1962.

Brundage, James A. *Medieval Canon Law and the Crusader.* Madison, Wis., 1969.

Chazan, Robert. *European Jewry and the First Crusade.* Berkeley and Los Angeles, 1987.

Cowdrey, H. E. J. "Martyrdom and the First Crusade." In *Crusade and Settlement.* Edited by P. Edbury, 46–56. Cardiff, 1985.

Erdmann, Carl. *The Origin of the Idea of Crusade.* Translated by Marshall W. Baldwin and Walter Goffart. Princeton, 1977.

Hamilton, Bernard. *Monastic Reform, Catharism and the Crusades, (900–1300).* Variorum Reprint CS 97. London, 1979. Several papers relate to the Crusades.

Mayer, Hans Eberhard. *The Crusades.* Translated by John Gillingham. New York and Oxford, 1972. See also the same author's bibliographies: *Bibliographie zur Geschichte der Kreuzzüge* (1960), supplemented by his "Literaturbericht über die Geschichte der Kreuzzüge" (1958–1967), in *Historische Zeitschrift,* Sonderband 3 (1969).

Prawer, Joshua. *Histoire du royaume de Jerusalem.* Translated by G. Nahon. Paris, 1969.

Riley-Smith, Jonathan. *The Crusades: A Short History.* New Haven, 1987.

Runciman, Sir Steven. *A History of the Crusades.* 3 vols. Cambridge, 1951–54. Still very readable, but particularly vols. 2 and 3 have been superseded by Mayer, Setton, and Riley-Smith.

Setton, Kenneth M. *A History of the Crusades.* 5 vols. Madison, Wis., 1969–85.

Sivan, Emmanuel. *L'Islam et la croisade. Idéologie et propagande dans les réactions musulmanes aux croisades.* Paris, 1968.

Southern, Sir Richard W. *Western Views of Islam in the Middle Ages.* Cambridge, Mass., 1962.

The Worms Agreements

Bernheim, Ernst. *Das Wormser Konkordat und seine Vorurkunden.* Breslau, 1906.

Büttner, Heinrich. "Erzbischof Adalbert von Mainz, die Kurie und das Reich in den Jahren 1118 bis 1122." In *Investiturstreit und Reichsverfassung,* 395–410.

Classen, Peter. "Das Wormser Konkordat in der deutschen Verfassungsgeschichte." In *Investiturstreit und Reichsverfassung,* 411–60. The essay is a significant contribution. I have adopted its conclusions without reservations.

Hoffmann, Hartmut. "Ivo von Chartres und die Lösung des Investiturproblems." *DA* 15 (1959):393–440.

Hofmeister, Adolf. *Das Wormser Konkordat: Zum Streit um seine Bedeutung.*

Neuausgabe mit Vorwort von Roderich Schmidt. Darmstadt, 1962. Includes an extensive bibliography: it also discusses manuscript transmission.

Speer, Lothar. *Kaiser Lothar III. und Erzbischof Adalbert I. von Mainz: eine Untersuchung zur Geschichte des deutschen Reiches im frühen zwölften Jahrhundert*. Dissertationen zur mittclalterlichen, Geschichte 3. Cologne and Vienna, 1983.

Sprandel, Rolf. *Ivo von Chartres und seine Stellung in der Kirchengeschichte*. Stuttgart, 1962.

INDEX

University of Pennsylvania Press
MIDDLE AGES SERIES
Edward Peters, General Editor

David Anderson. *Before the Knight's Tale: Imitation of Classical Epic in Boccaccio's* Teseida. 1988

F. R. P. Akehurst, trans. *The* Coutumes de Beauvaisis *of Philippe de Beaumanoir.* 1991

Benjamin Arnold. *Count and Bishop in Medieval Germany: A Study of Regional Power, 1100–1350.* 1991

J. M. W. Bean. *From Lord to Patron: Lordship in Late Medieval England.* 1990

Uta-Renate Blumenthal. *The Investiture Controversy: Church and Monarchy from the Ninth to the Twelfth Century.* 1988

Daniel Bornstein, trans. *Dino Compagni's Chronicle of Florence.* 1986

Betsy Bowden. *Chaucer Aloud: The Varieties of Textual Interpretation.* 1987

James William Brodman. *Ransoming Captives in Crusader Spain.* 1986

Otto Brunner (Howard Kaminsky and James Van Horn Melton, eds. and trans.). Land *and Lordship: Structures of Governance in Medieval Austria.* 1991

Robert I. Burns, S.J., ed. *Emperor of Culture: Alfonso X the Learned of Castile and His Thirteenth-Century Renaissance.* 1990

David Burr. *Olivi and Franciscan Poverty: The Origins of the* Usus Pauper *Controversy.* 1989

Thomas M. Cable. *The English Alliterative Tradition.* 1991

Leonard Cantor, ed. *The English Medieval Landscape.* 1982

Anthony K. Cassell and Victoria Kirkham, eds. and trans. *Diana's Hunt. Caccia di Diana. Boccaccio's First Fiction.* 1991

Brigitte Cazelles. *The Lady as Saint: A Collection of French Hagiographic Romances of the Thirteenth Century.* 1991

Willene B. Clark and Meradith T. McMunn, eds. *Beasts and Birds of the Middle Ages: The Bestiary and Its Legacy.* 1989

G. G. Coulton. *From St. Francis to Dante: Translations from the Chronicle of the Franciscan Salimbene (1221–1288).* 1972

Richard C. Dales. *The Scientific Achievement of the Middle Ages.* 1973

Charles T. Davis. *Dante's Italy and Other Essays.* 1984

George T. Dennis, trans. *Maurice's Strategikon.* 1984

Katherine Fischer Drew, trans. *The Burgundian Code.* 1972

Katherine Fischer Drew, trans. *The Laws of the Salian Franks.* 1991

Katherine Fischer Drew, trans. *The Lombard Laws.* 1973

Nancy Edwards. *The Archaeology of Early Medieval Ireland.* 1990

Margaret J. Ehrhart. *The Judgment of the Trojan Prince Paris in Medieval Literature.* 1987

Felipe Fernández-Armesto. *Before Columbus.* 1987

Patrick J. Geary. *Aristocracy in Provence.* 1985

Julius Goebel, Jr. *Felony and Misdemeanor: A Study in the History of Criminal Law.* 1976

Avril Henry, ed. *The Mirour of Mans Saluacioune.* 1987

J. N. Hillgarth, ed. *Christianity and Paganism, 350–750.* 1986

Richard C. Hoffmann. *Land, Liberties, and Lordship in a Late Medieval Countryside.* 1990

Robert Hollander. *Boccaccio's Last Fiction: "Il Corbaccio."* 1988

Edward B. Irving, Jr. *Rereading* Beowulf. 1989

C. Steven Jaeger. *The Origins of Courtliness.* 1985

William Chester Jordan. *The French Monarchy and the Jews: From Philip Augustus to the Last Capetians.* 1989

William Chester Jordan. *From Servitude to Freedom: Manumission in the Sénonais in the Thirteenth Century.* 1986

Ellen E. Kittell. *From* Ad Hoc *to Routine: A Case Study in Medieval Bureaucracy.* 1991

Alan C. Kors and Edward Peters, eds. *Witchcraft in Europe, 1110–1700.* 1972

Barbara Kreutz. *Before the Normans: Southern Italy Before the Ninth and Tenth Centuries.* 1991

Jeanne Krochalis and Edward Peters, ed. and trans. *The World of Piers Plowman.* 1975

E. Ann Matter. *The Voice of My Beloved: The Song of Songs in Western Medieval Christianity.* 1990

María Rosa Menocal. *The Arabic Role in Medieval Literary History.* 1987

A. J. Minnis. *Medieval Theory of Authorship.* 1988

Lawrence Nees. *A Tainted Mantle: Hercules and the Classical Tradition at the Carolingian Court.* 1991

Lynn H. Nelson, trans. *The Chronicle of San Juan de la Peña: A Fourteenth-Century Official History of the Crown of Aragon.* 1991

Charlotte A. Newman. *The Anglo-Norman Nobility in the Reign of Henry I: The Second Generation.* 1988

Thomas F. X. Noble. *The Republic of St. Peter: The Birth of the Papal State, 680–825.* 1984

Joseph F. O'Callaghan. *The Cortes of Castile-León, 1188–1350.* 1989

William D. Paden, ed. *The Voice of the Trobairitz: Essays on the Women Troubadours.* 1989

Kenneth Pennington. *Pope and Bishops: The Papal Monarchy in the Twelfth and Thirteenth Centuries.* 1984

Edward Peters. *The Magician, the Witch, and the Law.* 1982

Edward Peters, ed. *Christian Society and the Crusades, 1198–1229.* Sources in Translation, including The Capture of Damietta by Oliver of Paderborn. 1971

Edward Peters, ed. *The First Crusade: The Chronicle of Fulcher of Chartres and Other Source Materials.* 1971

Edward Peters, ed. *Heresy and Authority in Medieval Europe.* 1980

Edward Peters, ed. *Monks, Bishops, and Pagans: Christian Culture in Gaul and Italy, 500–700.* 1975

Clifford Peterson. *Saint Erkenwald.* 1977

James M. Powell. *Anatomy of a Crusade, 1213–1221.* 1986

Joel T. Rosenthal. *Patriarchy and Families of Privilege in Fifteenth-Century England.* 1991

Donald E. Queller. *The Fourth Crusade.* 1977

Michael Resler, trans. *EREC by Hartmann von Aue.* 1987

Pierre Riché (Jo Ann McNamara, trans.). *Daily Life in the World of Charlemagne.* 1978

Jonathan Riley-Smith. *The First Crusade and the Idea of Crusading.* 1986

Barbara H. Rosenwein. *Rhinoceros Bound: Cluny in the Tenth Century.* 1982

Steven D. Sargent, ed. and trans. *On the Threshold of Exact Science: Selected Writings of Anneliese Maier on Late Medieval Natural Philosophy.* 1982

Robert Somerville and Kenneth Pennington, eds. *Law, Church, and Society: Essays in Honor of Stephan Kuttner.* 1977

Sarah Stanbury. *Seeing the* Gawain-*Poet: Description and the Act Perception.* 1991

Susan Mosher Stuard, ed. *Women in Medieval History and Historiography.* 1987

Susan Mosher Stuard, ed. *Women in Medieval Society.* 1976

Ronald E. Surtz. *The Guitar of God: Gender, Power, and Authority in the Visionary World of Mother Juana de la Cruz (1481–1534).* 1990

Patricia Terry, trans. *Poems of the Elder Edda.* 1990

Frank Tobin. *Meister Eckhart: Thought and Language.* 1986

Ralph Turner. *Men Raised from the Dust: Administrative Service and Upward Mobility in Angevin England.* 1988

Harry Turtledove, trans. *The Chronicle of Theophanes.* 1982

Mary F. Wack. *Lovesickness in the Middle Ages: The* Viaticum *and Its Commentaries.* 1990

Benedicta Ward. *Miracles and the Medieval Mind.* 1982

Suzanne Fonay Wemple. *Women in Frankish Society: Marriage and the Cloister, 500–900.* 1981